Immigration and Identity in Beur Fiction

Berg French Studies

General Editor: John E. Flower

ISSN: 1354-3636

John E. Flower and Bernard C. Swift (eds), *François Mauriac: Visions and Reappraisals*

Michael Tilby (ed.), *Beyond the Nouveau Roman: Essays on the Contemporary French Novel*

Colin Nettlebeck, *Forever French: The French Exiles in the United States of America during the Second World War*

Bill Marshall, *Victor Serge: The Uses of Dissent*

Allan Morris, *Collaboration and Resistance Reviews: Writers and the Mode Rétro in Post-Gaullist France*

Malcolm Cook, *Fictional France: Social Reality in the French Novel 1775–1800*

W.D. Halls, *Politics, Society and Christianity in Vichy France*

David H. Walker, *Outrage and Insight: Modern French Writers and the 'Fait Divers'*

H.R. Kedward and Nancy Wood, *The Liberation of France: Image and Event*

David L. Looseley, *The Politics of Fun: Cultural Policy and Debate in Contemporary France*

Nicholas Hewitt, *Literature and the Right in Postwar France: The Story of the 'Hussards'*

Laïla Ibnlfassi and Nicki Hitchcott, *African Francophone Writing: A Critical Introduction*

Alex Hughes and Kate Ince, *French Erotic Fiction: Women's Desiring Writing, 1880–1990*

Jennifer E. Milligan, *The Forgotten Generation: French Women Writers of the Inter-war Period*

Immigration and Identity in Beur Fiction

Voices from the North African Immigrant Community in France

Alec G. Hargreaves

First published in 1991 by
Berg
Editorial offices:
150 Cowley Road, Oxford, OX4 1JJ, UK
70 Washington Square South, New York, NY 10012, USA

Updated paperback edition published in 1997.

Berg is the imprint of Oxford International Publishers Ltd.

British Library Cataloguing-in-Publication Data
Hargreaves, Alec G.
  Voices from the North African immigrant community
  in France: Immigration and identity in Beur
  fiction. – (Berg French studies)
  I. Title II. Series
  843

  ISBN 0 85496 649 8

Library of Congress Cataloging-in-Publication Data
Hargreaves, Alec G.
    Voices from the North African immigrant community in France:
  immigration and identity in Beur fiction / Alec G. Hargreaves.
      p. cm. – (Berg French studies series)
    Includes bibliographical references and index.
    ISBN 0 85496 649 8 (Cloth)
          1 85973 148 1 (Paper)
    1. North African fiction (French)–History and criticism.
  2. French fiction–20th century–History and criticism.
  3. Emigration and immigration in literature. 4. North Africans–
  France–Intellectual life. 5. North Africans in literature.
  6. Immigrants in literature. I. Title. II. Series.
  PQ3988.5.N6H37   1991
  843′.9140996044–dc20   91–321
                                                                 CIP
  ISBN 0 85496 649 8 (Cloth)
        1 85973 148 1 (Paper)

Printed in the United Kingdom by WBC Bookbinders, Bridgend, Mid-Glamorgan.

For Kate and Rose

Contents

Acknowledgements

I am extremely grateful to all the writers who gave so generously of their time during the preparation of this book, and who granted access to many unpublished materials. John Flower's interest and advice at an early point in my research were crucial in getting the project on the rails. David Bancroft and Annie Frolet facilitated that early spark and much else subsequently in their own inimitable way. My periodic migrations across the English Channel, together with a foray across the Mediterranean, were made possible by a grant from the British Academy.

In France I benefited greatly from the advice of Charles Bonn, Abdelkader Djeghloul and the late Annie Lauran. The staff at L'Harmattan, Mercure de France, Denoël, Sindbad and Seuil placed many useful materials at my disposal. Christiane Achour and Paul de Quincey provided invaluable help in Algeria.

I was fortunate to begin drafting the book against the backdrop of a series of seminars on francophone North African writers organised at the Institut Français in London by Philippe Daros and Ethel Tolansky during the winter of 1988–9. The distinguished speakers who led the seminars provided a deep well of wisdom on which I was able to draw. Wendelin Guentner saved my bacon by her rigorous reading of a decidedly undercooked first draft. François Desplanques, Sylvie Roberts and Charles Stivale also risked their taste-buds and made valuable comments. The proof of the pudding is, as ever, in the eating. For any errors or inadequacies which remain I am of course solely responsible.

AGH
Loughborough

Glossary of Foreign Terms

Terminological explanations are given on the pages indicated below:

Preface to the Second Edition

Since the first edition of this study, the corpus of writings published by second-generation Maghrebis (North Africans) in France, popularly known as 'Beurs', has grown considerably. The critical debate over this literature, which was only just beginning in the late 1980s, has also expanded rapidly, reflecting a steadily widening interest in what is now generally known as post-colonial writing. While retaining a certain practical utility, the word 'Beur' has itself become increasingly problematic. For this expanded edition, I have added a new chapter discussing these developments. I have also updated the bibliography to include a comprehensive list of narrative works by authors of Maghrebi immigrant origin up to 1996, together with the principal items of secondary literature published by scholars and critics in both French and English. The first four chapters are based on a corpus of 25 narrative works published during the 1980s by the earliest of these authors (17 in all) to enter print. Today, this core corpus remains highly representative of writings by second-generation Maghrebis in France. As is shown in chapter 5, recently published works confirm many of the trends discussed in the initial study, while at the same time indicating a number of new directions open to these writers.

AGH
Loughborough
November 1996

Introduction

During the last decade a new group of writers has appeared on the literary scene in France. They are part of the so-called 'Beur' generation. Beur is a name popularly applied to the sons and daughters of North African immigrants.[1] A longer-established label is that of 'second-generation immigrants', but as most of those concerned were born in France, this is something of a misnomer, for they have never migrated from one country to another. In their daily lives the Beurs have, however, been compelled to migrate constantly between the secular culture of France and the traditions carried with them by their Muslim parents from across the Mediterranean. These experiences have been explored by Beur writers in poems, plays and, above all, prose fiction. It is with this growing body of fiction that the present study is concerned.

This is the first full-length study to be devoted to these writers. It aims to cater both for the general reader and for those who already have some knowledge of the issues raised by the literary practices which have been stimulated by the interaction between Western and Third World cultures. To this end, it focuses on the key problematic which has preoccupied Beur writers: the articulation of a sense of personal identity, forged in the particular circumstances which are those of an ethnic minority in France. Running in parallel with the rise of the Beurs, there has in recent years been a growing concern with the concept of identity among politicians and academics in France. Jean-Marie Le Pen's extreme right-wing party, the Front National, has scored a series of spectacular electoral successes by playing on fears that immigrants of 'Maghrébin', i.e. North African, origin constitute a threat to French national identity. Scholars have focused less single-mindedly than Le Pen on the presence of these immigrants, but agree about the importance

---

1. The term was tormed by inverting the syllables which make up the word 'Arabe'. For a fuller explanation, see Section 1.3.

of the underlying issue: in a world of diversity, how can a sense of coherence be constructed and sustained?[2] For members of the immigrant community, this question constitutes neither a political football nor an academic debating point, but is part and parcel of their daily existence. For most of them, the question is less one of collective identity (how do nations or other groups build up and share in a sense of community?) than of personal identity (how can I fit together into a coherent whole the different parts of my experience, which often conflict with each other because of my participation in a mixture of communities and cultures?).[3] This uncertain sense of identity is the central theme in the writings of Beur authors.

The idea of personal identity is virtually synonymous with that of the self. Both are notoriously problematic concepts. The processes of change which every subjectivity undergoes by virtue of its constant movement through time and space clearly render untenable any simple idea of a fixed, unitary self. At any given moment the self is perhaps best understood as a mode of projection towards the future based upon a distillation of the subject's past. While that mode of projection may remain relatively constant over certain periods of time, it is always open to change.

If certain impulses are innate, the identity of an individual is nevertheless constructed to a very significant degree out of borrowings from others. Conflicts within the self may be stimulated by differences between the various others on whom we model our projections. My identification (i.e. feeling of affinity) with a particular individual or group may help to generate desires or expectations which cut across projects derived from other role-models. No subject is immune from conflicts of this kind. The Beurs are therefore by no means unique in experiencing a divided sense of identity. What is distinctive about the Beurs is the particular set of parameters within which these tensions arise, and the intensity which they sometimes acquire. While such conflicts may be experi-

---

2. Politically-oriented treatments of this theme include that of the right-wing Le Club de l'Horloge, *L'Identité de la France*, Paris, Albin Michel, 1985, and that of the more leftward-leaning Espaces Quatre-vingt-neuf, *L'Identité française*, Paris, Editions Tierce, 1985. Recent academic studies include Julia Kristeva, *Etrangers à nous-mêmes*, Paris, Fayard, 1988 and Tzvetan Todorov, *Nous et les autres*, Paris, Seuil, 1989.
3. A particularly influential theorist of personal identity has been Erik H. Erikson. Works such as Erikson's *Identity: Youth in Crisis*, London, Faber and Faber, 1968, have had a direct influence on important psycho-social studies of the Beurs, most notably Hanna Malewska-Peyre et al., *Crise d'identité et déviance des jeunes immigrés*, Paris, La Documentation Française, 1982.

enced most commonly in everyday personal relations, they are rooted in the juxtaposition of radically different cultural systems consequent upon large-scale international population movements. For the Beurs, the negotiation of personal identity is inseparable from the more or less overt confrontation of this wider socio-historical cleavage.

In the construction of a sense of self, no borrowings are more important than the signifying systems through which the subject thinks and speaks. Relations between those systems and individual subjects are complex and in many ways opaque. If unconscious elements are as fundamental to the psyche as Freud and his followers have suggested, what credence or importance are we to attach to the conscious articulation of ourselves? And if utterances are necessarily made in signifying systems which in many important respects are beyond the control of the speaker or writer, are the postmodernists right to conclude that the self is little more than a discursive fiction?[4]

It would be naïve to read any literary text, no matter how apparently autobiographical, as a direct and transparent representation of the author's self. Some may wish to quarry what they can from a text in an attempt to construct a picture of the author's identity, but that is not my concern. While some of my arguments are supported by biographical information, the main purpose of the present study is to assist in understanding the narrative works produced by Beur writers, and in particular to investigate their treatment of the theme of identity.

In some ways, these writings parallel the already substantial corpus of works by an older generation of authors from what we now call the Third World – and most obviously North Africa – who have chosen to write in French. By writing in the language of what, until thirty years ago, was the occupying power in the land of their birth, francophone North African authors have had to grapple with complex problems of identity and allegiance. In a number of cases – Driss Chraïbi, Mohammed Dib and Rachid Boudjedra are among the best known examples – they have written about the immigrant community, sometimes after taking up residence in France.[5] Yet their education sets these writers apart from

4. Cf. Michael Newman, 'Revising Modernism, Representing Postmodernism: Critical Discourses of the Visual Arts', in Lisa Appignanesi (ed.), *Postmodernism: ICA Documents*, London, Free Association Books, 1989, esp. pp. 114–24.
5. These works are discussed by Jean Déjeux, 'Romanciers de l'immigration maghrébine en France', *Francofonia*, vol. 5, no. 8, Spring 1985, pp. 93–111, and by Charles Bonn, 'Roman maghrébin, émigration et exil de la parole',

most North African immigrants. The great majority of first-generation immigrants were illiterate when they arrived in France to take up poorly paid, unskilled jobs. Such is their preponderance among the immigrant community that the word 'immigrés' is commonly applied solely to working-class foreigners; the small minority of professionally qualified incomers tend instead to be called 'étrangers'.[6] When educated North Africans have written about the immigrant community, they have inevitably done so from the outside, so to speak.

This also applies to French novelists such as Claire Etcherelli, Raymond Jean and Michel Tournier.[7] The controlling hand of their French editors is heavily present, too, in the life-stories of illiterate immigrants whose tape-recorded words were published in book form during the 1970s.[8] Having been brought up in France, the Beurs have all, in contrast with their parents, learned to read and write as an integral part of their passage through the state educational system. Unlike the older generation of North African writers, however, the Beurs have undergone their formative experiences as part of an ethnic minority within France, where they have shared through the family home in both the material disadvantages and the cultural traditions associated with first-generation immigrants. Beur authors have in this sense been the first to write from within the immigrant community itself.

Beginning with Hocine Touabti in 1981, close to twenty Beur writers have now found commercial publishers.[9] I include among them Bouzid Kara, though his father was a 'harki' rather than an

Annuaire de l'Afrique du Nord, vol. 24, Paris, CNRS, 1987, pp. 399–415. See also Christiane Achour, *Anthologie de la littérature algérienne de langue française*, Algiers, ENAP/Paris, Bordas, 1990, ch. 5, 'Ecritures de la migration', which includes a section on Beur authors.

6. See Abdelmalek Sayad's remarks in his interview with Thomas Ferenczi, 'Le Burnous sous le béret', *Le Monde*, 22–3 Dec. 1985.

7. Claire Etcherelli, *Elise ou la vraie vie*, Paris, Denoël, 1967; Raymond Jean, *La Ligne 12*, Paris, Seuil, 1973; Michel Tournier, *La Goutte d'or*, Paris, Gallimard, 1985. There has as yet been no systematic study of French fiction dealing with the immigrant community.

8. Works of this kind are among those discussed by Philippe Lejeune in *Je est un autre*, Paris, Seuil, 1980, pp. 229–315.

9. New works by Beur authors were being published throughout the period in which I conducted my research. Six volumes appeared in 1989 alone, two of them – Mehdi Charef's *Le Harki de Meriem* and Tassadit Imache's *Une Fille sans histoire* – during the autumn 'rentrée'. As my typescript was by then nearing completion, it has been possible to include in it only limited treatment of the most recently published narratives. Moussa Lebkiri's *Une Etoile dans l'œil de mon frère*, Paris, L'Harmattan, 1989, came to my attention too late for it to be included in my corpus of works. Scholarly studies of Beur literature are only

immigrant driven by 'classic' economic motives. The harkis were Muslim soldiers who fought on the side of the French during the Algerian war of independence, at the end of which they were 'repatriated' to France for their own safety. Because the harkis crossed the Mediterranean as political exiles, they are traditionally distinguished from 'immigrés', who came to France essentially for economic reasons. This distinction has been sustained by the habitual identification of the harkis with conservative political forces in France, in contrast with the generally more leftward-leaning sympathies of economically-motivated immigrants. Yet both groups have their origins in the least educated sections of North Africa's Muslim population, and in France they have shared equally poor employment and housing conditions. The children they have brought up in France have recognised these similarities, and have been increasingly inclined to disregard the old demarcation line between the two groups. This is seen most obviously in the prominent role played by youngsters from harki homes in what became known as the Marche des Beurs, a major political demonstration held in 1983 which forms the backbone of Bouzid's narrative, *La Marche*.[10]

Also included in the present study are the works of Leïla Houari, though her Moroccan parents emigrated to Belgium rather than France. The North African community in Belgium has a very similar status to that of its counterpart in France, and Houari ranks to all intents and purposes as a Beur. By contrast, Leïla Sebbar is not included here, despite the fact that she has written extensively

just beginning to appear. Monique Gadant, 'La Littérature immigrée', *Les Temps modernes*, nos 452–4, Mar.–May 1984, pp. 1988–99, is informed by considerable prescience, but as the bulk of Beur narratives were published later, they fall outside the parameters of Gadant's discussion. More recent but still brief surveys include Hédi Bouraoui, 'A New Trend in Maghrebian Culture: the Beurs and their Generation', *Maghreb Review*, vol. 13, nos 3–4, 1988, pp. 218–28; Jean-Michel Ollé, 'Les Cris et les rêves du roman beur', *Le Monde diplomatique*, Oct. 1988, p. 27; Abdelkader Djeghloul, 'L'Irruption des Beurs dans la littérature française', *Arabies*, May 1989, pp. 80–7. Lively collections of interviews and articles have been assembled in special issues of *Actualité de l'émigration*, 11 Mar. 1987, pp. 22–7, 'L'Expression "*Beur*": esquisse d'une littérature', and of *Hommes et migrations*, no. 1112, Apr.–May 1988, 'Le Livre et l'immigration'. The first doctoral thesis on the subject was completed in 1989: Jamila Boulal, 'Introduction à la littérature française d'expression immigrée', UER de Sciences des textes et documents, Université de Paris VII, 1989.

10. Bouzid, *La Marche*, Paris, Sindbad, 1984. It will be observed that the book was published under the author's first name only. As this appears to be Bouzid's wish, I have referred to him by this name throughout the present study.

about the Beurs. As Sebbar has acknowledged, she is not herself a Beur,[11] for she was born and brought up in Algeria, where her French mother and Algerian father worked as schoolteachers.[12]

In recent decades, literary theorists have tended increasingly to study texts independently of the lives and social circumstances of their authors, though as Charles Bonn has pointed out, the works of francophone North African writers were for many years by-passed by this trend:

> Un survol des recherches universitaires effectuées depuis vingt ans sur les littératures maghrébines confirme [que], du moins jusqu'à une époque récente[,] ces littératures ont longtemps été étudiées essentielle-ment comme des documents sur leur société d'origine, ou comme des prises de position politiques diverses. C'est-à-dire, dans les deux cas, comme un contenu. L'écriture de ces textes est rarement décrite comme une parole majeure, un dire émancipé. Car ce dire n'est considéré que par l'information qu'il livre à une mise en perspective en lieu autre: celui d'une lecture qui ne se fait pas dans le même espace que celui dans lequel le texte est censé être né. Dans ces conditions, le texte littéraire 'déco-lonisé' est traité comme un signifiant transparent dont le sens, qui seul importerait, est donné en dernier recours par l'ancienne métropole coloniale. Peut-on dans ce cas parler de littérature 'décolonisée', ou du moins d'une lecture non aliénante?[13]

While the immigrant community is situated on French rather than North African soil, it has a foreignness for most readers which is very much akin to that of the former colonies in which these immigrants have their origins. The subordinate position of these new ethnic minorities within France may indeed be seen as an adaptation of the old hegemonic relationships characteristic of the colonial period. Writing just before the explosion of Beur fiction, Bonn noted that literary representations of the immigrant com-munity, written and read almost entirely by non-migrants, effec-tively submitted those concerned to a similar hegemonic hold.[14]

11. Leïla Sebbar and Nancy Huston, *Lettres parisiennes*, Paris, Barrault, 1986, p. 125.
12. For similar reasons, Antoinette Ben Kerroum-Covlet, who was raised in Morocco by a Franco-Moroccan couple, is also excluded from this study, though her novel *Gardien du seuil*, Paris, L'Harmattan, 1988, features a Beur protagonist.
13. Charles Bonn, 'La Lecture de la littérature algérienne par la gauche française: le "cas" Boudjedra', *Peuples méditerranéens*, no. 25, Oct.–Dec. 1983, pp. 3–4.
14. Ibid., pp. 7–9.

Beur fiction aspires in many ways to be precisely the kind of 'dire émancipé' championed by Bonn. Lest it be considered that the use of biographical and historical information in parts of the present study constitutes in some sense a demeaning or reductive approach, a word of explanation seems advisable. Beur writing is such a recent phenomenon that very little published information. on its practitioners exists. Drawing on extensive unpublished interviews, Chapter 1 makes available for the first time detailed biographical portraits of these authors, and situates them in their socio-historical context.[15] This is not to say that their literary works are to be judged on some simple scale of social veracity or utility. The works of Beur writers cannot be reduced to the circumstances in which they were conceived and elaborated. But important aspects of the creative process can be properly understood only if we know something about the raw materials out of which these authors have fashioned their writings. Chapter 1 should therefore be seen as laying the groundwork for Chapter 2, where the basic constituents of the stories recounted by Beur writers are analysed and compared with the life experiences of the authors. We shall see that even in the most autobiographical of Beur narratives, significant elements of selection and invention enter into the construction of the stories which they recount.

Beyond this first step in the imaginative process (or, more probably, simultaneously with it), the author must apply his or her creative skills in many other ways. In the overall meaning of a text, the story is often matched and sometimes exceeded in importance by the manner of narration, i.e. the way in which the story is told. Who narrates the story? When, where and for whom? These and related questions are examined in Chapters 3 and 4. The division of labour between these two chapters corresponds roughly to that which separates the basic ontological axes of time and space. Chapter 3 examines the extent to which narrators and authors appear to position themselves 'within' or 'outside' particular groups, while Chapter 4 concentrates on the interplay between time at the level of narration and time within the flow of the story.

The intricacies of individual texts cannot be fully grasped

15. Throughout my study, except where otherwise indicated, all biographical information is derived from the unpublished interviews which I conducted with the authors concerned. These are listed in the bibliography, together with other unpublished materials on which I have drawn. Among my corpus of writers, the only one whom it proved impossible to pin down was Bouzid Kara; I therefore fell back on biographical information supplied by his mother.

without a clear conceptual framework. Taking as his starting point the distinction between what he calls diegesis and narration, i.e. between the story represented in the text and the manner of its depiction, Gérard Genette has developed a particularly fruitful system for classifying the spatio-temporal positions of narrators.[16] The theoretical tools fashioned by Genette are therefore drawn on in the analysis pursued in Chapters 3 and 4. The ideas of Mikhail Bakhtin, for whom the interplay between different narrative voices is of fundamental textual importance, are also used to illuminate the cultural tensions which frequently characterise the narration of Beur fiction.[17]

In human affairs, the physical axes of time and space are always overlaid by cultural constructions of this kind. Such constructions are fundamental to the patterns of meaning from which individuals derive a sense of identity. While the narratives studied here cannot be read as transparent self-portraits, they offer valuable insights into the bi-cultural condition within which each author, like the Beur generation as a whole, must seek to achieve a coherent sense of self.

---

16. See Gérard Genette, *Figures III*, Paris, Seuil, 1972; idem, *Nouveau discours du récit*, Paris, Seuil, 1983.
17. See M.M. Bakhtin, *The Dialogic Imagination*, trans. Caryl Emerson and Michael Holquist, Austin, University of Texas Press, 1981.

-1-

History and Biography

1.1 Worlds of Experience

The population movements in which Beur writers have their
geographical and historical origins may be traced back to the
colonial period, when North Africans first began emigrating to
France. For many decades, these men remained heavily outnum-
bered by immigrants of European origin, but the balance began to
change after the Second World War. In 1946 Algerians, Moroccans
and Tunisians together accounted for less than 3 per cent of
France's immigrant community. By contrast, in the 1982 census
the figure was not far short of 40 per cent. Algerians are now the
largest single national group among the foreign population in
France.[1]

Initially, almost all North Africans came to France on a temporary basis. They were working men whose families remained in
their country of origin, to which the breadwinners returned after a
few years. Since the 1950s, however, a growing number have been
joined by their families and have become more settled in France.
The relatively high birth rate prevalent in these families has, in the
space of a generation, transformed the North African immigrant
community. Dominated in the past almost exclusively by men of
working age, it is today characterised by a very high proportion of
young people of both sexes. Most first-generation immigrants

---

1. INSEE, *Recensement général de la population de 1982, sondage au 1/20, France
métropolitaine: Les Etrangers*, Paris, La Documentation Française, 1984, Table
R6. For a detailed account of these historical developments, see Gérard Noiriel,
Le Creuset français: histoire de l'immigration, xixe–xxe siècles, Paris, Seuil, 1988;
Larbi Talha et al., *Maghrébins en France: émigrés ou immigrés?*, Paris, CNRS,
1983; Magali Morsy (ed.), *Les Nord-Africains en France*, Paris, CHEAM, 1984;
Alain Gillette and Abdelmalek Sayad, *L'Immigration algérienne en France*, 2nd
edn, Paris, Entente, 1984; Jacqueline Costa-Lascoux and Emile Temime (eds),
Les Algériens en France: genèse et devenir d'une migration, Paris, Publisud, 1985.

were illiterate when they left their homeland, and their mastery of
written French remains shaky to this day. By contrast, the children
whom they have raised in France have all attended school as a
matter of course, thereby learning to read and write. Here lie the
seeds from which a new generation of writers has grown.

In the overwhelming majority of cases, first-generation immigrants have been unskilled workers occupying the lowest ranks in
French society, as indeed they did in their country of origin. They
came mainly from rural areas, most notably Kabylia, a mountainous region to the east of Algiers. Unable to sustain a living there,
they sought employment in the expanding industries of metro-
politan France. What they found were invariably the dirtiest, most
dangerous and least well paid jobs – those which the French
themselves did not want to do.

On the eve of the First World War, there were only a few
thousand North Africans in France. During the war, France was to
draw heavily on the reserves of manpower available to her in the
colonial territories across the Mediterranean. Between 1914 and
1918, approximately 250,000 Algerians were brought over to
France, together with smaller numbers of Moroccans and Tunisians. Some came as civilian workers, while others were drafted
into the army to assist directly in the French war effort. Most of
them returned to North Africa when the war ended. Numbers
were to fluctuate considerably during the next two decades. In
total, as many as 500,000 may have crossed the Mediterranean
during the inter-war period, but the number present in France at
any one time was always very much smaller than that, for this was
the heyday of the so-called 'rotation' system. Under this system,
men would spend a few years working in France before returning
to their country of origin, whence they would be replaced by a
fresh contingent of workers, often from the same village if not
indeed from the same family. In some cases, sons followed fathers
or nephews replaced uncles.

North Africans were again recruited into the French armed
forces during the Second World War. However, large-scale emigration really began to take off after 1947, when a new statute
granted to Algeria in the hope of binding the country more closely
to the colonial motherland gave Algerians the right to move freely
in and out of France. Agreements reached in 1963 with Morocco
and Tunisia (which had gained their independence in 1956) also led
to a big increase in immigration from those countries in response to
the labour shortages being experienced in France during the post-
war economic boom. In 1946 the North African community in

France had numbered just 40,000. By 1982 the figure stood at more than 1,400,000. Similar developments occurred in Belgium during this period. As late as 1961, only a few hundred North Africans were resident there. Twenty years later there were well over 100,000 North Africans in Belgium, most of whom originated in Morocco.[2]

The family origins of the writers studied here reflect these broad historical trends. In France, commercially published Beur writers are without exception of Algerian descent. As the settlement of Moroccans and Tunisians is a relatively recent phenomenon, their children are in general not yet sufficiently mature to have produced a comparable body of work. Several Beur authors can trace ancestors back to the early stages of the North African presence in France. A great-uncle of Mehdi Lallaoui, for example, was among the Algerians enlisted into the French armed forces during the First World War. Lallaoui's maternal grandfather, born in Kabylia in 1904, spent much of his life working in a glass factory in Levallois, in the north-west suburbs of Paris, where he died of a lung disease in 1947. Abdelkader Lallaoui, Mehdi's father, first worked in France during the late 1930s, and did forced labour for the Germans during the Nazi Occupation. After the war he returned to Algeria and got married. His wife Zohra remained behind when he headed back across the Mediterranean once more in search of work. Abdelkader spent several years in France on his own, making occasional visits to his family when he could afford it. By the time he decided to bring them to France, in 1955, three sons had already been born in Algeria. A fourth was born soon after their arrival. Their fifth son, Mehdi, was born in Argenteuil, not far from Levallois, in 1957, and six more children followed. They were supported by what their father earned on the assembly line of the Simca car factory at Poissy, further to the west, and later in a metal-working firm at Argenteuil.

The father of the oldest Beur writer, Kamal Zemouri, left his village in Kabylia during the 1920s. He worked initially in a coking factory and later helped to lay railway track in the Marseilles area. Unusually for the period, he was joined in France by his wife. They settled in Saint-Denis, another industrial suburb just north of Paris, and had three children. The youngest of them, Kamal, was born there in 1941. Kamal's father was employed for a time in a sewage

2. For an overview of developments in Belgium, see J.P. Grimmeau, 'Les Derniers Immigrés? Maghrébins et Turcs en Belgique: quelques considérations géographiques et démographiques', *Tribune immigrée*, no. 21, Dec. 1986, pp. 5–9.

treatment plant. His last job was in a silver-plating factory, which his family blame for the cancer which killed him in 1961.

Jean-Luc Yacine's father, Saïd, also hailed from Kabylia. He was just fourteen years old when he arrived in northern France with his own father in 1932. The pair of them worked in the coal-mines there. Saïd had a spell in the French army during the Second World War, at the end of which he married a French woman, Madeleine Istace, and settled in Arras. Jean-Luc, the third of their six children, was born in Arras in 1950.

Another of our authors, Ahmed Kalouaz, is the son of Abdelkader Kalouaz, who left his home near Oran, in north-western Algeria, to join the French army in 1937. After serving in the Second World War, Abdelkader returned to Algeria in 1945. Like Lallaoui's father, he married there and then went back to France to find work, visiting his wife Yamina when the money he earned as a miner near Grenoble permitted it. A few months after the birth of their second child, Ahmed, in the town of Arzew in 1952, Abdelkader brought the family over to France, where nine more children were born. Ahmed's father moved from the mines to work as a labourer on hydro-electric dam construction sites near Grenoble, and finished his working life in a plastics factory there.

Until the 1950s, very few immigrant workers brought their wives and children with them from North Africa. When the Algerian war of independence broke out in 1954, there were only 6,000 families of Algerian origin in France. Among them were the families from which five Beur writers come: those of Ahmed Kalouaz, Kamal Zemouri, Jean-Luc Yacine, Akli Tadjer and Hocine Touabti. Zemouri's parents were one of the very few Algerian couples to have established themselves in France during the inter-war period. Saïd Yacine's marriage to a French woman in 1944 was also rare for the time. The parents of Akli Tadjer settled in Paris soon after the war. Akli, the fourth of their seven children, was born in 1954. Hocine Touabti was born near Sétif, a town just to the south of Kabylia, in 1949. Together with his two older brothers, he was brought to France a few months after his birth. Two younger sisters were born after the family settled in the industrial town of Saint-Chamond, not far from Saint-Etienne.

A wave of Algerian families settled in France during the war of independence, carrying the total from 6,000 at its inception to 30,000 when the conflict ended in 1962. Among them were the families of nine Beur authors: Azouz Begag, Farida Belghoul, Sakinna Boukhedenna, Tassadit Imache, Bouzid Kara, Mohammed Kenzi, Nacer Kettane, Mehdi Lallaoui and Mustapha Raïth.

Bouzid Begag left the village of El-Ouricia, near Sétif, in 1949 to work on building sites in the Lyons area. It was not until 1955 that his wife and children left Algeria to join him in France. Azouz, the fifth of seven children, was born in Lyons in 1957. The movements of Mehdi Lallaoui's family, which have already been described, followed a similar pattern, except that they settled in the Paris area. Nacer Kettane's family followed an almost identical itinerary. Nacer was born in the Kabyle village of Kebouche in 1953. The boy's father had been working in Paris since the end of the Second World War (during which he had been a French army conscript); the family, which eventually numbered ten children, joined him there in 1958. Similarly, Mohammed Kenzi was eight years old when, in 1960, he and his mother left the village where he had been born near Maghnia, a small town in north-west Algeria with a long history of emigration, to join the boy's father in Nanterre. Farida Belghoul's father, Brahim, first came to France in 1947, returning to his native Kabylia four years later. After marrying in 1953, he emigrated once more, and was joined in Paris by his wife a year or two later. Farida, the first of their five children, was born in 1958. Tassadit Imache, the daughter of a mixed marriage contracted early in the Algerian war, was born in Argenteuil in 1958. Her Kabyle father and French mother had met while working in a nearby factory.

Sakinna Boukhedenna was born in Mulhouse, in eastern France, in 1959. All but one of her six older brothers and sisters had been born before the family left Kabylia; two other children were later born in Mulhouse. Mustapha Raïth, the sixth in a family of thirteen children, was born further north, in Hautmont, in 1960. Raïth's father had left the village of Aïn Bessem, on the edge of Kabylia, on the eve of the Algerian war, and had been joined in France by his wife shortly afterwards. Bouzid Kara was born in a small village near Constantine, in north-eastern Algeria, in approximately 1958. As his father was a harki, the family fled to France with the advent of Algerian independence in 1962, settling near Aix-en-Provence, where a total of nine children were eventually raised.

Family emigration from North Africa accelerated further after 1962, but most of the children concerned are of course still too young to have begun writing seriously. Only three of our authors are from families that have settled in Europe since that date. Mehdi Charef, who was born in Maghnia in 1952, came to France in 1963. In the same year, the family of Messaoud Bousselmania, who is known to the public by the pen-name of Maya Arriz Tamza, which he has recently contracted to Arriz Tamza, left the village of Oued

Tamza, where he had been born six years earlier, and moved to Marseilles. Leïla Houari, the oldest of seven children, was born in Casablanca in 1958. Her family moved from Morocco to Belgium in 1965.

While they belong in the main to the earliest wave of family immigration, the circumstances of their upbringing make the formative years of Beur writers typical of this still burgeoning generation. The families of almost all these authors have their origins in rural areas, and the majority are from Kabylia, which has been the single most important region for Algerian emigration in general. Tamza's native region is the Aurès, a mountainous area not unlike Kabylia but further to the south. Indeed most of its inhabitants, like those of Kabylia, are Berbers, i.e. descendants of North Africa's original population prior to the arrival of the Arabs in the seventh century. In both Kabylia and the Aurès, the Berber language, rather than Arabic, is still predominant.

Houari is unusual in having been born in a large North African city, Casablanca. Her father was the son of a wealthy and well educated landowner in the town of Guercif, in north-east Morocco. Her origins are in this respect untypical of the Beurs. But the family arguments which led Houari's father to emigrate forced him to earn his living doing odd jobs in Brussels, where the living conditions of his family matched those of the immigrant community in general. His children were brought up in typically run-down parts of the city inhabited by large numbers of foreign workers and their families.

Like the North African immigrant community in general, the families of Beur writers are heavily concentrated in the industrial areas of France and Belgium. Belghoul, Charef, Imache, Kenzi, Kettane, Lallaoui, Tadjer and Zemouri were all raised in the Paris conurbation, while the adopted home of Houari is Brussels. Begag hails from Lyons, France's second largest city. Kalouaz and Touabti were brought up not far away, in Grenoble and Saint-Chamond respectively. Most of Tamza's childhood and adolescence were spent in Marseilles, a southern port with heavy concentrations of North African immigrants, and Bouzid was raised in the nearby town of Aix-en-Provence. Arras and Hautmont, the home towns of Yacine and Raïth, are in the old industrial heartland of northern France, while Mulhouse, the birthplace of Boukhedenna, is part of a similar complex in the east of the country.

The families of most first-generation North African immigrants are very much larger than the average French family unit, but as most of the breadwinners have poorly paid unskilled jobs their incomes are much lower. This has forced them into the lower end of the housing market. Some immigrant families found apartments in decaying inner-city areas, but during the 1950s and 1960s many had no alternative but to live in 'bidonvilles'. These were collections of ramshackle buildings thrown up on spare land around the edges of major cities. For both Charef and Kenzi, their first home in France was in one of the many bidonvilles that sprawled across Nanterre, in the western suburbs of Paris.[3] A dilapidated house near a rubbish tip bought by Begag's father in Villeurbanne, a suburb of Lyons, in 1955 became the core of a bidonville in which the family lived until 1966. These shantytowns had none of the usual facilities (neither mains gas nor electricity, tarmaced roads nor a proper sewerage system) enjoyed by the bulk of the population in France. For their water supply, hundreds and sometimes thousands of houses, or, to be more accurate, huts, would share a single standpipe.

Government initiatives to clear these slums eventually led to the creation of 'cités de transit', which mushroomed during the 1970s. These were meant to be temporary dwellings, pending the provision of proper housing. They were built of somewhat better materials than the bidonvilles, and basic facilities were provided. Nevertheless, they fell far short of the standards expected by most French citizens, and their 'temporary' status proved to be far longer-lived than originally anticipated. Charef, for example, spent ten years in a cité de transit. Asked what the difference was between that and a bidonville, he replied sardonically: 'Aucune, sinon que dans les cités de transit, on paie.'[4] When the authorities eventually rehoused the families who had moved into cités de transit, their low incomes once again greatly limited the relocation choices open to them. Most had to settle for low-grade HLM estates (the French equivalents of British council estates and American housing projects) on the outskirts of the big cities. Those estates and cheap private apartments in run-down inner-city districts are where most immigrant families live today.

3. A graphic collection of documents relating to these bidonvilles was assembled by Monique Hervo and Marie-Ange Charras, *Bidonvilles*, Paris, Maspéro, 1971.
4. Charef's comment was made in his interview with Bernard Cuau, 'Mehdi Charef: La tendresse dans le béton', *Jeune Afrique Magazine*, May 1985, p. 27.

1.2 Marks of Identity

The children of immigrants, like children everywhere, internalise certain habits of mind in the process of growing up. Shared habits of this kind are characteristic of a culture, which serves as a bridge between past experiences and future projections. However, the material conditions outlined in the previous section are such that the Beurs find themselves participating in different and sometimes conflicting cultures. Prior to the French colonisation of North Africa, and the more recent tide of emigration in the opposite direction, these cultures were geographically separate from each other. Today they live cheek by jowl in many parts of France. While each culture serves as a bridge of continuity to those within it, others who, like the Beurs, cross from one culture to another often face chasms of alarming proportions.

Eight of our writers were born in North Africa. Four of them – Bouzid, Kalouaz, Kettane and Touabti – came to France at a very young age and consequently remember nothing of their early months or years in Algeria. The other four were, however, old enough to carry with them childhood memories of their homeland. Tamza was aged six, while Houari was seven and Kenzi was eight when the move came. Charef emigrated at the age of eleven. Because they had already begun to put down roots in North Africa, the move to Europe came as a profoundly disorienting experience, for the thread of continuity between the past and the future was suddenly severed. 'Oui, j'ai vécu le fait de venir en Europe comme un déchirement,'[5] Houari stated in an interview. Her words are paralleled by those of Charef, for whom 'la rupture fut de larmes.'[6]

Quite apart from the dreadful material conditions into which Charef was thrust – he remembers moving straight from the sun-filled skies of his home town, Maghnia, to a wintry bidonville in Nanterre – there was the huge emotional wrench of leaving behind friends and members of his extended family. Making new friends in a foreign country is not necessarily easy for a child. Charef was fortunate in that he had at least learned some French in Maghnia, though his schooling had been badly disrupted by staff losses during the Algerian war, and his command of the written language was poor. Houari knew no French at all when she left Morocco: her father only began to teach her the rudiments of the

5. Interview with Leïla Houari, 10 June 1988.
6. Mehdi Charef, 'Mères patries', *La Croix*, 25 Nov. 1983.

language during the train journey to Belgium. During her early years Houari, like all children, had gradually mastered the basic rules of the cultural system prevailing in her homeland. Her life there had a coherence that was lost with the move to Europe. Instead of serving as a bridge by which to communicate with the society around her, Houari's first language, Arabic, cut her off from people in Belgium. A new learning process and many re-adjustments would be necessary before she could re-establish a coherent sense of her place in the world.

For children born in Europe, similar problems were liable to occur in reverse if the family returned to North Africa. Akli Tadjer remembers feeling very unhappy during family holidays spent in his parents' village in Kabylia:

J'arrivais dans le village avec mes parents. Il y avait des gosses de mon âge. Ils parlaient tous kabyle ou arabe, et moi je n'y comprenais rien du tout. J'étais exclu. C'était pas drôle, les vacances. Tandis que quand je partais en colonie de vacances avec mes copains d'école en France, c'était mieux; il y avait une continuité, quoi.[7]

That feeling of continuity, characteristic of cultural coherence, was fractured for Ahmed Kalouaz when his family spent several months in Algeria during the school year of 1961–2. It was the first time he had been back there since leaving the country as an infant. For Kalouaz, far more disturbing than the war of independence, then in its final stages, were his feelings of cultural estrangement. Having spent all but the first few months of his life in France, where he had been at school for several years, he suddenly found himself expected to cope with lessons in Arabic. The result was a bitterly unhappy school year. When the family returned to Algeria for a summer holiday in 1967, Kalouaz felt so ill at ease that he scarcely ventured out of the house at all; he has never been back since.

Feelings of discontinuity are by no means confined to overseas journeys of this kind. The Beurs move every day between the culture which their parents attempt to sustain within the family home and that which they encounter beyond its walls. As most immigrants speak Arabic or Berber at home, that is the first language learned by their children. But when they begin school, the language of instruction is French, which is of course also the

---

7. Interview with Akli Tadjer, 26 Apr. 1988. The words 'kabyle' and 'berbère' are often used interchangeably to denote the dialect spoken in Kabylia.

language of non-immigrant schoolfriends, as well as of television, street signs and every other major public medium. As the use of their mother tongue declines under these outside influences, a common pattern within the home is for children to start replying to their parents in French, even when addressed in Arabic or Berber. As fathers, too, and to a lesser extent their wives start picking up more French in the course of their work or in other forms of contact with non-immigrants, the parents sometimes switch to French at home, especially when conversing with their children. This was the experience of Zemouri, for instance, as well as of Tadjer. By the time Zemouri first set foot in Algeria at the age of twenty-one, he had forgotten virtually every word of Berber that he had learned as a child. Some parents, anxious to improve their children's chances at school, positively encourage the use of French. Boukhedenna, for example, recalls that while her parents spoke to each other in Arabic, from her earliest years they used only French with her.

Parents have often been far less willing to see their children renounce other aspects of North African culture. The most important sticking point is Islam. Unlike European immigrants, who came from countries which shared with France a long history of Christian, mainly Catholic, belief, virtually all North African immigrants are Muslims, and they are usually keen to have their children share their faith. It is not simply a matter of abstract belief. On the contrary, Muslims hold that concrete signs of belief should be seen everywhere: in prayers recited in the direction of Mecca five times a day, for example, in strict dietary regulations including fasting during the month of Ramadan, and in the organisation of major aspects of family life. Immigrant parents attempting to transmit their Islamic heritage have been hampered by the fact that until recently, Muslims have had very little organisational infrastructure in France. During the childhood and adolescence of Beur writers in the 1950s and 1960s, parents had few opportunities of providing their children with any formal religious instruction. It was not until the late 1970s that the Islamic community in France really began to get organised.[8] Today there are well over a thousand recognised places of worship. But very few of these are purpose-built mosques. Most are converted buildings or simply rooms, often of very modest dimensions, tucked away in odd corners of housing estates or in the hostels that still house 'single'

---

8. On the development and organisation of Islam in France, see Gilles Kepel, *Les Banlieues de l'Islam*, Paris, Seuil, 1987.

male immigrants. Koranic schools are still only very patchily developed.

The obstacles to the transmission of Islamic teachings have been vividly described by Tadjer:

> Pour nos parents, l'Islam c'était très concret. Le problème, c'est que l'Islam est difficilement transmissible aux mômes nés en France. Pour eux c'est abstrait. L'Islam est facilement transmissible quand tu nais dans un berceau islamique – quand il y a une mosquée, quand il y a un imam, quand il y a toutes les valeurs religieuses dans un village. Ici en France il n'y a aucun de ces points-là, aucun de ces repères. Une mosquée, moi je ne visualisais pas ce que c'était. Une église, je voyais bien ce que ça voulait dire. Des choses qui ne sont pas à la télé, qui ne passent pas dans les journaux, c'est abstrait. Même le message, il n'est pas dans l'environnement, il ne s'inscrit pas. C'est dur de tourner vers La Mecque quand tu es dans le métro. Mes parents ne pouvaient pas expliquer les versets du Koran. Ils pouvaient te réciter, mais ils ne pouvaient pas vraiment expliquer. Comme pratiquement tous les immigrés ils étaient complètement incultes, c'est-à-dire qu'ils ne pouvaient pas lire le Koran, ils étaient analphabètes. Ils avaient comme seuls repères de l'Islam ce que toi, tu peux apprendre en trois jours. Eux, ils avaient ça pour toute leur vie à gérer – faire le ramadan, parce que . . ., ne pas manger de porc, ils ne savent pas pourquoi, il ne faut pas boire d'alcool, les rudiments, quoi. Mais maintenant va leur demander de rentrer en profondeur, ils ne savent pas. Ils savent réciter la prière, ils peuvent même te traduire un peu ce qu'il y a dans le texte, mais ils ne peuvent pas t'expliquer ça.[9]

In Algeria, Islamic precepts have been perpetuated through countless channels of everyday social intercourse. The imam (preacher) in the local mosque reinforces through his detailed knowledge of the Koran a basic message that is already familiar to peasants in the fields, even if they have were denied access to literacy when young. Major aspects of family life are regulated by Islamic law, and since independence the state-controlled schools and mass media have been able to carry the message of the Koran into every classroom and home on a daily basis. In France, most of those channels are closed to the Islamic community. The main means of mass communication carry altogether different messages. Secular values, overlaying a long heritage of Christian belief, are to the fore. In the streets and at school, the children of immigrants pick up habits and

---

9. Interview with Akli Tadjer, 26 Apr. 1988.

expectations which are sometimes seriously at odds with those of their parents. Ruptured lines of cultural continuity may threaten basic family relationships and instil within individuals painful conflicts of loyalty. Charef has described these tensions thus:

> Ce qui me dérange avec la génération des premiers immigrés, c'est que la majorité d'entre eux voudrait que leurs enfants soient ce qu'ils sont ou ce qu'ils ont été. A la maison, c'est tout le temps: 'Attention, ne fais pas ci, parce que tu es Arabe . . . Ne fais pas ça . . . N'oublie pas que tu es musulman!' Dans la rue, le gosse se retrouve carrément dans un autre monde que les parents ignorent. Il est déchiré et c'est ce déchirement qui me dérange. C'est ce déchirement qui fait souffrir les jeunes.[10]

These comments again echo Houari's description of the move from North Africa to Europe as a 'déchirement', but it would be very short-sighted to reduce this to a mere geographical divide. Where the Beurs are concerned, the split is effectively between two different parts of the self: one which identifies with the secular values of contemporary France, and one which, through the family home, remains engaged with the Islamic traditions of North Africa.

The strongest areas of conflict are apt to revolve around the regulation of relations between the sexes. Islam assigns a dominant role to men, and forbids public signs of female sexuality. Teenage girls with 'liberated' French schoolfriends often resent the restrictions placed upon them by their Muslim parents. The traditional right of such parents to choose spouses for their sons as well as their daughters is not uncommonly resisted by youngsters who feel they should enjoy the same personal freedoms as their French peers. Family quarrels provoked by these and other tensions sometimes end in a serious breakdown of relations. In some cases, for example, girls run away from home to avoid arranged marriages.

Imache was saved from an arranged marriage at the age of thirteen when her French mother refused to go along with the plans being made by the girl's Algerian father. Belghoul achieved personal independence only by resorting to subterfuge: she pretended she was continuing her education hundreds of miles away from her parents' home in Paris, when in reality she was living with a friend in a neighbouring district of the city. When Zemouri returned to Algeria in 1962, his family there immediately tried to marry him off

10. Charef's remarks were made in his interview with Farida Ayari, 'Le Thé au harem d'Archi Ahmed de Mehdi Charef', Sans Frontière, May 1983, p. 37.

to a cousin. Zemouri's refusal to accept her hand and his decision a few years later to take a bride of his own choice led to an almost total breakdown in relations with his family. Kalouaz was deeply shocked when an older brother was married off by his parents in the late 1970s to a young woman brought over from Algeria, who was a total stranger to her husband. When a younger sister ran away from home to escape similar parental pressures in 1981, Kalouaz severed all relations with his mother and father, and it was not until five years later that they began to mend their bridges.

The ruse to which Belghoul resorted was motivated by the desire to secure her personal freedom without at the same time hurting her parents. As a consequence, she found herself living 'une double vie qui conditionn[ait] un personnage double . . . mais unique'.[11] The cohabitation within the Beurs of conflicting aspirations derived from their bi-cultural condition makes the construction of a coherent sense of personal identity a highly problematic process. Certain choices involve the Beurs in long-term commitments indicative of an attachment to one culture rather than another. Engagements of this kind would appear to be signalled, for example, by their choice of marriage partners, places of residence and countries of citizenship. Yet few if any of these choices entirely resolve the inner tensions felt by those concerned.

Several Beur writers – among them Begag, Kalouaz, Lallaoui and Yacine – live with French spouses or companions. Others, such as Charef, Houari, Kettane and Zemouri, are married to partners of Algerian or Moroccan nationality. Intimate personal relations of this kind normally presuppose some basic similarity of outlook. The case of Mustapha Raïth shows the need for caution, however, in taking sexual relations as an index of cultural affinities. Raïth left home in his late teens and bummed around France, experimenting with drugs and scrounging a living as best he could. In 1980 he married a young French woman, Corinne Buil. The following year he raped another woman, also French. He was sentenced to twelve years imprisonment. While serving his sentence, Raïth was divorced by Corinne. At the same time, he became profoundly committed to Islam, a religion which he had rejected during his youth. In 1986 he described his divided sense of identity in a letter written from his prison cell in France to *Algérie-Actualité*, one of Algeria's leading news magazines:

---

11. Belghoul made this comment in her interview with Khadidja Bachiri, 'Le Produit des circonstances', *Cinémaction*, no. 24, 1983, p. 127.

A qui dois-je m'adresser en particulier pour attirer, ne serait-ce qu'un semblant d'attention sur mon cas, qui est aussi celui de tant de milliers de jeunes issus de cette fameuse 'seconde génération'?

Est-il nécessaire de rappeler la lutte désespérée que nous menons, à la quête constante d'une identité qui trop souvent nous échappe?

Comment donc parvenir à démêler l'écheveau de l'identité culturelle et psychologique si la bobine de la morale nous apparaît insaisissable, hors série? La perturbation, aussi incompréhensible soit-elle, est inhérente; et c'est comme ça que dès l'adolescence, les premiers symptômes de la folie se font ressentir et inévitablement c'est la chute fatale: dépression, internement, schizophrénie, mal-être, délinquance. [. . .]

Lorsque je suis revenu à la réalité, ce fut celle d'un monde clos: la prison! Ce fut donc là le prix de mon affranchissement des problèmes de l'identité contre lesquels j'ai lutté des années durant, optant définitivement pour la culture arabe que, certes, je connais très mal.

[. . .]

Si je vous parle de cette question, c'est tout simplement parce que je souhaiterais que vous me fassiez rêver, désirant m'installer définitivement en Algérie, pays que je n'ai visité que sur cartes postales . . .[12]

The wild fluctuations in Raïth's behaviour and attitudes are particularly extreme, but the conflicting impulses which underlie his instability are shared in varying degrees by many among the Beur generation. In these circumstances, no single deed or display of emotion, no matter how dramatic or apparently binding, can be regarded as a definitive indicator of personal identity. Raïth's apparent desire to live in a country whose culture he admits to knowing little about has all the marks of an escapist fantasy, rather than of a serious long-term commitment.

Several Beur writers, and many other members of their generation, have tried to make a reality of Raïth's dream. Almost all have failed.[13] Zemouri is alone among our authors in having resettled permanently in North Africa. He was assisted in that by an exceptional combination of personal and historical circumstances. Zemouri's adolescence was spent amidst intense racial animosity generated against the immigrant community in France during the Algerian war. His father died in 1961, and when independence came the following year, Zemouri seized the opportunity to start a

12. Mustapha Raïth, 'Seconde Génération: les problèmes d'identité, la crise, le rêve', *Algérie-Actualité*, 21 Aug. 1986, p. 2.
13. The problems encountered by the Beurs in Algeria have been vividly documented by François Lefort and Monique Néry, *Emigré dans mon pays*, Paris, CIEM/L'Harmattan, 1985.

new life in Algeria. He arrived there during the euphoria of the independence celebrations, and was soon joined by his mother (who died shortly afterwards) and brothers. Zemouri now had no remaining family ties in France. Algeria was desperately short of professionally skilled personnel, and although Zemouri had no formal qualifications, the basic education he had received in France enabled him to find a schoolteaching job. Later he made a career in journalism. It is highly doubtful whether such opportunities would have come his way had he remained in France.

The heady days of 1962 are now long gone, and the hard realities of life in contemporary Algeria offer far less scope for the idealism that once fired Zemouri. A variety of explanations has been offered for the riots which rocked the country in October 1988, among them material shortages, political corruption and insufficient personal freedoms. What is beyond dispute is that young people were at the forefront of the rioting and bore the brunt of the hundreds of casualties inflicted during the authorities' repression of the unrest. Before those events, youths from immigrant families across the Mediterranean had, on returning to the land of their parents, experienced similar frustrations and made parallel complaints to those which were to be voiced by the young rioters in the streets of Algiers in 1988. The Beurs, like their parents, are uniformly proud of Algerian independence, but they are often highly critical of the policies pursued by those in authority since 1962. Early in 1979, at the age of twenty-one, Lallaoui tried to resettle in Algeria, inspired by the patriotic sentiments instilled in him by his father and by the hope that a fresh start would offer a way out of life's problems in France. Before the year was out, he had given up and headed back across the Mediterranean. Upon returning home he immediately applied to take French citizenship.

Existing nationality laws provide basically that any child born of foreign parents on French soil automatically acquires French citizenship upon reaching the age of majority. The position is, however, complicated by France's colonial legacy. Unlike Tunisia and Morocco, which had the legal status of protectorates rather than of outright colonies, Algeria was regarded as an integral part of French territory until independence in 1962. That year, Algerian immigrants opted *en masse* for Algerian citizenship, and their children were deemed to have the same nationality. But French law regards children born to Algerian immigrants since 1 January 1963 as French from birth, on the grounds that their parents, too, were French in the period prior to independence. Algeria refuses to recognise this claim, and regards all the children of its citizens (regardless of when and where they were born) as Algerian. In practice, children born to Algerian immigrants up to 1962 – which includes all our writers with the exception of Houari – are effectively Algerian unless they decide to apply for French citizenship, whereas those born in France since then automatically receive French papers unless they specifically opt for Algerian ones.[14]

Passive acquiescence in the nationality bestowed upon Beur authors does not necessarily indicate a strong level of attachment to the country concerned. Lallaoui's decision to take French nationality, like Kalouaz's in 1980 and Begag's in 1988, is a much more convincing indicator. Significantly, all three men live with or are married to French partners. Yet none would in any sense wish to deny or devalue their Algerian roots. Moreover, Begag explained his decision in terms of sheer practicality: with border formalities for the citizens of member-states set to be phased out within the European Community, he had no desire to find his freedom of movement blocked by Algerian papers.[15] Nacer Kettane took French citizenship in 1989 for similar reasons. Down on his luck at about the same time, Hocine Touabti gave serious consideration to the possibility of switching to French citizenship in the hope that this might improve his employment prospects. Clearly, their choice of nationality has come to be viewed by the Beurs in an increasingly functional light, rather than as a fundamental expression of political allegiance.

Little more than a year after Raïth's letter was published in *Algérie-Actualité*, the author was shaken to learn that under new procedures introduced by the conservative government in power from 1986 to 1988, he would be expelled from France to Algeria upon completing his prison sentence. In an appeal against the move, Raïth wrote:

A présent TOUT S'ECROULE. IL NE ME RESTE PLUS RIEN.
– Plus de réinsertion sociale,
– Plus d'amis,
– Plus de permissions,

14. On this complex issue, see Jacqueline Costa-Lascoux, 'L'Immigration algérienne en France et la nationalité des enfants d'Algériens', in Talha et al., *Maghrébins en France*, pp. 299–320; Abdelmalek Sayad, 'Les Immigrés algériens et la nationalité française', in Smaïn Laacher (ed.), *Questions de nationalité*, Paris, L'Harmattan, 1987, pp. 156–8.
15. Begag gave this explanation for his decision in the television debate 'Les Dossiers de l'écran: Les Beurs parlent aux Français', Antenne 2, 3 Nov. 1987. His formal change of papers took place the following year.

Plus que des larmes et le désespoir d'être expédié sans emballage dans un pays où JE N'AI JAMAIS MIS LES PIEDS. Je n'ai même pas de passeport, juste des pièces d'identité portant la nationalité de mes parents et que je n'avais pas songé à modifier parce que . . . parce que je n'y avais tout simplement pas songé!
Je suis attaché à une terre, pas à un bout de papier.[16]

This is a very different line from the one Raïth had taken a year earlier. Algeria is now revealed for what it is: a foreign country of which he knows virtually nothing. The rehabilitation to which he aspires is clearly within French society. His prison sentence prevented Raïth from changing to French citizenship, but had this not been the case there is little doubt that he would have made the switch, for this would have nullified the expulsion order against him. Here again nationality appears in an essentially functional light.

A more revealing indicator, as Raïth himself suggests, is the choice of where to live. Most Beur writers are equally at liberty to reside on either side of the Mediterranean. The fact that all save Zemouri have chosen to live in Europe[17] leaves little doubt as to where they see their long-term future. Yet if their future lies in France (or, in the case of Houari, Belgium), the roots of these writers are in a very real sense in North Africa, and their sense of identity is always in some measure stretched between these poles. Algeria or Morocco served as constant reference points in the homes where they were raised. Raïth is alone among our writers in having never set foot in North Africa. The others have all spent time there, usually on family holidays, and sometimes at their own initiative. Even those who appear to have no interest in making further visits, and who in some cases have had serious differences with their parents, remain at the very least respectful towards the older generation, and in almost all cases a powerful emotional bond still exists. Not uncommonly, the Beurs are in fact rediscovering the language and culture of their parents. Several Beur authors have dabbled in Arabic, though none is able to write fluently in the language. Belghoul, like Raïth, has become very serious in her commitment to Islam after disregarding it in her youth. Lallaoui,

16. The unpublished typescript of this appeal by Raïth, headed simply 'Mémoire', is dated 15 Dec. 1987.
17. When Kenzi was expelled from France in 1974, he went to live in Switzerland. As soon as the opportunity arose, he returned to France. This was made possible by the election in 1981 of President François Mitterrand, who abrogated the banning order against Kenzi.

one of the first to make a deliberate switch to French nationality, has also done more than any other Beur writer to retrace his Algerian roots through extensive archival research.

1.3   Into Print

Like it or not, every Beur has a foot in two cultures, and this is a situation with which he or she must learn to live. Historically, legally and logically those two cultures are in many respects at odds with each other. They can be reconciled only by the invention of new solutions or compromises. At an everyday level, these may involve white lies or other forms of play-acting. Begag told a seminar in England that he was not a Muslim, but added that he would never tell his father this because it would be too painful for him to hear.[18] Belghoul resorted to a more elaborate subterfuge in order to secure her personal freedom without hurting her parents unduly (she lied to them about her whereabouts and the reason for her absence). To ease inner conflicts within themselves, the Beurs sometimes practice forms of self-deception. Raïth's escapist fantasy of a new life in Algeria is a case in point. On an altogether different scale, the creative works of Beur writers and artists may be read as attempts to bridge the gaps and contradictions which characterise their creators' lives.

Reflecting on the tensions caused by his sudden removal to France, Charef remarked: 'Si j'étais resté en Algérie, j'aurais été peut-être bien, je n'aurais peut-être pas eu besoin de m'exprimer . . .'[19] It was the mental turmoil provoked by the failure of Lallaoui's attempt at resettling in Algeria that prompted him to write the first draft of his novel *Les Beurs de Seine*. Houari had undergone an almost identical experience two years before him. In May 1977 she took a job in Casablanca, hoping to resettle there. Within six months, Houari realised that she simply did not fit into Moroccan society. She returned to Brussels and threw herself into a whole range of creative activities designed to make sense of and revalorise the immigrant experience in Belgium. She gave adult literacy classes, helped stage plays and musical events in collaboration with other young members of the North African community, and eventually wrote her first novel, *Zeida de nulle part*.

The powerful forces unleashed by these creative tensions were

18. Seminar held at Loughborough University, 22 Nov. 1988.
19. Interview with Ayari, '*Le Thé*', p. 37.

vividly described by Charef shortly after the publication of his own first novel, *Le Thé au harem d'Archi Ahmed*, in 1983:

> Toujours tiraillés entre deux sociétés qui, en même temps, nous oublient – mais qu'est-ce que l'Algérie a fait pour nous, les jeunes? – et veulent nous enrôler, peu tentés par le retour en Algérie, poussés, au contraire, je dirais même condamnés à vivre en France, écorchés vifs, les jeunes de la migration pensent que maintenant le meilleur moyen de s'affirmer, c'est de vivre tels qu'ils sont, de se poser en fils de migrants vivant en France, en mettant en valeur ce qui a pu être sauvé de la culture d'origine, mais en affirmant aussi qu'ils appartiennent déjà et de plus en plus à la société française.
> [. . .]
> Le meilleur moyen de s'affirmer, c'est de s'exprimer, de parler. Les médias nous en ont longtemps dénié le droit, en laissant entendre qu'un bougnoule était incapable de s'exprimer et qu'il n'avait que le droit de se taire. Cette réflexion, à propos de mon bouquin, je l'ai souvent entendue.
> Maintenant, la condamnation au silence, c'est fini. Les jeunes veulent parler, dire ce qu'ils ont sur le cœur, dialoguer. Pour eux, mon livre, c'est normal. Mais il n'y a pas que le livre, il y a le chant, le théâtre. Il y a aussi la radio. Quel succès pour 'Radio-Beur', par exemple! Ils parlent, tous ces jeunes, ils chantent, ils expliquent leurs problèmes, leurs situations, et c'est ainsi qu'une nouvelle culture prend racine.[20]

The first sizeable wave of youths from North African backgrounds in France began to reach adulthood during the 1970s, which brought the earliest significant stirrings of creative output among them. Amateur theatre groups were among their earliest activities. Drama requires literacy of neither performers nor spectators, and a number of troupes run by first-generation immigrants were already in existence when their children began to get involved during the mid-1970s. The older generation saw their plays mainly as a means of preserving their original culture while articulating grievances over conditions in France. Arabic and Berber predominated, but plays were sometimes performed in a mixture of these languages and French. As the younger generation became more involved, different priorities and perspectives were brought into play. These youngsters were more concerned with charting a way through life's problems in France than with preserving the traditions of their

---

20. Mehdi Charef, 'La Nouvelle Culture des migrants: d'abord ne pas oublier', *La Croix*, 3–4 July 1983.

parents. They began to set up their own troupes, performing mainly in French with a smattering of Arabic or Berber.[21] Very few of these plays were published,[22] and they seldom reached audiences beyond the immigrant community itself. Similar limitations applied where young poets were concerned. Their works began to appear in small private editions and in immigrant magazines from the mid-1970s onwards, but as none was published commercially they had no impact on the general public.[23]

Among Beur writings, prose forms alone have found commercial publishers in significant numbers, and even the first of these – Touabti's novel *L'Amour quand même* – passed virtually unnoticed when it came out in 1981. Within two years the climate was to change markedly, however. When Charef's *Le Thé au harem d'Archi Ahmed* appeared in 1983, it became a bestseller almost overnight. Kalouaz and Tadjer brought out their first novels the following year, which also saw the publication of Kenzi's *La Menthe sauvage*. In 1985 it was the turn of Houari and Kettane to enter print, and in 1986 no fewer than seven Beur novels were published.

This upsurge in the creative output of the Beurs and the growth of public interest in it cannot be fully understood without reference to important changes in the political climate during this period. In 1981 the Socialists came to power in France under President François Mitterrand. Among their first actions was the abolition of a law which had previously forbidden foreigners from organising any kind of association without the prior approval of the Ministry of the Interior. The Socialists also made public funds available to the immigrant community on an unprecedented scale. The result was a veritable explosion of new organisations set up and run by members of the immigrant community, particularly the younger generation. To the theatre troupes and other associations already established during the late 1970s were added many new groups, working in virtually every medium from rock music and fashion to radio and film.[24]

21. This transition is valuably documented in the unpublished doctorat d'état of Frédéric Maatouk, 'Le Théâtre des travailleurs immigrés en France', UER Sciences de l'Homme, Université François-Rabelais, Tours, 1979.
22. The first Beur plays to be made widely available in France were those collected by Chérif Chikh and Ahsène Zehraoui, *Le Théâtre beur*, Paris, Arcantère, 1984.
23. See Jean Déjeux, 'A la recherche d'une expression poétique', *Hommes et migrations*, no. 1112, Apr.-May 1988, pp. 19–31. Kalouaz and Yacine both brought out private editions of poems in this way before finding commercial publishers for their narrative works.
24. For an overview of this cultural upsurge, see Michel Laronde, 'La "Mouvance

Another early reform by the Socialists opened up the air waves to scores of privately run local radio stations. Among these was Radio Beur, which began broadcasting in the Paris area at the end of 1981. Its appearance marks the first recorded usage of the word Beur. This term is itself a striking illustration of the creative capabilities of those whom it denotes. The word initially entered circulation during the 1970s as a mode of self-designation among younger members of the North African immigrant community in the Paris area. It is a piece of 'verlan', this being a form of slang practised originally by members of the French underworld and more recently by urban youths. Verlan has served both as a code in which to discuss shady activities without being understood by those in authority and as a means of promoting fellow-feeling among socially marginalised groups. Youngsters from immigrant backgrounds have become keen practitioners, to the point indeed where, when a sociolinguist recently embarked on a study of verlan, she took as her prime informant a thirteen-year-old school-boy of Algerian origin named Saïd. For Saïd, verlan was not simply a functional device:

> Saïd prend un plaisir évident à raconter ses 'petites histoires', à manier un langage dont il est maître, à égarer ses auditeurs dans un univers à l'envers; puis à aller les chercher en retournant ses mots à l'endroit pour qu'ils puissent suivre . . . Cette fonction poétique est peut-être aussi importante que sa fonction référentielle.[25]

Verlan functions by inverting the first and last syllables of words. The word verlan is itself an example of this process, for it is an inversion of [à] l'envers'. 'Beur' is derived by a similar process of inversion from 'Arabe', as Nacer Kettane, the President of Radio Beur, has explained:

> Beur vient du mot 'arabe' inversé: *arabe* donne *rebe*, qui, à l'envers, donne *ber* et s'écrit *beur*. Mais il n'a rien à voir avec la signification académique du mot 'arabe'. Beur renvoie à la fois à un espace

---

beure": émergence médiatique', *French Review*, vol. 62, no. 4, March 1989, pp. 661–8. This upsurge is also discussed in the context of related political activities by Adil Jazouli, *L'Action collective des jeunes maghrébins de France*, Paris, CIEMI/L'Harmattan, 1986.

25. Vivienne Mela, 'Parler verlan: règles et usages', *Langage et société*, no. 45, Sept. 1988, p. 70.

géographique et culturel, le Maghreb, et à un espace social, celui de la banlieue et du prolétariat de France.[26]

Partly as a consequence of the Algerian war, the word 'Arabe' has often carried pejorative connotations in French ears. Public opinion polls have indeed consistently shown Arabs, especially Algerians, to be the least liked foreigners in France.[27] Few Frenchmen are aware that many North African immigrants – Kettane's family is a case in point – are not Arabs at all, but Berbers; all are seen simply as Arabs. By inventing an alternative form of self-designation, young members of the immigrant community were able to expunge from their own discourse the stigma attaching to the term 'Arabe'. Initially confined to usage among youths in the Paris conurbation, the word Beur was picked up slowly by the press in 1982, and gained national currency the following year through media coverage of what became known as 'la Marche des Beurs'. This march took place across the length of France during the closing months of 1983 in response to a dramatic worsening in the political climate that year. The Socialists' sympathetic approach to the immigrant community had given their opponents the opportunity to play on xenophobic sentiments in the campaign for the local elections held in March 1983. Those elections brought the first successes of Jean-Marie Le Pen's extreme right-wing Front National. Le Pen was to succeed in holding immigration at the forefront of political debate throughout the rest of the decade. Media coverage of this debate stimulated widespread interest in the whole issue of immigration, and Beur writers in search of publishers undoubtedly benefited from this.

The 1983 march was the first national demonstration by younger

26. Nacer Kettane, *Droit de réponse à la démocratie française*, Paris, La Découverte, 1986, p. 21. The word 'Maghreb', which is of Arabic origin, is now widely used in France to denote the former colonial territories of North Africa. A number of commentators have suggested that rather than being a piece of verlan, 'Beur' may be a contraction of 'Berbères d'Europe': see, for example, Jean Déjeux, 'Romanciers de l'immigration maghrébine en France', *Francofonia*, vol. 5, no. 8, Spring 1985, p. 103 n. 44; Hédi Bouraoui, 'A New Trend in Maghrebian Culture: the Beurs and their Generation', *Maghreb Review*, vol. 13, nos 3–4, 1988, p. 219. There is, however, no evidence to support this view from within the immigrant community itself. It is true that Kettane, like most of the other founding members of Radio Beur, is of Berber origin, but all agree that the self-designation 'Beur' is a verlanesque adaptation of 'Arabe'.

27. See, for example, 'Attitudes des Français à l'égard de l'immigration étrangère: nouvelle enquête d'opinion', *Population*, vol. 29, no. 6, Nov.–Dec. 1974, esp. pp. 1032–3; 'Les Français et le racisme', *Le Point*, 29 Apr. 1985, p. 47.

members of the immigrant community. Its official title was 'la Marche pour l'égalité et contre le racisme', but reporters quickly dubbed it 'la Marche des Beurs'. As the march was originally conceived by young activists in Lyons and had its starting point in Marseilles, there was some indignation among those involved at seeing their efforts subsumed under a label which was not of their making. One of the leading spokesmen for the march was Bouzid, who joined the demonstration when it passed near his home in Aix-en-Provence. In his account of the march, he specifically rejects the word Beur as a Parisian invention.[28] Its popularisation by the mass media was to induce a similar unease among a considerable number of those to whom it was applied elsewhere in France. Were they once again being manipulated by the hegemonic forces which had traditionally spurned or marginalised the North African immigrant community? Speaking to me in Dijon, Boukhedenna remarked:

> On nous a dit que ce sont les jeunes issus de l'immigration eux-mêmes qui ont choisi ce mot. Mais on nous a tellement fait comprendre qu'on est des gens à l'envers qu'on a fini par comprendre ce que les gens veulent de nous. On peut mettre les choses à l'endroit en disant: 'Laissez-moi être Arabe.' Moi, si je dis le mot 'Beur', c'est comme si on reconnaît qu'on est encore colonisé.[29]

The spirit of autonomy and indeed subversion which was originally attached to the word Beur precisely because it lay beyond the comprehension of most Frenchmen has inevitably been largely neutralised by its popularisation. While aware of the understandable misgivings felt by some of those concerned, I have nevertheless adopted the word here for several reasons. Firstly, it is now in general circulation (with entries in both the *Petit Larousse* and the *Petit Robert* to prove it), and it is widely understood in a relatively value-free sense. Secondly, no concise alternative exists; used continuously, 'youths of North African immigrant origin' and similar periphrases are apt to become wearisome to the reader. Thirdly, in spite of the misgivings felt in some quarters, it remains true that the word was originally adopted and is still used as a mode of self-designation by significant numbers among the younger generation of the immigrant community.

28. Bouzid, *La Marche*, Paris, Sindbad, 1984, p. 14.
29. Interview with Sakinna Boukhedenna, 21 Apr. 1988.

While the word Beur has its origins in popular street-culture, the springboard which has enabled young men and women of immigrant origin to enter the more elite sphere of the printed word has been the French educational system. In general, the Beurs suffer from high failure rates at school. Their low levels of educational achievement are very similar to those of children from French working-class backgrounds.[30] This is hardly surprising, considering that the Beurs come from similarly disadvantaged backgrounds, with the added handicap of parents who are generally unable to read or write and who understand little of what goes on in a French school. All this, combined with racial prejudice among some employers, puts the Beurs in a very weak position in the job market.

Almost by definition, those who have produced literary works capable of attracting commercial publishers tend to have surmounted these obstacles more successfully than others. Roughly half our corpus of writers have had some form of higher education, a far higher proportion than among the Beurs in general. However, in several cases this has taken the form of part-time study only. Moreover, relatively few have progressed as far as degree level. Belghoul and Lallaoui have each completed a maîtrise in economics. Kettane is a qualified doctor, while Begag's doctoral thesis on the immigrant community in Lyons was the stepping stone to a career as a researcher with the prestigious Centre National de la Recherche Scientifique. The educational qualifications and career profiles of most other Beur writers remain comparatively modest. Boukhedenna progressed only as far as the CAP, one of the lowest certificates awarded in French secondary schools, and works as a cleaning lady. Raïth reached the slightly more advanced BEPC, but never had a serious job of any description before landing his twelve-year prison sentence. Houari and Imache have done various kinds of social work, while Tamza and Yacine are male nurses (the latter specialising in psychiatric care). Lallaoui is a schoolteacher. Touabti worked for many years as a welder. Since starting to write he has tried to support himself by a variety of odd jobs, but life has been tough for him as it has been for most of those who have dropped out of full-time employment in order to spend more time

30. Pierre Mondon, 'Effectifs et scolarité des enfants d'immigrés', *Cahiers de l'Education Nationale*, June 1984, pp. 7–10. For a wider discussion of the educational experience of the Beurs, see Abdel Aissou, *Les Beurs, l'école et la France*, Paris, CIEMI/L'Harmattan, 1987; Serge Boulot and Danielle Boyzon-Fradet, *Les Immigrés et l'école: une course d'obstacles*, Paris, CIEMI/L'Harmattan, 1988.

writing. Belghoul gets by thanks to temporary secretarial jobs.

Very few Beur writers have succeeded in making full-time careers out of their creative talents. Tadjer has become a scriptwriter for French television, while Zemouri is a journalist with *Algérie-Actualité*. The biggest success story is undoubtedly that of Charef. For more than ten years he worked on a lathe sharpening tools in a Paris factory. Then he had an extraordinary series of lucky breaks. Ever since being a child, Charef had dreamed of making films. In his spare time he wrote several screenplays, but he had no contacts in the film world and those to whom he sent his scripts showed no interest in them until the writer Georges Conchon replied that if Charef turned one of the screenplays into a novel he would try to get it published by Mercure de France. Conchon was as good as his word, and in February 1983 *Le Thé au harem d'Archi Ahmed* appeared on the bookstalls. By this time, media interest in matters relating to immigration was becoming intense, and the publicity machine of Mercure de France, one of the most prestigious publishers in modern French literature, was ideally placed to capitalise on this. *Le Thé au harem d'Archi Ahmed* was quickly reviewed – often with great enthusiasm – by leading writers and critics in all the main French dailies and news magazines.[31]

A number of radio and television appearances were also secured for Charef. Much the most important of these was his appearance on Bernard Pivot's 'Apostrophes', the most popular literary programme on French television. Mercure de France placed advertisements in all the main national newspapers on the morning of April 1, to ensure the largest possible audience for Charef that evening. The modesty and sincerity which he displayed in response to Pivot's questions won him many friends. Thereafter, media coverage mushroomed. Charef's next stroke of luck came shortly afterwards when the film-makers Costa-Gavras and Michèle Ray began looking for suitable material on which to base a film about immigration. When Ray began her research, almost the first press cutting she came across was an enthusiastic review of *Le Thé au harem d'Archi Ahmed* by the respected pied-noir author Jules Roy. She and Costa-Gavras read the novel and immediately invited Charef to adapt it for the screen. Initially, Charef was engaged

---

31. See, for example, Louis Gardel, 'Mehdi Charef: délinquance bronzée', *Le Quotidien de Paris*, 22 Feb. 1983; Georges Conchon, 'A bon tourneur salut!', *Le Matin*, 23 Feb. 1983; François Nourissier, 'Mehdi Charef: cinéma-vérité', *Le Figaro Magazine*, 5 Mar. 1983, p. 18; Jules Roy, 'Ahmed sortit à cinq heures', *Le Nouvel Observateur*, 22 Apr. 1983, pp. 88–9.

simply to write the screenplay: the intention was that Costa-Gavras would direct and Ray would produce the film. But they found Charef had such clear ideas about how the film should look (hardly surprising, perhaps, bearing in mind that the novel had originally been conceived as a film-script) that they offered him the position of director. Charef took a couple of weeks to think over the offer, for it meant leaving his secure if unfulfilling factory job. He accepted, went on to make a highly successful first film, and now makes a full-time living as film-maker.

Odd quirks of chance have inevitably played a role in the publishing fortunes of more than one Beur writer. Touabti must have thought himself lucky to get into print in 1981, especially after *L'Amour quand même* had been turned down by no less than 13 publishers.[32] Yet in a sense, the break came too early, for there was at this time little public interest in the Beur generation (the word itself had yet to enter general circulation), and Touabti's publisher, Belfond, seems to have done little to promote his novel. Kalouaz might have beaten Touabti into print, had it not been for a last-minute disagreement over the title of his first novel, 'Le pluriel d'espoir n'est-ce pas désespoir . . .', which was to have been brought out by a small publisher in Grenoble; it remains unpublished to this day. Five years passed before Kalouaz made his commercial debut with a completely different narrative entitled *L'Encre d'un fait divers*. A disappointment suffered in 1983 turned out to be a blessing in disguise for Begag. That year he entered the first draft of *Le Gone du Chaâba* in a competition for youths from immigrant backgrounds run by a small publisher in Lyons, which promised to publish the winning manuscript. The company went out of business before a winner could be picked. Undeterred, the young author decided to try his luck with a mainstream publisher in Paris. A friend put him in touch with a contact at Seuil, who eventually published a much revised version of the manuscript. Thus, instead of slipping into print in an obscure provincial backwater, Begag sailed straight out onto the high seas under the flag of one of the nation's most prestigious publishing houses.

With the exception of *Le Thé au harem d'Archi Ahmed*, no other Beur narrative has aroused as much attention as *Le Gone du Chaâba*, which came out in 1986. Within two years of its publication, Charef's novel had chalked up sales of 25,000,[33] a healthy figure for

32. Salim Jay, 'Hocine Touabti: *L'Amour quand même*', *L'Afrique littéraire*, no. 70, Oct. 1983, p. 90.
33. Thierry Leclere, 'Mehdi Charef: Contre-plongée dans l'univers des HLM', *Murs, murs*, Mar. 1985, p. 38.

a first work. Some 15,000 copies of *Le Gone du Chaâba* were sold in just six months,[34] and sales were given a further boost in 1988 by national media coverage of a row over the decision by a schoolteacher in Lyons to use Begag's novel with her pupils.[35] The parents of some of the children, egged on by Front National supporters, complained that *Le Gone du Chaâba* was pornographic, and therefore totally unsuitable reading for adolescents. The complaints were based on a couple of pages in the novel describing the naïve efforts of the pre-adolescent protagonist to mime the sexual act.[36] Far from being pornographic, the offending pages are a humorous celebration of sexual innocence. The controversy did, however, confirm the old adage that there is no such thing as bad publicity. Pleased with the rise in sales (which totalled more than 30,000 by the end of 1988),[37] Seuil converted their initially vague interest in publishing a sequel by Begag into a firm commitment. This second narrative, *Béni ou le Paradis Privé*, was rushed out at the beginning of 1989, with an appearance by the author on 'Apostrophes' as the centrepiece of the launch campaign.

Four more volumes of imaginative prose by Beur writers were to appear before the year was out, carrying the total since 1981 to well over twenty. While there can be no guarantee that publishers will maintain their present level of interest, the pace of literary composition shows no sign of slackening. Touabti and Charef, the first to be commercially published, are, with the single exception of Zemouri, the oldest Beur writers. As those who have followed them into print were also born during the relatively early stages of family immigration from North Africa, there is no reason to expect a fall-off in the literary output of this still growing generation.

34. Michel Cressole, 'Le Gone de Chaâba réédite ses exploits', *Lyon-Libération*, 25–6 Oct. 1986.
35. See, for example, Pascale Robert-Diard, 'Azouz contre Racine', *Le Monde*, 25 Feb. 1988; 'Le Livre du scandale', *Lyon-Matin*, 8 Mar. 1988; Daniel Licht, 'Les Parents d'élèves chassent la prof, à cause d'un roman beur', *Libération*, 9 Mar. 1988; 'La Prof enseignait le porno', *Minute*, 16 Mar. 1988, pp. 8–9.
36. Azouz Begag, *Le Gone du Chaâba*, Paris, Seuil, 1986, pp. 120–1.
37. Information given to me by the author on 22 Nov. 1988.

–2–

Autobiography and Fiction

2.1 Names and Titles

Traditionally, the main constituents of a novel are summarised or in some way announced in its title.[1] In many of the best-known novels in the Western canon, the protagonist's name serves as the title of the narrative. Familiar examples include *Le Père Goriot, Madame Bovary, David Copperfield, Anna Karenina,* etc. Although most narratives by Beur authors focus on a single main character, in only a handful of cases is s/he named in the title of the work. A proper name is generally thought of as a mark of individuality, but as most names are selected from within a repertoire which is specific to a particular language or culture, they also serve to situate their referents within such a culture. This helps to explain why Beur writers have been reluctant to name their protagonists in the titles of their works. By placing a culturally-specific name on the title page, the author would run the risk of inducing in the reader premature or simplistic ideas which would run entirely counter to the central thrust of Beur fiction, where the main emphasis is on the protagonist's uncertain sense of identity.

In Azouz Begag's second novel, *Béni ou le Paradis Privé,* the narrator-protagonist hates his real name:

> Je déteste qu'on m'appelle Ben Abdallah, même si c'est le nom de mon ancêtre mort du typhus à Sétif au début du siècle. Je préfère encore tous les petits noms que Nordine a conçus pour me faire plaisir: Big Ben, gros sac, gros porc, gros tas de merde, gras-double. Mais j'aime surtout quand on m'appelle Béni, parce que là, on voit pas que je suis arabe. Pas comme Ben Abdallah que je suis obligé de porter comme une djellaba toute la journée en classe.[2]

---

1. The issues involved here are discussed at length by Serge Bokobza, *Contribution à la titrologie romanesque: variations sur le titre 'Le Rouge et le Noir',* Geneva, Droz, 1986, and by Gérard Genette, *Seuils,* Paris, Seuil, 1987, pp. 54–97.
2. Azouz Begag, *Béni ou le Paradis Privé,* Paris, Seuil, 1989, p. 40.

Just as a djellaba, a hooded smock of North African design which covers the wearer from head to toe, functions as an all-embracing visual sign of foreignness in French eyes, so the protagonist feels that the name given to him by his parents reduces him to an ethnic stereotype at odds with his own sense of selfhood. The nick-names invented by his brother Nordine, even though many of them appear insulting, offer release from that trap. The polyphonic qualities of Béni make it the protagonist's preferred name: 'Béni c'est moi, "mon fils" dans la langue du Prophète, béni dans celle du Christ, anagramme de bien dans celle du Petit Robert.'[3] Through the inventiveness seen at work in word-play of this kind, Béni's adopted name enables him to straddle two different worlds: that of France, with its Christian heritage and modern secular culture, and the Islamic traditions of his parents. A fanciful engagement with a third cultural field, that of the English-speaking world, is alluded to in the nickname Big Ben. The protagonist plays upon this Anglo-Saxon dimension and adds a further element of ambiguity when a French girl to whom he is attracted asks him where the name Béni comes from. To maximise his chances of impressing her he replies: 'De partout. Mon père est africain et ma mère anglaise!'[4] In French, the term 'africain' is generally applied to Black Africans alone; North Africans are more commonly referred to as 'Maghrébins'. By surrounding his name with (Black) African and English accretions, Béni effectively conceals the whole of his family background from the girl.

The protagonist's real name is spelt out in the title of only two Beur novels. In each case it is qualified in such a way as radically to undercut the stabilising function normally associated with proper names. In the title of Leïla Houari's *Zeida de nulle part*, instead of the protagonist's first name being anchored to a patronymic it is suspended almost literally in mid-air, surrounding the eponymous heroine with a sense of mystery. Nacer Kettane, the author of *Le Sourire de Brahim*, may appear at first sight to present the reader with a more reassuring title, but Brahim's smile is in fact used explicitly throughout the novel to symbolise an essential but concealed part of the protagonist's identity.[5]

Two Beur novels display entirely false names in their titles. Readers who open Mehdi Charef's *Le Thé au harem d'Archi Ahmed* in the expectation of some exotic divertissement are in for a rude

3. Ibid., p. 35.
4. Ibid., p. 44.
5. Nacer Kettane, *Le Sourire de Brahim*, Paris, Denoël, 1985, pp. 19, 23, 44, 68, 81, 120, 147, 156, 178.

shock. There is no harem and no Ahmed, for the title is simply a malapropism for 'le théorème d'Archimède' ('Archimedes' Principle') coined by a teenager of North African origin amid the boredom of a maths lesson in a suburban Paris schoolroom.[6] In *Georgette!*, the apparently simple title chosen by Farida Belghoul couples a false name with a sardonic exclamation mark. Georgette is a name which the young protagonist imagines being thrown at her dismissively by her Muslim father as a mark of estrangement from her family roots.[7] We never learn the girl's true name, i.e. the one given to her by her Muslim parents, and this omission is emblematic of the way in which her constantly shifting sense of identity slips for ever through the reader's fingers.

The names of the protagonists are displayed in the titles of two volumes of short stories by Arriz Tamza, *Lune et Orian* and *Zaïd le mendiant*. These characters are, however, mythical figures of the type encountered in *A Thousand and One Nights*, and as such they are very untypical of Beur writing. In *Ombres*, the contemporary setting of which is much more in line with the bulk of Beur fiction, Tamza leaves most of the main characters nameless, and the shadowy way in which they are represented in the text is clearly alluded to in the title of the novel. Akli Tadjer builds a similar elusiveness into the title of *Les ANI du 'Tassili'*. Some readers may know that 'Tassili' is the name of a mountain in southern Algeria. Many will be unaware before opening the novel that it is also the name of a car-ferry which plies between Algeria and France. None will know the meaning of 'ANI', for this is a mock acronym invented specifically for the novel. The letters stand for 'Arabe Non Identifié',[8] a playful adaptation of OVNI ('Objet Volant Non Identifié'), the French for UFO ('Unidentified Flying Object'). By incorporating this acronym, the title directly reflects the uncertain sense of personal identity felt by Beurs such as the protagonist, Omar, in their constant movement between the cultures of France and North Africa.

The protagonists are alluded to in the titles of several other Beur novels but are not explicitly named, as, for example, in Mehdi Lallahoui's *Les Beurs de Seine*, which features a trio of main characters. The title of Tassadit Imache's *Une Fille sans histoire* has an

6. Mehdi Charef, *Le Thé au harem d'Archi Ahmed*, Paris, Mercure de France, 1983, p. 99.
7. Farida Belghoul, *Georgette!*, Paris, Barrault, 1986, p. 148. In an interview on 26 Sept. 1988, the author told me she had deliberately chosen the name Georgette as the most alien she could think of in Arab ears.
8. Akli Tadjer, *Les ANI du 'Tassili'*, Paris, Seuil, 1984, pp. 23–7.

ostentatiously anonymous ring. In his second novel, *Le Harki de Meriem*, Mehdi Charef explores the experiences of a range of characters, all of whom are related to the harki Azzedine by family ties or military comradeship. Yet instead of highlighting Azzedine in the title of the novel, Charef casts him as the nameless appendage of his wife Meriem. Similarly, in the working title of Farida Belghoul's unpublished second novel, 'La Passion de Rémi', the unnamed young woman at the centre of the story is almost entirely displaced by her lover, Rémi.

The title of Azouz Begag's first novel, *Le Gone du Chaâba*, describes but does not name the hero, and is likely to appear somewhat enigmatic to most readers. Those outside Lyons may well be unaware that 'gone' is a local slang-word for 'enfant'.[9] Readers will find this explanation in a glossary at the back of the book, but there is no comparable entry for 'Chaâba'. Although we learn in the opening pages of the novel that this is the name of the bidonville where the protagonist, Azouz, lives in a suburb of Lyons, no etymology of the term is given. It certainly sounds Arabic, and has apparently been given to the bidonville by its Algerian inhabitants, but in the absence of a translation the word remains in some degree impenetrable to the average French reader.[10] This mixture of French and Arabic in the title situates Azouz at one and the same time in relation to his disadvantaged material circumstances (he is a shantytown kid) and at the junction of rival cultural systems between which the novel shows him to be torn. By alluding to the protagonist through this combination of terms, instead of naming him directly, the author builds into the very title of the novel the personal tensions and uncertainties which are fundamental to the text.

Although the title of Kamal Zemouri's *Le Jardin de l'intrus* contains no foreign or slang words, it in some ways parallels *Le Gone du Chaâba*. In each case the protagonist is referred to by a common

9. Many reviewers consequently felt obliged to begin their notices by explaining the meaning of the word 'gone' for the benefit of readers outside Lyons. See, for example, the reviews in *La Bretagne à Paris*, 31 Jan. 1986, p. 7, and in *La Vie nouvelle* (Chambéry), 18 Apr. 1986, p. 12.

10. In a part of the manuscript deleted from the published text of the novel, 'Chaâba' is described as a word 'qui peut provenir du mot "peuple" en arabe mais auquel on avait collé l'image de "bout du monde"'. In the Arabic dialect spoken in Algeria, 'Chaâbi' means 'people', i.e. ordinary folk; it is possible that the spelling adopted by Begag reflects the Sétif accent of his parents and of most of the other inhabitants of the shantytown. In contemporary Algerian slang, 'Chaâba' is also used to denote the idea of untidiness; the ramshackle nature of the shantytown would fit with this.

noun ('intrus' and 'gone' respectively) rather than by his proper name, and he is situated in relation to a designated but somewhat mysterious place. There is no garden in *Le Jardin de l'intrus*; indeed the words used in the title never appear in the text. The reader is obliged to piece together the meaning of the title from the various experiences which the protagonist, Lamine, undergoes in the course of the novel.[11]

Uncertainty is built into the title of two other works by the use of personal pronouns. Who is being apostrophised in the title of Leïla Houari's *Quand tu verras la mer . . .*? The reader (who may initially wonder whether s/he is implicated) must wait until the penultimate of the five stories assembled in the book before learning who is designated by the 'tu' in the title.[12] Who is the referent of the demonstrative pronoun in Ahmed Kalouaz's collection of short stories, *Celui qui regarde le soleil en face . . .*? The story which gives its name to the collection quotes a saying, explicitly described as mysterious in character, according to which 'celui qui regarde le soleil en face devient aveugle'.[13] This has the ring of a proverb, and when the demonstrative pronoun is used in sayings of this kind it designates a class of persons rather than a particular individual. Yet we cannot help feeling that there is a specific connection between this saying and the male protagonist, who is fatally injured after a police chase on the main highway from Paris to Marseilles. As we are reminded in the final sentence of the tale, that highway is popularly known as 'l'autoroute du soleil'.[14] The story has to do essentially with mistaken identities. The protagonist, a perfectly law-abiding citizen, has been wrongly taken for a kidnapper by the police. It appears that a pretty young hitch-hiker to whom he has

11. When I interviewed Zemouri on 1 Oct. 1988, he told me that the title reflected his divided sense of belonging. As a child in France the author, like his fictional counterpart in *Le Jardin de l'intrus*, had been basically happy in his immediate home environment, but had felt less at ease when he had wandered further afield: 'Quand je dis "jardin" je fais référence un peu à *Candide*, au jardin de Candide. Finalement, sa vie, son petit paradis, c'est le jardin qu'on se cultive soi-même, on a des fleurs, on est chez soi, on est heureux. Mais on était quand même des intrus. Je n'étais pas chez moi, je le sentais. Quand j'étais à l'école, les maîtres étaient très gentils et tout ça, mais j'apprenais des choses qui n'avaient rien à voir avec ma culture. Je sentais que j'étais moins concerné par ces choses-là que les autres, que j'avais une autre culture, un autre pays, le pays de mes racines.'
12. Leïla Houari, *Quand tu verras la mer*, Paris, L'Harmattan, 1988, p. 83.
13. Ahmed Kalouaz, *Celui qui regarde le soleil en face. . . .* Algiers, Laphomic, 1987, p. 52. In an interview on 13 June 1988, Kalouaz told me he believed this saying to be of Arabic origin.
14. Ibid., p. 54.

given a lift has telephoned the police for kicks, claiming that she has been abducted. Because she is the daughter of a wealthy newspaper magnate, the police take the young woman at her word, and as she dies in the ensuing car chase it seems unlikely that her misrepresentation of the unfortunate driver can ever be corrected. An earlier version of the story gives the man's name as Ken, but this is omitted from the text as published in book form.[15] The absence of a proper name helps to reinforce the message that his true identity and purpose in driving south (he was in fact in the process of deserting his lover) will never be known to the millions of television viewers who hear the news broadcast quoted at the end of the story.

In *Le Pacte autobiographique*, Philippe Lejeune defines autobiography essentially as that class of retrospective narratives in which the author, narrator and protagonist all share the same name, and consequently the same identity.[16] If we accept this definition, very few, if any, Beur narratives rank as autobiographies. Only in Begag's *Le Gone du Chaâba*, Sakinna Boukhedenna's *Journal. 'Nationalité: immigré(e)'*, Mustapha Raïth's *Palpitations intra-muros*, and Bouzid's *La Marche* do the author, narrator and protagonist have in common the same name. Even these cases, however, do not necessarily fall within Lejeune's categorisation. Bouzid's narrative focuses in the main on his recent experiences during the Marche des Beurs, rather than on a retrospective account of his whole life. As the title of Boukhedenna's narrative implies, it often reads like a diary, written contemporaneously with events, rather than from the retrospective vantage point which, in Lejeune's definition, is characteristic of autobiography. Moreover, although the author shares her first name, Sakinna, with the narrator-protagonist, the family name of the latter is not explicitly given, and it is technically possible that this may be other than Boukhedenna. Even if we disregard the question of when the text is narrated, it ought strictly, by Lejeune's criteria, to be classed as a 'roman autobiographique'. This would place it alongside works such as *A la recherche du temps perdu*, where although the author and narrator share the same first name and many other features, they are nevertheless seen as distinct from each other. *Palpitations intra-muros* also falls outside the strict letter of Lejeune's criteria for, as we shall see presently, the title page of this novel contains not one

---

15. Compare ibid., pp. 51–2, with Ahmed Kalouaz, 'Celui qui regarde le soleil en face devient aveugle', *Plurielle*, nos 5–6, July–Dec. 1987, p. 29.
16. Philippe Lejeune, *Le Pacte autobiographique*, Paris, Seuil, 1975, pp. 14–15.

but two names in the space normally occupied by the author. Among Beur narratives, *Le Gone du Chaâba* alone meets all Lejeune's criteria. The story is recounted retrospectively, and the narrator, protagonist and author all share the same full name, Azouz Begag. Yet the title page of *Le Gone du Chaâba* describes it as a novel!

Most, though not all, Beur narratives may be loosely described as autobiographical novels, for there is a strong but never complete resemblance between the stories represented in them and events experienced in real life by their authors. Lejeune evinces no interest in resemblances of this kind. In his analyses, autobiographical novels (which are defined as such by their relationship with the world outside the text) are passed over in favour of 'pure' autobiographies, where Lejeune argues that extra-textual realities may be ignored thanks to the identity of author, narrator and protagonist.[17] The guarantee of that identity is the name which they all share within the text, assuming that we include within this the title page and/or cover bearing the author's name.

Yet when, in *Le Pacte autobiographique*, Lejeune invokes that name as a guarantee of the identity shared by three different personae, he confines the word 'identité' to a purely technical sense which sidesteps most of the substantive issues at stake. It is true that the name of all three personae is the same ('identical'), but in what sense, if any, does this guarantee their sameness as people? In a more recent work, Lejeune has acknowledged the complexities of this problem much more fully. Personal identity is not a fixed entity, but at best 'une *relation constante* entre l'un et le multiple',[18] a way of conceiving many different and sometimes contradictory experiences and feelings as somehow part and parcel of one and the same person. Proper names certainly act as emblems of unified personal identity, but the guarantees they offer are far from total, as Lejeune recognises in the following observations on narrator-protagonists who designate themselves in the first person:

Le nom est le garant de l'unité de notre multiplicité: il fédère notre complexité dans l'instant et notre changement dans le temps. Le sujet de l'énonciation et celui de l'énoncé sont bien 'le même', puisqu'ils portent le même nom! Nous voilà substantivés, unifiés. Le vertige ne reprendrait que si nous réalisions que nous ne sommes peut-être que . . . notre propre homonyme, ou que si nous prenions conscience de 'l'arbitraire'

17. Ibid., pp. 25, 35–41.
18. Philippe Lejeune, *Je est un autre*, Paris, Seuil, 1980, p. 35; Lejeune's emphasis.

du nom (qui ne se définirait alors que par l'intersection des énoncés où il figure) . . .[19]

The issues raised here by Lejeune render highly problematic the idea of some neatly defined personal identity corresponding to a particular proper name. Lejeune's differentiation between 'l'énonciation' and 'l'énoncé' corresponds to Genette's distinction between narration and diegesis.[20] In a retrospective autobiographical narrative there is often a pronounced distinction between the narrating 'I' and the diegetic 'I', despite the fact that they share the same name and are jointly designated in the first person. From his later vantage point in time, the narrator may ridicule or find incomprehensible earlier parts of his life. He may forget or repress certain experiences altogether. It would clearly be foolish to regard the narrating 'I' as literally identical to (i.e. the same as) the diegetic 'I', beyond the purely technical sense in which they both share the same name.

Raïth shows an acute awareness of these problems in *Palpitations intra-muros*. The text is narrated by a prisoner whose fundamental concern is to come to terms with and in some sense transcend the rape for which he was given his jail sentence. He seeks to understand and accept responsibility for an act which now horrifies him; while acknowledging it as part of his past, he wishes to be and in some sense already is a different person. This cohabitation of two different people in one is conveyed by varying both the names and the grammatical persons used in designating himself.

Ordinarily, a narrator who is also the protagonist speaks of himself in the first person. However, in most of *Palpitations intra-muros*, including the whole of Part I (which represents the events leading up to and including the rape), the narrator refers to himself in the third person. Later in the text the first person comes to the fore, as the main focus shifts to the narrator-protagonist's predicament in prison, which he clearly finds less difficult to acknowledge than his past wrong-doings. That both grammatical persons ultimately designate the same human being is made clear from the outset in the following prefatory note:

Un jour, Mustapha entra dans la cellule et fixa longuement son double dans le miroir. Alors tout s'assombrit autour de lui, un tourbillon

19. Ibid., p. 35.
20. On the distinction between narration and diegesis, cf. Introduction.

violent l'emporta loin, loin vers les coteaux de son enf...ice et de sa vie de zonard.

Il se mit doucement à raconter son histoire comme si l'autre n'existait plus que dans la fiction. Parce qu'il faut, disait-il, tuer ton passé, mourir symboliquement pour renaître, perdre ta propre importance pour être.

Voilà pourquoi cet ouvrage, rédigé avec toute la maladresse d'un niveau BEPC, est avant tout destiné à ces milliers d'enfants d'immigrés nés en France qui, un jour ou l'autre, se retrouvent en prison, victimes de la mal-vie.

Amour, sexe; drogue, violence: comment démêler l'écheveau de l'identité lorsque la bobine de la morale est hors série?

C'est la prise de conscience physique, avec les tripes, de ce déracinement fatalement irrémédiable qui entraîne une lutte sans merci et délirante contre l'inattaquable réalité du 'syndrome d'abandon'.

Tout dans ce livre a de l'importance même si fréquemment le sens des commentaires perd sa direction dans le délire. Les éclaboussures, pour ceux qui ne font pas de fixation sur les 'mal-dits', sont celles d'un Algérien qui, à une phase déterminante de son adolescence, a perdu le contrôle de sa bicyclette mentale. Il le retrouvera en prison où, au prix de douze ans de réclusion criminelle, il paie les dégâts causés sur sa route.

C'est donc de ce monde carcéral que, dans l'attente de la cassation du procès, j'envoie mon bip-bip de détresse . . .

Mouss[21]

If we equate the 'je' of the final paragraph with Mouss, he may, as the narrator, appear to be distinct from Mustapha, who is designated in the third person. Yet it is made clear in the opening paragraphs that the narrator of the story we are about to read, Mustapha, is in an identical situation to that of Mouss, i.e. one of imprisonment. It is equally clear that Mustapha feels simultaneously compelled to face and efface the story he is going to tell – that of his own self. These contradictory impulses of self-disclosure and self-effacement make it sensible for the reader to conclude that Mouss and Mustapha, 'je' and 'il', are different representations of one and the same individual.

These different personae are in fact fused momentarily at the end of the second paragraph. This junction is effected through the combined use of the second person and the 'style indirect libre'. Intimate conversations with oneself are commonly conducted in the 'tu' form. Imaginary conversations of this kind often take place

21. Mustapha Raïth, *Palpitations intra-muros*, Paris, L'Harmattan, 1986, pp. 7–8.

when the speaker is divided in his or her own mind on some question. This is clearly the case where Mustapha is concerned. 'Il' would ordinarily designate someone entirely separate from the speaker, but in the extract quoted above, the distinctions between the first, second and third persons become blurred by the use of the 'style indirect libre'. Mustapha's inner monologue is presented neither in direct speech (there are no quotation marks) nor in the form of reported discourse (which would have required changes of grammatical persons and of tenses). In reported speech the words originally used are subordinated to a discursive framework imposed by the narrator, while in direct speech the narrator is temporarily supplanted by the speaker of the words which appear in quotation marks. In free indirect speech, these neat grammatical divisions are eroded, and the demarcation lines between the different personae become blurred.[22] Thus in the sentence with which we are concerned, the designation of one and the same referent by 'il' and 'tu' blurs the distinction between the two different speakers, Mouss and Mustapha. Although the first person does not appear explicitly here, each speaker implicitly occupies this role: Mouss is the implicit 'je' who designates Mustapha as 'il', while Mustapha is the implicit 'je' who addresses another part of himself as 'tu'. Except when direct speech is being quoted, normal grammar precludes the possibility of the first person singular denoting two different people within the same sentence. By removing the grammatical markers which would ordinarily distinguish them, this sentence all but merges Mouss and Mustapha into one.

In the main body of the text, the protagonist is generally called Mouss, but we are told that this is a diminutive of Mustapha.[23] The fact that Mouss and Mustapha are one and the same person is confirmed unequivocally in the closing stages of the novel, where we read: 'Quand Mustapha eut fini de raconter l'histoire de son double, il rentra dans la peau de Mouss.'[24] In a notebook, the imprisoned narrator-protagonist writes:

Dans l'ailleurs et en cage, Mouss et Mustapha ne font qu'un: Moi.
Ensemble nous avons raconté,
Ensemble rédigé ces mots.
Il fallait que je raconte Mouss,

22. For a fuller discussion, see Brian McHale, 'Free Indirect Discourse: A Survey of Recent Accounts', *PTL*, vol. 3, 1978, pp. 249–87.
23. Raïth, *Palpitations*, p. 58.
24. Ibid., p. 222.

Pour mourir dans le passé,
Re-naître dans le présent,
Espérer dans le futur.[25]

Mustapha and Mouss are identified not only as the narrator and protagonist of the text, but also as its author. Unusually, both names appear on the title page, which is headed:

Mustapha Raïth

'Mouss'

Palpitations intra-muros

That this is the same Mustapha/Mouss as the narrator-protagonist is clear from a reference to his family-name, Raïth, early in the text.[26] It is not difficult to show that the book is autobiographical in a factual sense, for having visited Raïth in prison and seen official documents, I know from external sources that he was sent there in exactly the circumstances described in the narrative. It is also autobiographical in the narrower, technical sense that we find identical names designating the protagonist, narrator and author. But far from these names encapsulating his identity, they are in fact a mark of its instability. The very fact that two different names feature on the title page (instead of a single one, as in Lejeune's model) reflects the impossibility of reducing the life-experiences of the author-narrator-protagonist to an unequivocally unified whole.

The identity of Mustapha/Mouss is, we are told in the prefatory note quoted above, a tangled web which defies understanding. The author clearly attributes these complexities to his immigrant background. His faults are those of 'un Algérien qui, à une phase déterminante de son adolescence, a perdu le contrôle de sa bicyclette mentale', and his account of them is 'avant tout destiné à ces milliers d'enfants d'immigrés nés en France qui, un jour ou l'autre, se retrouvent en prison, victimes de la mal-vie'. The implication is that the bi-cultural condition of youths from immigrant backgrounds constitutes a potentially explosive threat to their mental stability. For Mustapha/Mouss, as he reflects on all this in prison, the death of the past, the newness of the present and the

25. Ibid., p. 222.
26. Ibid., p. 63.

uncertain hopes of the future make for a highly problematic continuum; yet without such a continuum, there can be no authentic sense of self.

Autobiographical though it is, Raïth's narrative appears to its writer like a work of fiction, the story of someone other than himself, for the imprisoned narrator feels in many ways distant from and puzzled by his past. Even when this feeling of alienation is absent, there is always an element of fantasy involved in the reconstruction of the past. Lejeune recognises this when he writes of 'les erreurs, les déformations, les interprétations consubstantielles à l'élaboration du mythe personnel dans toute autobiographie'.[27] Omissions, inventions and transpositions in the recreation of his or her past are an inevitable consequence of the author's sense of self at the time of writing. Many distortions of this kind can be recognised as such only by comparing the text with external sources of information. Lejeune clearly believes these distortions are significant, but as he claims to have no interest in the world beyond the text it is difficult to see how he can detect or measure them. While few if any Beur narratives rank as autobiographies in the narrow sense, most display close but never complete similarities with the life experiences of their authors. By making comparisons of the kind that Lejeune eschews, it is not my intention to 'reduce' these texts to their biographical origins. On the contrary, it is precisely in the gap between raw experience and the finished text that the creative process operates, and it follows that the achievements of Beur writers cannot be fully appreciated without some consideration of that divide.

More often than not, the works of Beur authors converge thematically in a shared preoccupation with the conflicts between rival cultural systems, and in particular with the difficult choices faced by those who stand astride such cultures. It is not difficult to see that if these writers have made tensions of this kind their central theme, this is because of the great importance which such conflicts have had in their own lives. As we shall see in the remainder of this chapter, however, there is no one-to-one relationship between the life experiences of Beur authors and the diegetic fabric of their works. Each has selected autobiographical elements in his or her own particular way, combining them with materials borrowed from elsewhere or of a wholly invented nature.

27. Lejeune, *Le Pacte*, p. 40.

2.2 Time and Space

If we plot their basic parameters in time and space, the diegetic constituents of Beur narratives quickly reveal close parallels with the life experiences of their authors. Almost without exception, these works are confined to the same historical epoch as that through which their authors have lived, i.e. essentially the period from the 1950s to the present day. Arriz Tamza's short stories, *Lune et orian* and *Zaïd le mendiant*, are unique in using mythical settings outside the confines of historical time. The principal characters in most other Beur narratives are members of the immigrant community in contemporary France or Belgium, with the second generation consistently to the fore. Thus in the majority of cases, the age group to which the protagonist belongs is one through which the author has already passed.

With the exception of Mehdi Lallaoui's as yet unpublished second novel, 'La Colline aux oliviers', none of these works extends significantly beyond a period of thirty years, and the time-span is often very much shorter than that. Some Beur novels depict episodes in the protagonist's life stretching right the way through from infancy to early adulthood, though the whole of that time-span is not always evenly covered. Narratives featuring this kind of chronological spread include Mohammed Kenzi's *La Menthe sauvage*, Nacer Kettane's *Le Sourire de Brahim*, Kamal Zemouri's *Le Jardin de l'intrus*, and Tassadit Imache's *Une Fille sans histoire*. While spanning a similar period, novels such as Mehdi Charef's *Le Thé au harem d'Archi Ahmed*, Leïla Houari's *Zeida de nulle part* and Mustapha Raïth's *Palpitations intra-muros* are much more obviously selective in their coverage of events. In each case, however, the protagonist's experiences are closely based on the author's own life-history.

The main action in most Beur novels extends over a period of no more than four or five years, and in some cases it lasts as little as twenty-four hours. Sakinna Boukhedenna's *Journal. 'Nationalité: immigré(e)'* covers about five years, mainly in the late teens of the narrator-protagonist, and Ahmed Kalouaz limits himself to a similar period in the life of the young woman at the centre of *L'Encre d'un fait divers*. Azouz Begag's first novel, *Le Gone du Chaâba*, covers roughly four years in the late childhood and early adolescence of the protagonist; most of the sequel, *Béni ou le Paradis Privé*, is devoted to a period of less than a year in the life of the teenage Béni. Hocine Touabti's *L'Amour quand même* covers two years in the early manhood of the unnamed protagonist, and most of the text is devoted to a period of just three months. The same author's unpublished 'Rue de la rive' spans the first twelve years of the protagonist's life, but concentrates mainly on the last two years of this. Jean-Luc Yacine's unpublished 'Les Années de brume' focuses on an almost identical period in the childhood of the protagonist. A few months is almost all we see in the lives of the young men featured in Yacine's *L'Escargot* and Bouzid's *La Marche*. Most of Akli Tadjer's *Les ANI du 'Tassili'* focuses on a period of no more than a few weeks in the life of the 23-year-old protagonist, Omar, and the main action spans a single day; Ahmed Kalouaz strikes a similar balance in *Point kilométrique 190*, as does Farida Belghoul in her depiction of the seven-year-old protagonist in *Georgette!*. All these works, except for those of Kalouaz and to a lesser extent Yacine's *L'Escargot*, feature protagonists whose experiences closely resemble those which the authors themselves underwent at a similar age.

The spatial limits of Beur fiction coincide almost exactly with the areas which the authors themselves know best. They are confined almost entirely to France and to a lesser extent Algeria (or, in the case of Houari's works, Belgium and Morocco). The narratives published by Kenzi, Kettane, Zemouri, Lallaoui, Belghoul and Imache[28] are set mainly, and in some cases exclusively, in the working-class suburbs of Paris where these authors were brought up. Kenzi, Kettane and Lallaoui also present briefer portraits of Algeria based on personal experiences there. Charef's first novel, *Le Thé au harem d'Archi Ahmed*, follows a similar pattern.

Touabti, although not a native of Paris, set the whole of *L'Amour quand même* in the French capital after living there for several years. Most of his second novel, 'Rue de la rive', takes place in an unnamed town between Saint-Etienne and Lyons clearly modelled on Saint-Chamond, where the author's own family lived. Although the protagonist in *L'Escargot* originates in Paris, almost all the action takes place in Arras, where Jean-Luc Yacine was born and brought up. The same author's unpublished 'La Messe dans la porcherie' uses heavily fictionalised characters and locations, but 'Les Années de brume' retraces with great fidelity part of Yacine's childhood in Arras together with a brief period which he spent in Paris. Azouz Begag's narratives are confined almost entirely to his native Lyons. Arriz Tamza, who was raised in Marseilles, uses this city as the

28. I refer here to Tassadit Imache's novel, *Une Fille sans histoire*, Paris, Calmann-Lévy, 1989. Her short story for children, *Le Rouge à lèvres*, Paris, Syros, 1988, uses mainly fictional locations and events.

principal location for his novel *Ombres*. Mustapha Raïth's *Palpitations intra-muros* ranges more widely across France, in line with the wanderings of the author himself. Bouzid's *La Marche* naturally follows the 1,000 kilometre route of the 1983 Marche des Beurs through much of southern and eastern France en route to Paris; we also briefly glimpse a trip to Algeria which the author made six years earlier. Boukhedenna's *Journal* zig-zags between provincial France and Algeria, faithfully reflecting the author's own movements during the period concerned. The sea-crossing between Algiers and Marseilles which occupies almost the whole of *Les ANI du 'Tassili'* is based on a similar journey made by Tadjer just a few months before he wrote the novel. With only minor exceptions, all Houari's stories are divided between Brussels, where she has lived since the age of seven, and her native Morocco.

In most Beur novels, the main characters live in bidonvilles, cités de transit, HLM estates and crumbling inner-city apartment blocks similar to those in which the authors themselves were raised. After the family home, the most important locale in Beur fiction is school. *Le Gone du Chaâba* and *Georgette!* are divided almost equally between these two locations. School also plays an important role in novels such as *Le Sourire de Brahim*, *Le Thé au harem d'Archi Ahmed* and *Le Jardin de l'intrus*. Between school and home is the street, and a number of associated spaces open to a range of people and activities. The street is the principal meeting place and playground of the young friends featured in *Le Thé au harem d'Archi Ahmed* and *Béni ou le Paradis Privé*. The café is a favourite locale in *Les Beurs de Seine*, and also features significantly in *L'Escargot* as well as in Houari's stories. Prison, a place of retribution for those who go astray in the street, is the central locale in *Palpitations intra-muros* and an important *lieu de passage* in the later stages of *La Menthe sauvage*; it also beckons forbiddingly at the end of *Le Thé au harem d'Archi Ahmed*. In practically every case, these locales are modelled directly on places with which the authors were personally acquainted.

Veritable rarities in Beur fiction are places of work. Bearing in mind the fundamental role of employment in attracting immigrants to France in the first place, this is a striking lacuna. The marginal role of work is, of course, a reflection of the age group to which most of the protagonists belong. Most are teenagers, and few of them are very much older than twenty; some are not yet even in their teens. The majority of Beur narratives deal therefore with the period which precedes entry into working life. It is a time of preparation for adulthood, in which youngsters learn what is expected of them by others, what their own temperament might incline them towards in life, and how they might go about realising their objectives. Typically, Beur fiction takes the form of a 'roman d'apprentissage' or 'Bildungsroman', in which the line of the plot follows the learning curve of the protagonist.

To make his or her way through life, the protagonist must understand and in some degree participate in one or more cultures. Each of the locales mentioned above is a culturally defined space. When children first enter school, they find new demands are made of them. While these demands sometimes come as a surprise, they are usually found in the fullness of time to complement what the children have already learned inside the family home. Where the children of immigrants are concerned, however, conflicts are far more evident. The language they have acquired at home – the fundamental key to the cultural codes of their parents – denies them access to what they must learn at school. Similarly, the religious beliefs which permeate daily life at home are by law excluded from state schools. Whole new codes must be learned and – if the child wishes to gain the esteem of his peers and superiors – acted upon. Open conflicts between the two orders may be avoided as long as they remain spatially divided. But when one invades the territory of the other, the results may be catastrophic.

Azouz Begag furnishes vivid examples of this in *Le Gone du Chaâba*, all of them closely modelled on his own childhood. The narrator-protagonist, Azouz, loves his friends and family in the bidonville where he is brought up, but he is also determined to do well at school. Success at school is measured by mastery of the French language and by conformity with the moral precepts transmitted by the teacher. When Azouz proudly displays these talents during a police-raid on the bidonville, he unwittingly betrays the whole community there. An uncle of his has been operating an unlicensed hallal abattoir within the bidonville, slaughtering sheep in the manner prescribed by Islamic teachings on land for which Azouz's father is legally responsible. The slaughtering of sheep in this way is a respectable, indeed honoured practice among Muslims, but it places them at fault in the eyes of the French authorities. When the police arrive to enforce the law, the grown-ups pretend they cannot understand French, and are therefore unable to assist in the hunt for the slaughter-yard. The police inspector decides to enlist the help of a child, and picks on Azouz, whose education at the local primary school has equipped him not only with fluent French but also with firm convictions about the need to support law and order. Without a moment's hesitation he leads the police to the spot which they are seeking. Stiff fines are imposed on Azouz's father and uncle, who also suffer the ignominy of having their wrong-doings reported in the local press. Azouz had failed to appreciate that the rules he had learned at school might conflict with the conventions applied at home. Frightened and humiliated, his father and uncle quarrel, and the bidonville never again regains its community spirit.[29]

Later in the same novel, we see the blurring of territorial and cultural demarcations at school. On enrolling at a new school after the removal of his family to a city-centre apartment, Azouz decides it will be easier to make new friends if he pretends he is Jewish, like two of his classmates. When his mother unexpectedly arrives in full Algerian costume to collect him at the end of the school day, the boy is forced to disown her in order to sustain the illusion of his Jewishness. As a consequence, she and Azouz both suffer profound feelings of shame and humiliation.[30]

Far from being isolated incidents, events of this kind are just the tip of the iceberg. The different cultural traditions to which the Beurs are heirs simply cannot be held in separate territorial compartments. The secular values of modern France penetrate directly into the family home through powerful media such as television. Again, *Le Gone du Chaâba* provides a revealing illustration. After a family row, Azouz's father, Bouzid, returns home to find his wife and children watching a film on television. He sits down with them, and their reconciliation seems assured until a love scene in the film climaxes with a passionate kiss. Bouzid's sense of decency is outraged by this display of Western mores within the family home. According to Islamic teachings, such acts ought not to be seen in public. He therefore rips the plug of the television set out of its socket, fusing all the lights in the apartment and at the same time setting back his reconciliation with the family through this fresh display of ill-temper.[31]

A similar incident occurs early in Mehdi Charef's *Le Thé au harem d'Archi Ahmed*. The protagonist, Madjid, is asked by his mother, Malika, to go and look for his father. Madjid ignores her and retires to his room to play a record of the British rock group The Sex Pistols at full volume, thereby drowning out his mother's words. When she stops the record player Madjid claims not to understand what Malika is saying because of her poor French accent. She has even less effect on him when she lapses into Arabic,

29. Azouz Begag, *Le Gone du Chaâba*, Paris, Seuil, 1986, pp. 122–63.
30. Ibid., pp. 190–3.
31. Ibid., pp. 198–200.

threatening to send her son back to Algeria to do his military service. Madjid wishes to surround himself inside the family home with cultural practices which he has learned outside its walls. Malika may try to exclude those influences, but the fact is that her son has internalised them, and they are carried with him wherever he goes. Speaking in Arabic, she warns Madjid that if he fails to do his military service in Algeria he will be denied Algerian papers and refused entry into the country or thrown into prison there:

> – T'auras plus de pays, t'auras plus de racines. Perdu, tu seras perdu.
> Parfois Madjid comprend un mot, une phrase et il répond, abattu, sachant qu'il va faire du mal à sa mère:
> – Mais moi j'ai rien demandé! Tu serais pas venue en France je serais pas ici, je serais pas perdu . . . Hein? . . . Alors fous-moi la paix!
> [. . .]
> Elle quitte la chambre et Madjid se rallonge sur son lit, convaincu qu'il n'est ni arabe ni français depuis bien longtemps. Il est fils d'immigrés, paumé entre deux cultures, deux histoires, deux langues, deux couleurs de peau, ni blanc ni noir, à s'inventer ses propres racines, ses attaches, se les fabriquer.[32]

For first-generation immigrants such as Malika, there is an un-equivocal sense of belonging fundamentally to Algeria. As Madjid observes, the younger generation have been robbed of such a sentiment by the migration of their parents. Brought up in France by parents who still speak of Algeria as their home, the Beurs carry within themselves conflicting cultural imperatives which make it impossible for them to feel unequivocally rooted in a single terri-torial base.

In several narratives, the protagonists attempt to escape from the frustrations which they experience in Europe by travelling to North Africa. The aspirations which they carry with them are, however, so conditioned by the land in which they have been brought up that it is impossible to satisfy them on the other side of the Mediterranean. Exasperated by the racism to which she is subjected as an Arab in France, Sakinna, the narrator-protagonist in Boukhedenna's *Journal*, decides to seek a new life in Algeria. Her experiences there bring bitter disillusion. The personal indepen-dence to which she has become accustomed in France makes her quite unwilling to comply with the subordinate role expected of women in Islamic countries:

32. Charef, *Le Thé*, pp. 14–15.

Si la culture arabe, c'est de réduire la femme à l'état où elle est, je ne veux pas de cette arabité [. . .] Alors j'ai pris l'avion pour la France. La France est raciste, mais en France je peux vivre seule sans mari, sans père, mère, et la police ne m'épie pas tous les jours. Je peux crier, 'non' au racisme, 'non' à l'exploitation de la femme, je me sens un peu plus libre que sur ma terre.[33]

Sakinna may still think of Algeria as her homeland ('ma terre') but she was born in France, and in the final analysis she feels more at ease (or at any rate less ill at ease) there than on the other side of the Mediterranean.

Brought up in France by fiercely nationalist immigrant parents, the eponymous protagonist in Kettane's *Le Sourire de Brahim* feels 'algérien à fond'.[34] While training in Paris to become a doctor, Brahim decides, as the author himself did at a similar age, to spend the summer vacation as a volunteer medic in Algeria. It is with great excitement that he flies to a land of which he has no more than hazy childhood memories: 'Pour lui, l'Algérie, ce n'était ni plus ni moins que la France avec du soleil. Il avait du mal à imaginer comment pouvait être ce pays.'[35] Brahim is completely unprepared for the social order he finds there. Administrative inefficiency, political bombast and intolerance and the oppressive weight of Islam produce a rude awakening in him, and there is no mistaking the sense of relief with which he boards the return flight to Paris at the end of the summer.[36]

Omar, the narrator-protagonist in Tadjer's *Les ANI du 'Tassili'*, boards the car-ferry back to France in an almost identical frame of mind.[37] He had hoped to stay in Algeria indefinitely, but lasted less than three weeks. Aware of the possible difficulties, he had immersed himself as far as possible in the cultural life of the immigrant community in Paris before making the trip, but his preparations proved to be in vain: 'Toute cette somme de travail, de recherches et d'efforts pour en conclure que l'Algérie, c'est autre chose qu'un plat de couscous, deux disques, un livre de géographie et de littérature.'[38] He knows only a few words of Arabic and has no interest in Islam. Algeria may be his homeland in a mythical

---

33. Sakinna Boukhedenna, *Journal. 'Nationalité: immigré(e)'*, Paris, L'Harmattan, 1987, pp. 100–1.
34. Kettane, *Le Sourire*, p. 80.
35. Ibid., p. 86.
36. Ibid., pp. 93–121.
37. Tadjer, *Les ANI*, p. 20.
38. Ibid., p. 42.

sense, but in all practical respects Omar's home is in the suburbs of Paris, and he is glad to be returning there: 'Eh oui! je suis heureux de partir de "chez moi" pour rentrer "chez moi". Heureux de savoir que, de l'autre côté de la grande bleue, en banlieue parisienne, dans une cité de HLM comme il en existe des milliers, mes parents, mes amis m'attendent.'[39]

The action in Houari's *Zeida de nulle part* is divided equally between Belgium and Morocco. In Part I, we see the adolescent Zeida fleeing and then returning to the family home in Brussels where her father wishes to impose upon her the traditional discipline expected of Muslim girls. Torn between respect for the cultural heritage of her parents and the desire for personal freedom, including the right to explore her own sexuality, Zeida decides to return to Morocco: 'Ce n'était qu'une fuite, elle le savait, mais vivre autre chose et ailleurs, cela pouvait peut-être l'aider à échapper à toutes les contradictions dont elle souffrait.'[40] The aged aunt with whom she goes to stay in an isolated Moroccan village in Part II could not be kinder, nor could her neighbours. Zeida is even allowed to spend time in the company of boys, but this is only because she is seen as a temporary visitor, exempt from the sexual segregation normally imposed on local adolescents. Such concessions serve only to mark her as an outsider, and Zeida is clearly unwilling to comply with the constraints that would make her an authentic part of village life. Coming to Morocco has solved nothing, for her problems reside above all in her own divided mind, rather than in this or that piece of territory: 'Le choix de s'être retirée totalement de tout ce qui pouvait lui rappeler l'Europe n'avait fait qu'accentuer les contradictions qui l'habitaient.'[41] The last we see of Zeida is as she boards a plane back to Europe.

Bouzid, whose parents had taken French nationality after fleeing Algeria in 1962, describes a similar but much crueller experience in *La Marche*. During his adolescence, he was taken back to Algeria on a family holiday. He was initially exhilarated by a sense of release from the racist attitudes to which he had been exposed in France, but the euphoria did not last long:

Un jeune, qui aurait pu être mon frère, me traita avec mépris de 'fils de Française' . . . comme d'autres se sont faits traiter de 'carte jaune'. J'aurais pu me sentir français, à ce moment-là. Pas du tout! Je me suis

39. Ibid., p. 20.
40. Leïla Houari, *Zeida de nulle part*, Paris, L'Harmattan, 1985, p. 41.
41. Ibid., p. 74.

profondément senti immigré. J'étais immigré où que j'aille. J'aurais pu aller en Chine sur-le-champ; même là-bas j'aurais été un immigré. L'éternel immigré, c'était moi, coucou!
J'eus l'impression que tous les pays me claquaient leur porte au nez. Ils étaient privés. Il fallait la carte pour entrer. J'étais condamné à vivre dans les *no man's lands* que j'imaginais comme des couloirs froids où le vent soufflait à tout rompre . . .
En pensant à tous ceux qui se trouvaient dans mon cas, j'imaginai de construire un vaisseau spatial assez grand pour tous nous contenir. Et en avant! Direction: l'espace sidéral, à la recherche d'une planète habitable. Nous pourrions l'appeler 'Dignité', par exemple.[42]

Bouzid's feeling of being neither French nor Algerian, of belonging in a sense nowhere, is closely echoed in the extract from *Le Thé au harem d'Archi Ahmed* quoted earlier, and in the following remarks from the preface to Boukhedenna's *Journal*: 'C'est en France que j'ai appris à être Arabe[; c]'est en Algérie que j'ai appris à être l'Immigrée.'[43] Like Bouzid, Boukhedenna dreams of an imaginary territorial solution to her problems. In her case, it takes the shape of an artificial island halfway between Marseilles and Algiers for all those who, like her, may be classed as neither French nor Arab, and whose passports should therefore read: 'Nationalité: Immigré(e)'.[44]

At the end of Begag's second novel the narrator-protagonist, Béni, is excluded from a French nightclub. Smarting under a mixture of humiliation and rage, he imagines a ghostly figure carrying him up into the heavens. Asked to explain this dénouement, the author commented that for Béni the apparition could represent 'Allah qui le rappelle, ou la drogue qui lui fait tout oublier. Coincé dans un problème à deux dimensions, il s'en tire dans la troisième dimension.'[45] The two-dimensional problem in which Béni is stuck is that of his dual cultural heritage. The protagonist may dream of a third dimension as the solution to his problems, but neither Begag nor any other Beur writer regards fantasies of that kind as anything more than a parenthetical diversion from the dilemmas which they and their peers face. This is not to deny any role to the imagination. On the contrary, the Beurs are in a sense condemned to invent new amalgams out of the diverse traditions which they inherit. But those among them who have

42. Bouzid, *La Marche*, Paris, Sindbad, 1984, pp. 35–6.
43. Boukhedenna, *Journal*, p. 5.
44. Ibid., p. 103.
45. Begag's comments were made in an interview with Michel Cressole, 'Béni soit un Beur obèse', *Libération*, 10 Jan. 1989.

explored these issues with their pens have always kept in view the culturally-specific constraints of time and space to which they are subjected. If, as we shall see in the next section, they have drawn on their imagination to go beyond the bare bones of their own lives, it is almost always with the intention of illuminating those underlying constraints.

2.3   Borrowings and Inventions

Even in seemingly 'pure' autobiographies, there are always elements of invention. An obvious example is the use of direct speech. No one can remember the exact words used in conversations that took place five, ten or twenty years earlier. As noted in Section 2.1, indirect or reported speech has the effect of subordinating what was originally said to a discursive framework imposed by the narrator. Direct speech seems to offer a much more vivid impression of the original dialogue, yet the human memory is such that a large part of what seems to be quoted speech must in fact be invented. Belghoul casts *Georgette!* in the form of an interior monologue by a seven-year-old girl. Even if every event in the novel could be shown to have a direct counterpart in the author's own childhood, the words of the narrator-protagonist (which, as an interior monologue, constitute one long, uninterrupted self-quotation) must in the nature of things be invented by Belghoul. The four Beur narratives which, by Lejeune's criteria, might be classed as autobiographies – those published by Boukhedenna, Bouzid and Raïth, together with Begag's first novel – all contain verbatim accounts of conversations which in certain cases date as far back as the author's childhood. The artifice involved in the (re?-)creation of these conversations is paradoxically designed to make the narratives appear more authentic.

We can see this aspect of the imaginative process at work in the manuscripts of *Le Gone du Chaâba*. This is without doubt one of the most 'purely' autobiographical of Beur narratives. All the characters are based on people known to the author (including, most importantly, the author himself), and their original names are retained. The times and more especially the locations of events are generally identified with great precision; all correspond exactly with the childhood itinerary of Begag. The text nevertheless incorporates significant imaginative elements. One of the most widespread of these is invented dialogue. In the earliest version of the manuscript, a retrospective narrative viewpoint predominates and the tone is often heavily analytical. Each phase in Azouz's child-hood is described in general terms, with occasional references to particular incidents as illustrations of these broad trends. In the final, published version, the balance is reversed. The main emphasis is on the recreation of events as experienced at the time of their occurrence, with only occasional moments of retrospective analysis. A major part of this transformation is effected by the wholesale invention of dialogue.

This is by no means the only element of artifice in *Le Gone du Chaâba*. In a number of cases, a single character in the finished text is made up of elements from what in earlier drafts were several separate personae. For instance, in the original manuscript Begag recalls having had at least three different teachers at his first primary school, the Ecole Léo Lagrange. In the book, we meet only one, M. Grand. A woman teacher represented in the initial drafts of several important incidents is replaced by M. Grand in the final version of these events. He is evidently a composite character, incorporating elements drawn from what in reality were several different teachers.

Similar processes operated on a much more systematic scale in the composition of Tadjer's *Les ANI du 'Tassili'*. The text consists mainly of Omar's conversations with his fellow-passengers on board the *Tassili* as it sails from Algiers to Marseilles. These individuals amount to a cross-section of all the main groups which have been involved in the Franco–Algerian relationship during the lifetime of the author. The characters include first-generation 'single' male emigrants, Beurs such as Omar, French social workers (an important point of contact between the French state and the immigrant community), rapatriés (former white settlers in North Africa, also known as 'pieds-noirs') who have been on a return journey to the land they left in 1962, and members of Algeria's post-independence élite. For much of the time these characters are more loquacious than Omar, whose interventions are confined to occasional comments or asides. These interventions are, however, sufficient to indicate Omar's complex and at times contradictory feelings towards his various interlocutors, feelings which, in the final analysis, constitute the main thread of the novel. Despite various differences on points of detail (Omar is younger than Tadjer, for example, and hails from a north-western suburb of Paris, whereas his creator has lived mainly in the centre and south of the capital), there is a very close resemblance between the author and the protagonist. Through Omar's shifting levels of identification with his different interlocutors, the author is clearly dramatising his own divided sense of self. He does this, however, through characters and dialogue which to a very large extent are invented.

The ship on which Tadjer returned to France in September 1983 contained many of the types incorporated in the novel. To turn them into fully fledged characters, however, and to shape the dialogue in such a way as to illuminate subtly but persistently the position of Omar, Tadjer drew widely on many different individuals (not all of whom were on that particular sailing) and additional invented elements where necessary in order to create characters of a composite nature. As the dialogue between them and Omar occupies most of the text, it is clear that, despite the broad resemblance between the author and the protagonist, *Les ANI du 'Tassili'* is to a very significant extent fictional.

Even the portrayal of Azouz, in *Le Gone du Chaâba*, involves similar processes, albeit on a more limited scale. The original working title of the narrative was 'Les Gones du Chaâba'. Many of the early passages depicted Azouz and his friends as a largely undifferentiated group, and the protagonist was scarcely individualised at all. In the published version, many words and acts originally attributed to the children of the bidonville in general are reassigned specifically to Azouz, and at times this clearly takes the author beyond the bounds of strict veracity. For example, early in the novel we see Azouz rummaging through a rubbish heap next to Le Chaâba. The original manuscript (reproduced on the left, below), depicts this as a habitual activity engaged in by all the children, whereas the published text (on the right) focuses on Azouz:

On trouvait des vêtements, des jouets surtout, des bouteilles aux formes bizarres, des illustrés, des cahiers à moitié écrits, et aussi des médicaments sous forme de pillules que l'on prenait bien souvent pour des bonbons.	Les manches retroussées jusqu'aux épaules et le pantalon jusqu'au nombril, j'exhume du tas d'ordures des vêtements, de vieilles paires de chaussures, des jouets surtout, des bouteilles, des bouquins, des illustrés, des cahiers à moitié écrits, des ficelles, des assiettes, des couverts . . .
Après quelques dizaines de minutes d'investigation soignée, les enfants rentraient chez eux, les mains riches de leurs butins,	

la tête pleine de projets de jeux et
de bricolage, mais horriblement
sales et puants.
Parfois, quelques-uns
s'écorchaient sur des boîtes de
conserves éventrées ou sur des
tessons de bouteille. Personne
n'était à l'abri de graves
maladies, bien que nous n'ayons
jamais décelé de choses graves.
Quand l'un d'entre nous s'était
blessé, tous les autres lui criaient
qu'il allait bientôt mourir de la
maladie des remblais – pour qu'il
laisse sa place. Rien n'y faisait![46]

En tirant vigoureusement sur un
pneu de vélo que plusieurs
cartons recouvraient, ma main
s'écorche sur une boîte de
conserve éventrée. A quelques
mètres, Rabah aperçoit ma
blessure et me crie que je vais
mourir de la maladie des remblais
si je ne rentre pas chez moi pour
recevoir des soins. Je devine qu'il
veut s'approprier mon coin.
Aussi rien n'y fait: je reste sur
mon trésor.[47]

Using the imperfect tense, the original manuscript describes these events as a regular occurrence in which all the children participated in a more or less undifferentiated mass. By eliminating certain adverbs ('bien souvent', 'parfois', 'jamais') and switching to the historic present, the author turns the finished text into a description of one specific incident in which Azouz assumes a leading role. No individual children are named in the initial draft, and Azouz's own participation is given no special significance. At no point does he single himself out by using the 'je' form. His involvement is indicated by the use of the 'nous' form on two occasions in the second paragraph, but this is heavily outweighed by the predominance of the third person, firstly in the shape of the indefinite pronoun 'on', and later in a variety of formulations ('les enfants rentraient chez eux', 'il allait bientôt mourir', etc.) which scarcely implicate the narrator at all. The use of the first person makes the narrator-protagonist the principal actor in the revised version, where our attention becomes focused on Azouz's battle of wits with his friend Rabah. In the details of this apparent reconstruction of the author's personal past, there is clearly a significant element of adaptation.

In *Le Gone du Chaâba*, Begag retained the real-life names of the people on whom his characters were based, in the expectation that they would be flattered to see themselves depicted in print. He was

46. Unpublished draft of *Le Gone du Chaâba*.
47. Begag, *Le Gone*, pp. 38–9.

soon to realise that this had been a mistake. Louisa, for example, the kind-hearted but somewhat eccentric old lady who had opened up her house to Azouz and his young friends, complained that it was humiliating for her to be shown scavenging alongside them in the rubbish heap.[48] It was partly in order to avoid complaints of this kind that Begag used mainly fictional names in his second novel, *Béni ou le Paradis Privé*.

Nevertheless, when *Béni ou le Paradis Privé* came out, it was widely seen as a direct sequel to Begag's first novel. 'On retrouve avec intérêt le jeune héros du *Gone du Chaâba*',[49] wrote one reviewer. Strictly speaking this is incorrect, for the protagonist in the second volume shares neither the name nor the physique of his counterpart in the first. Unlike Azouz, Béni is fat. He is in this respect a composite character, for while in temperament he is based essentially on the author, his physique is modelled on that of a fat Italian neighbour in the HLM estate, La Duchère, where Begag lived as a teenager. This invented, or to be more accurate, borrowed trait is, however, used by the author to reinforce rather than to dilute the basic predicament with which the narrative is concerned, which is closely based on Begag's personal experience at this age: social exclusion through the prejudices of others. 'Gros plus arabe, mon personnage est handicapé à deux points de vue',[50] said Begag.

The girl at the centre of Béni's dreams is much the most mythical creation in either of Begag's narratives. Her very name, France, is obviously designed to make a symbol of her, and the coincidental circumstances of some of her meetings with Béni bear all the hallmarks of a literary contrivance. France personifies the land of acceptance and integration dreamed of by Béni. The anger with which Béni's father speaks of her is real enough, but as he has never met the girl it is clear that what he objects to is the culture she represents – and its threat to the perpetuation of his own values and beliefs – rather than anything of an individual nature. France flits elusively in an out of the text, for ever beyond Béni's grasp. It is she whom Béni has arranged to meet in the nightclub to which he is refused admittance at the end of the novel. Her mythical status, unique in Begag's narratives, is ultimately appropriate to the underlying problematic in *Béni ou le Paradis Privé*.

48. These complaints are mentioned by Begag in his interview with Michel Cressole, 'Le Gone de Chaâba réédite ses exploits', *Lyon-Libération*, 25–6 Oct. 1986.
49. Review of *Béni ou le Paradis Privé* in *Nord-Eclair*, 22 Feb. 1989.
50. Interview with Cressole, 'Béni soit un Beur obèse'.

That problematic is at root a continuation and development of the tensions experienced by Azouz in *Le Gone du Chaâba*, to which *Béni ou le Paradis Privé* is indeed an only thinly disguised sequel. Much of the early material in the second novel had in fact originally formed the final part of the first, from which it was removed before publication. After an introductory passage on childhood memories of Christmas, the second book takes up the story of Béni at almost exactly the point where the first, in its final, truncated version, left Azouz: with the installation of his family in the La Duchère housing estate. In both cases, the father is a bricklayer from Sétif. Béni, like Azouz, received most of his primary schooling at the Ecole Léo Lagrange, and he has shown himself to be a gifted child at secondary school. These and other parallels far outweigh the physical differences between Azouz and Béni and the fictionalising of certain names. Moreover, most of the events in *Béni ou le Paradis Privé* are, like those in the first volume, closely modelled on the author's own formative years, and the nightclub incident in particular is based directly on a very similar experience which left a deep emotional scar on Begag.

While some borrowings and inventions are of considerable significance, it would be tedious to attempt an exhaustive list of all the ways in which the stories represented in Beur narratives differ from the life experiences of their authors. Changes of name are often little more than precautionary measures to avoid the kinds of difficulties to which the veracity of *Le Gone du Chaâba* exposed Begag. Other details are sometimes changed for fairly incidental reasons. Zemouri, for example, has two brothers, but in place of them he gave his fictional counterpart in *Le Jardin de l'intrus* a sister because, as a child, he had always wanted one. Some changes contribute more substantively to the main thrust of the narratives. For instance, while most of the action in *L'Escargot* is set in Arras, where Yacine was born, his fictional *alter ego*, Amar, hails from Paris. Amar's departure from the capital early in the story and subsequent arrival in a town he does not know enable the author to dramatise the 'immigrant' status of the protagonist despite his having been born in France. The second half of Houari's first novel draws heavily on a visit which the author made as a teenager to a well-to-do grandfather in the town of Guercif. The displacement of the visit in its fictional form (Zeida goes to live with an aunt in a very poor and remote village) heightens the dramatic contrast between the heroine's urban environment in Europe and the conditions she encounters in Morocco.

The Algerian war has gripped the imagination of several Beur writers in ways which have taken them significantly beyond the bounds of autobiography, but important underlying parallels with their own experiences are none the less present. A children's story by Tassadit Imache, *Le Rouge à lèvres*, recounts the quest for vengeance by an Algerian woman who saw her parents killed by a French army unit when she was seven years old. She catches up with the lieutenant responsible for the massacre thirty years later, by which time he too has a seven-year-old daughter, who serves as the narrator of the story. Imache is the daughter of neither a French army officer nor a massacred Algerian peasant. Her own childhood in France was, however, badly disrupted by the Algerian war, during which her immigrant father and French mother were repeatedly harassed by the police. The fictional events recounted in *Le Rouge à lèvres* clearly parallel in spirit the emotional turmoil through which the author passed during this period.

The harki characters at the centre of Charef's *Le Harki de Meriem* are not in any sense directly autobiographical. The main action concerns their experiences as soldiers in Algeria during the war of independence, when the author himself was only a child. Indirectly, however, autobiographical material plays an important part. The main events take place in an area close to Tlemcen, in western Algeria, where Charef lived as a child during the Algerian war. His personal memories of that period undoubtedly contribute significantly to the portrayal of it in the novel.[51] Moreover, the narrative repeatedly emphasises the parallels between the fate of the harki community and that of 'economic' immigrants and their families. We are told, for example, that by enlisting in the French army Azzedine, the main harki character, submits himself to a form of exploitation directly comparable to that suffered by factory workers: 'Il s'était enrôlé comme on embauche à l'usine, pour la solde à

51. Charef has spoken of these memories in his interviews with Salim Jay, 'Mehdi Charef: *Le Thé au harem d'Archi Ahmed*', *L'Afrique littéraire*, no. 70, Oct.–Dec. 1983, p. 107; Chafika Kadem, 'La France irisée de Mehdi Charef', *Le Quotidien de Paris*, 2 May 1985; Olivier Schmitt, 'L'Homme qui marche', *Le Monde*, 29 Dec. 1987; Reda Karakchou, 'Mehdi Charef: le rêve réalisé', *Jeune Afrique*, 2 Mar. 1988, p. 53. Most of *Le Harki de Meriem* is narrated anonymously in the third person, but exactly half way through the novel a short passage using the first person appears in quotation marks: Charef, *Le Harki de Meriem*, Paris, Mercure de France, 1989, pp. 98–100. The equally anonymous narrator of this passage recalls how, as a seven-year-old child, he met one of the harkis featured in the story. Charef himself was exactly the same age in 1959, when this part of the story takes place. In positioning this personal testimony at the very centre of the text, the author would appear to be highlighting its autobiographical dimension.

la fin du mois, il savait désormais qu'il lui faudrait lutter pour sa survie.'[52]

The life-and-death situations into which Azzedine is thrust during the war of independence are more obviously dramatic than the everyday experiences of a factory worker, but the manipulative nature of the underlying forces to which both are subjected enables us to perceive in the harki a close cousin of the economic immigrant. A sizeable part of *Le Harki de Meriem* is devoted to the experiences of Azzedine's family in France during the period since 1962, and in particular to the racist killing of his son, Sélim, during the 1980s. Although these events are set in Rheims, they closely parallel similar incidents which took place in areas of Paris with which Charef was directly acquainted. No matter where they live, and whether their fathers be harkis or economic immigrants, younger members of the North African community in France have fallen victim to the same material disadvantages and racial prejudices to which Charef was himself exposed during his formative years.

Most of the fictional elements in Kettane's *Le Sourire de Brahim* are of relatively minor importance, compared with the generally close correlation between the life of the protagonist and that of his creator. However, the opening section of the novel constitutes a major exception to this. Here we see a brother of the young Brahim killed in his mother's arms during a demonstration which took place in Paris towards the end of the Algerian war. It is a matter of historical record that the demonstration was staged, as we are told in the novel, on 17 October 1961 by tens of thousands of unarmed Algerian immigrants to protest against a curfew which had been imposed upon them by the chief of police in Paris. The police responded with a massive display of force, arresting many thousands of demonstrators. An unknown number of immigrants were killed, in some cases after being brutally interrogated, and scores of bodies were found floating in the Seine. News of these events was largely suppressed by the French media, and it was not until a quarter of a century later that the full scale of police violence was brought home to the French public in a spate of printed and broadcast narratives, among them Kettane's.[53] His account of these events is based on historical fact, but unlike the protagonist in *Le*

---

52. Charef, *Le Harki*, p. 110; cf. pp. 45, 165, 167, 169, 178.
53. The French writer Didier Daeninckx incorporated these events into a detective novel, *Meurtres pour mémoire*, Paris, Gallimard, 1984. A television adaptation followed in 1985. The same year brought the publication both of Kettane's novel and of a documentary study by Michel Levine, *Les Ratonnades*

Sourire de Brahim, the author was not himself present during the
demonstration, nor was a brother of his killed in it.

More than twenty years later Kettane was, however, among the
100,000 people who marched through Paris on the final day of the
Marche des Beurs. Unlike the older generation, who had been so
brutally repressed in 1961, the Beur demonstrators were given star
treatment by the media and warmly greeted by no less a figure than
President François Mitterrand. A slightly fictionalised account of
the Beurs' triumphant arrival on the political scene provides the
dénouement of *Le Sourire de Brahim*. It constitutes a dramatic
counterpoint to the opening chapter of the novel. That Kettane was
anxious to achieve this contrast is clear from his decision to begin
the narrative with what is practically the only genuinely invented
episode in Brahim's life (all the others are modelled more or less
directly on the author's own experiences). From that day on,
Brahim never smiles again until the final page of the novel. His
'missing' smile is used as an emblem of a hidden or repressed part
of his identity, which can fully surface again only if the unequal
balance of power between the French and immigrant communities
is redressed. Kettane's evocation at the beginning of his novel of
events long ignored or suppressed by the mass media in France
constitutes, like the Marche des Beurs, precisely such a reversal.

A similar dynamic lies behind the much more extensive inventions in Mehdi Lallaoui's unpublished second novel, 'La Colline
aux oliviers'. The initial impetus for the novel came from a visit
which Lallaoui made to the French Pacific colony of New Caledonia in 1983. He was intrigued and deeply moved to learn that more
than a hundred years earlier, Algerians opposed to French rule had
been deported to the island following an uprising in 1871. Lallaoui
set out to discover what he could of this largely forgotten or, to be
more accurate, suppressed page in the history of the Algerian
people. So sensitive is the subject that many official files on it are still
closed to researchers. Long and painstaking detective work in archives
held by both France and Algeria eventually enabled Lallaoui to piece

---

d'octobre: un meurtre collectif à Paris en 1961, Paris, Ramsay, 1985. The Paris-
based Amicale des Algériens en Europe later brought out a collection of
documents entitled *17 octobre 1961: 'Mémoire d'une communauté'*, Paris,
Actualité de l'émigration, 1987. Further research has been conducted by
Jean-Luc Einaudi, 'Un Jour d'octobre à Paris', *Le Genre humain*, Autumn
1988, pp. 25–36. Briefer references to these events are made in the narratives
published by several Beur writers. See, for example, Tadjer, *Les ANI*, p. 121;
Raïth, *Palpitations*, p. 83; Mehdi Lallaoui, *Les Beurs de Seine*, Paris, Arcantère,
1986, pp. 158–60. They are given more extended treatment in Imache, *Une
Fille*, pp. 20–45.

together the deportees' story. In the process he began writing 'La Colline aux oliviers'. The unnamed Beur protagonist is entrusted by his grandfather Baba Mous (a former emigrant) with the task of finding out the fate of the old man's uncle, who disappeared without trace many years before Baba Mous was born. Mixing established historical facts, archival discoveries and authorial inventions, 'La Colline aux oliviers' retraces the history of the Algerian community in France as the fictional characters work their way back through time generation by generation, finally discovering that the missing uncle had been among those deported to New Caledonia. In this way, the story serves to expose some of the more shocking aspects of the colonial period and to underline the long history of exploitation which has characterised French dealings with Algeria.

Attitudes inherited from the colonial period continue to weigh upon the Algerian community in France, which has been the target of many racist attacks. One of the factors which prompted the political mobilisation of the Beurs was a spate of racist killings during the summer of 1983 directed particularly against younger members of the immigrant community. Ironically, one of the worst attacks took place after the Marche des Beurs had started. On the night of 14 November 1983, three young Frenchmen off to join the Foreign Legion set upon a young Algerian, Habib Grimzi, in a train travelling from Bordeaux to the Italian border town of Ventimíglia. After beating him up, they threw Grimzi to his death as the train hurtled along at 140 kilometres an hour. It should perhaps be pointed out that Grimzi was not of immigrant origin. He had lived practically all his life in Oran, and was on his way back there via Marseilles when the attack took place. None of these details were of any interest to his drunken assailants, for whom the simple fact of Grimzi's North African appearance was sufficient to trigger their ferocious attack. This murder and the attitudes of those present constitute the core of the second novel published by Ahmed Kalouaz, *Point kilométrique 190*.

The author himself had no direct connection with these events. The first he knew of them was a television news report similar to the one quoted at the beginning of the novel. Kalouaz is in fact unique among Beur writers in having almost completely avoided autobiographical material in his published narratives. He is also one of the most prolific, sharing with Arriz Tamza the distinction of having published three volumes of imaginative prose. A major source of inspiration for Kalouaz lies in what the French press call 'faits divers' (the phrase itself is incorporated into the title of his first novel, *L'Encre d'un fait divers*). 'Faits divers' are generally small items of news without any obvious political or ideological significance. Road accidents, robberies and murders are typical examples. Kalouaz delights in applying his imagination to these and more substantive news stories to produce narratives of an altogether more subtle kind. The title story of *Celui qui regarde le soleil en face . . .*, discussed earlier, is a case in point. It is inspired in part by the real-life story of Patty Hearst, the American newspaper heiress kidnapped in 1974 by an organisation styled loosely on the Black Panther movement. Photographs of her subsequent involvement in bank raids organised by her captors left a major question mark over Hearst's role: was she a willing accomplice, or had she been forced to participate? In Kalouaz's story, error and ambiguity surround not only the fictional counterpart of Hearst, but also her supposed kidnapper. Behind the five-line television report on which the story concludes, with its simple labels of 'ravisseur' and 'kidnapée',[54] the reader sees a far more enigmatic pair of characters.

Neither character is of immigrant origin, but their misrepresentation by the media closely parallels the oversimplifications from which ethnic minorities often suffer on television and in the press. These are sometimes invoked by groups such as Hearst's kidnappers to justify their violent assaults on existing power structures. Kalouaz is no advocate of violence, but his story certainly helps to undermine simplistic or dismissive ideas of the Other. This and a related concern to explore human subjectivities other than his own are the most persistent features of Kalouaz's works.

The bulk of his characters are of French or North African origin, but they are seldom if ever modelled on himself. There are nine stories in *Celui qui regarde le soleil en face. . . .* The old lady at the centre of the first of these, 'La Vieille dame au chapeau de paille', is an entirely fictional creation. 'Penalty', which depicts a professional footballer turned crook, is based on a combination of 'faits divers'. The original events concerned both a convicted armed robber and two former French internationals (one of them of Black African origin) found guilty of various swindles. All the main locations in the third story, 'L'Ascenseur', are based on real places which anyone who has visited the city will immediately recognise as Grenoble, where the author himself lives. The lift which gives the story its title is indeed inspired by one in the very apartment block where Kalouaz has his home. Karin Moulin, the main female character, is based on a stranger Kalouaz bumped into and

54. Kalouaz, *Celui qui regarde*, p. 54.

recognised in the street one day more than six months after they had happened to sit near each other in the theatre without exchanging a word. The most important parts of the plot – Karin's sudden departure to the West Indies and the subsequent mental derangement of her lover – are, however, entirely fictional. 'Demain' is built upon an equal if not more substantial imaginative process, with its gripping evocation of the mind of a terrorist bomber; the shop he is preparing to bomb seems to have been based on Tati, the Paris department store blown up in September 1986 by a man the police believed to be an Arab terrorist. 'Comme Caussimon sous sa casquette' tells the tale of a Vietnamese soldier who, after enlisting in the French army, was involved in massacring Muslim prisoners during the Algerian war. The heavily fictionalised story draws in part on newspaper reports published in 1982 following the discovery of a mass grave dating back to the Algerian war at Kenchela, near the Tunisian border.[55] 'Le Regard noisette de Doris' mixes the fictional story of three French characters caught in the eternal triangle with details of the real-life killings of young blacks in Atlanta, Georgia, between 1979 and 1981, about which Kalouaz had read in a French translation of James Baldwin's book *The Evidence of Things not Seen*.[56]

The longest text in the collection, 'La Mémoire du couteau', is described as a monologue. It is in fact a substantially reworked adaptation for the stage of Kalouaz's first, unpublished novel, 'Le Pluriel d'espoir n'est-ce pas désespoir . . .' The original novel is very much more autobiographical than anything Kalouaz has since written. The author and the narrator-protagonist share the same first name, Ahmed, and very nearly the same date of birth. Both originate from the Oran region of Algeria, and the working and living conditions of the protagonist in France closely replicate those of Kalouaz during the 1970s. In its description of events in the Oran region during the closing stages of the Algerian war, the novel also draws closely on the author's own experiences there during the winter of 1961–2. Nevertheless, even in the original draft of the novel, Ahmed differs in a number of very significant respects from the author.

In the novel, the protagonist is the son of a harki, which Kalouaz is not. While his father is working for the French, Ahmed finds

---

55. The most important of these reports appeared in *Libération*, 3 June 1982 and 4 June 1982.

56. James Baldwin, *The Evidence of Things not Seen*, New York, Rinehart and Winston, 1985; published in French as *Meurtres à Atlanta*, trans. James Bryant, Paris, Stock, 1985.

himself compelled to join the Front de Libération Nationale (FLN) in their fight for Algerian independence after a largely accidental brush with the police; again, this has no autobiographical basis. These inventions serve two main purposes. One is to broaden the scope of the novel beyond the immigrant community to a much more wide-ranging picture of Franco–Algerian relations. A major theme running through 'Le Pluriel d'espoir n'est-ce pas désespoir . . .' is the exploitative nature of that relationship from colonial times to the present. We see this, for example, in the fate of Ahmed's grandfather, who was blinded at Verdun after being conscripted into the French army during the First World War; forty years later the old man is shot by French troops during the Algerian war for failing to answer their questions satisfactorily. Similarly, the manipulation of Ahmed's father for the benefit of the French during the war of independence is paralleled by the protagonist's poor living and working conditions in contemporary France, which are typical of the immigrant community in general. At the same time, Ahmed's personal predicament is rendered especially problematic by his status as the son of a harki, which greatly strengthens a second thematic strand. This is the powerful feeling of displacement and dispossession which characterises his sense of self. The feeling that others are manipulating and misrepresenting him, already set in motion by his harki background and almost chance engagement in the FLN, is rendered acute by a further brush with the French police in the late 1970s. This time Ahmed is mistaken for an armed robber, and released only after hours of interrogation designed to extract a confession from him. This last incident parallels a similar incident which befell a younger brother of Kalouaz's at about this time. As one Arab is apt to look very much like another in the eyes of the French police, the latter were convinced – quite wrongly – on the basis of the description given by a witness that Kalouaz's brother was the man they were hunting.

'La Mémoire du couteau' retains most of the essentials from the original novel, but presents them in a highly condensed and often elliptical form. For much of the time, Ahmed addresses his monologue to a mirror. This is an obvious visual image of his quest for self-understanding and inner peace amidst the powerful manipulative forces to which he has been subjected. As Ahmed observes, the harki community has at root been exploited as mercilessly as the emigrants who left Algeria for economic reasons:

Peuple d'incertitudes, et de mains, et de bras, exportés comme des oranges, comme nous. On a la même gueule, mais leurs chiens bien dressés, mordent avant d'apprendre à lire nos papiers. Quelle différence . . .

Moi le Français fictif, ou vous les authentiques. Moi l'Arabe réel, ou moi le simulacre.[57]

The harkis and their families were given French nationality when they fled to France in 1962 to escape possible reprisals in Algeria. They are the 'nous' with whom Ahmed identifies himself here. But the French, including the police, often view them in the same domineering spirit which is commonly displayed towards Algerian immigrants, shipped across the Mediterranean like boxes of oranges to meet the needs of the French economy. What, the harkis and their descendants may wonder, is the meaning of their official status as French citizens, compared with the widespread French perception of them for all practical purposes as foreigners and underlings? Unlike the French audience ('vous') to whom he turns at the end of this extract, Ahmed seems, as the son of a harki, permanently dispossessed of an authentic sense of identity.

In 'La Mémoire du couteau', despite its general relevance to the Algerian community in France and consequently to Kalouaz, the specifically autobiographical elements originally incorporated into 'Le Pluriel d'espoir n'est-ce pas désespoir . . .' are reduced to little more than minor details. Perhaps the nearest thing to an autobiographical story in *Celui qui regarde le soleil en face . . .* is 'Pablo sera à l'hôpital'. In it, a professional footballer, Pablo, is taken to hospital with a suspected heart attack. He becomes obsessed with a news story about a racist killing in Nice, and after stealing a car drives off to kill the fathers of those responsible. It is unclear whether he succeeds in this or whether he merely imagines the newspaper report of their deaths with which the story concludes. Kalouaz wrote the story in a hospital bed after suffering a heart attack in August 1987. The author, like the protagonist, was hospitalised in the Atlantic seaside town of La Baule. As Kalouaz began to recover he had at his bedside a news magazine report on the death of a Tunisian immigrant worker, Amar Abidi, in a Nice alleyway at the hands of half a dozen French youths.[58] A grey Volvo glimpsed outside the hospital became the vehicle in which Pablo set out on

57. Kalouaz, *Celui qui regarde*, p. 92.
58. Caroline Brizard, 'Nice: ils étaient six à cogner', *Le Nouvel Observateur*, 7 Aug. 1987. pp. 30–1.

his mission of retribution. Despite the incorporation into the text of these and many other elements drawn from Kalouaz's hospitalisation, it will be observed that even here, the most important part of the plot (Pablo's act of revenge) is entirely fictional. While the text clearly reflects the author's anger over the murder of Abidi, Kalouaz has never been one to promote or condone violent responses to racial intolerance.

In recreating the killing of Habib Grimzi in *Point kilométrique 190*, Kalouaz drew on a wide range of documents. Press cuttings were an important source of information. They in fact provided the germ from which the most important character in the novel (apart from Grimzi) grew. She is Sabine, a journalist who, obsessed with trying to understand what Grimzi went through, replicates his journey by taking the same train a year after his death. Sabine is a composite character based partly on Marie-Christine Jeanniot, who retraced Grimzi's final journey for the Catholic weekly *La Vie*,[59] and partly on Chantal Longo, who, after the arrest of Grimzi's assailants, took photographs of them for the local newspaper.[60] Besides consulting these materials, Kalouaz corresponded with one of the murderers in prison and obtained a sound recording made by a regional television station on the stretch of line where the attack took place so that he could listen to it while writing the narrative.

Yet the finished novel is anything but documentary in approach. Far less important than the clinical details of where and when things happened are the subjective responses of the characters, and these are evoked in what might ordinarily be called an intensely lyrical style, were it not for the fact that they revolve around the brutal killing of a man. Kalouaz wanted above all to somehow recreate Grimzi's consciousness, and in doing this he drew on a number of literary sources, in addition to the journalistic materials already mentioned.

The original idea of the novel had been conceived during a railway journey which the author happened to make one night shortly after the murder. It was strengthened by an allusion to Grimzi incorporated into a play by the Moroccan writer Tahar Ben Jelloun which Kalouaz saw performed in Metz in April 1984: 'Et si un jeune homme parmi nous vient à manquer, [. . .] défenestré d'un train qui va vite, qu'on maintienne sa voix vive, éternelle.'[61]

59. See Marie-Christine Jeanniot, 'Un Soir, un train, un mort', *La Vie*, 23 Nov. 1983, pp. 49–50.
60. See especially the photographs by Longo in *La Dépêche du midi*, 17 Nov. 1983 and 2 Dec. 1983.
61. Tahar Ben Jelloun, *La Fiancée de l'eau* suivi de *Entretien avec Monsieur Saïd*

As he was about to begin writing, Kalouaz came across a lyrical prose poem, *La Nuit remonte la mémoire/l'autre pays*, recently published by Danusza Bytniewski, the daughter of a Polish immigrant.[62] (Kalouaz was to learn later that Bytniewski's father had at one point been employed in the same coal mine where his own father had worked.) In Bytniewski's poem, the narrator attempts to recapture the voice of a now dead traveller; in the traveller's journey through the night we may see an image of the migratory passage of the author's own father, as well, perhaps, as an echo of deportations to concentration camps during the Nazi occupation of Poland. Kalouaz was struck by the sombre parallels with his own recreation of the fate of Habib Grimzi, and incorporated into *Point kilométrique 190* a number of images drawn from *La Nuit remonte la mémoire/l'autre pays*. The title of Bytniewski's poem is clearly alluded to by Sabine when, describing her attempt to relive Grimzi's final journey, she says: 'Je remonte une mémoire.'[63] Bytniewski's narrator also serves in part as the model for Hélène, the girlfriend who, in Kalouaz's account of events, Grimzi is on his way to visit in Marseilles.[64] Alix, a mutual friend of Grimzi and Hélène, is loosely modelled on Alix Cléo Roubaud, wife of the poet Jacques Roubaud, whose journal Kalouaz had recently read.[65]

Granted that the author is a man, one of the most striking features of Kalouaz's narratives is their frequent use of female narrators. The principal narrator in *Point kilométrique 190* is Sabine. It is she who tries to imagine what may have been Grimzi's thoughts during the final minutes of his life. In the process, Sabine becomes an important character in her own right, for her obsession with Grimzi's death bites deep into her own personal life. The first novel published by Kalouaz, *L'Encre d'un fait divers*, is the story of Naïma, a young Algerian woman brought to France by her husband Driss after an arranged marriage. Exasperated by the subservient role expected of her, Naïma stabs Driss to death. The novel was inspired by Kalouaz's shock at the arranged marriage of one of his brothers to a complete stranger brought over from Algeria, and by the subsequent refusal of a younger sister to agree to her parents'

Hammadi, ouvrier algérien, [Arles], Actes Sud/Théâtre Populaire de Lorraine, 1984, p. 19.

62. Danusza Bytniewski, *La Nuit remonte la mémoire/l'autre pays*, Le Chambon-sur-Lignon, Manier-Mellinette, 1983.

63. Ahmed Kalouaz, *Point kilométrique 190*, Paris, L'Harmattan, 1986, p. 36.

64. Several remarks attributed to Hélène are taken directly from Bytniewski's poem. Compare, for example, *Point kilométrique 190*, p. 56, with *La Nuit*, pp. 11–12, and *Point kilométrique 190*, p. 66, with *La Nuit* p. 18.

65. Alix Cléo Roubaud, *Journal 1979–1983*, Paris, Seuil, 1984.

arrangement of a similar marriage for herself. The text of *L'Encre d'un fait divers* takes the form of a journal addressed to a French friend, Céline, by Naïma during the prison sentence imposed on her for killing her husband. Here, as in *Point kilométrique 190*, Kalouaz has set himself the task of attempting to write from the point of view of a woman and, moreover, a woman in extremely unusual circumstances. To assist in writing the narrative, Kalouaz corresponded with several women prisoners, and shut himself up in a confined space in order to simulate the conditions in which Naïma composes her journal.

In his narratives, Kalouaz shows a preoccupation with diverse types of bigotry and in a more general sense with the forms of human consciousness generated by unequal social relations. Coming from an ethnic minority background, the author has every reason to sympathise with the victims of inequality and intolerance. By choosing protagonists and narrators foreign in some measure to himself (by virtue of their gender or other characterists) in preference to ploughing a 'safe' autobiographical furrow, Kalouaz imposes upon himself precisely the kind of imaginative effort which is required if such divisions are ever to be reduced or transcended. Their foreignness is, paradoxically, an important part of Kalouaz's own sense of self.

2.4 Attenuations and Omissions

Despite their heavy autobiographical content, Beur narratives are often silent about important aspects of their authors' lives. Omissions of this kind are most readily apparent when the finished text is compared with external sources of information, but the reader is often conscious of gaps at a purely intra-textual level. In Tadjer's *Les ANI du 'Tassili'*, for example, although Omar is present throughout the narrative, and is in a literal sense at the centre of all the conversations represented in the text (since the remarks of all the other characters are addressed to him), he remains in many ways a mystery to us. Apart from a few rudimentary details, we know very little indeed about his life in France prior to the visit to Algeria from which he is now returning. Omar is in fact positively reluctant to talk about himself, and even when he agrees to answer the questions of Nelly, a French social worker, towards the end of the novel, his words are deliberately evasive on many issues and still leave us with huge gaps in his curriculum vitae. Omar is clearly of the opinion that gaps of this kind are salutary to the extent that they prevent his listener from concluding that life experiences as complex as those of the Beurs can be reduced to some neat, simplistic formula. There can be little doubt that the author himself shares this view. In addition, Omar's evasiveness on certain issues arises from an unwillingness to re-live some of his unhappier memories. As we shall see later in this section, a similar sensitivity attaching to certain areas of experience appears to have played a significant role in inhibiting their depiction in the works of many Beur writers.

It would, of course, be impossible for any author to represent within the covers of a single book the totality of his or her life experiences. Even in the most openly autobiographical of narratives, a system of priorities must inevitably operate. Granted that the author is limited to a finite number of pages, the inclusion of certain materials necessarily implies the exclusion of others. As noted in Section 2.2, Beur writers often confine their stories within relatively short periods of time. In selecting these periods, the authors have naturally focused on particularly significant or revealing events. In doing so, they have cast their narratives in the metonymic mode which is characteristic of realist fiction.

Almost all Beur fiction operates within a realist aesthetic, i.e. the reader is meant to regard the events recounted in it as if they have actually happened, rather than as mere fantasies. Fantasies may, of course, tell us something about the real world, but they do so in an indirect way. Through animal fables, for example, the reader may learn certain lessons by recognising similarities between events in the story and aspects of the human world. In this respect, non-realist fiction functions in what is basically a metaphoric mode, i.e. by transferring elements from one sphere of meaning into another quite separate field. By contrast, as Roman Jakobson argued in a seminal article,[66] realist fiction adopts a metonymic idiom. Whereas a metaphor establishes a connection between things which are quite separate in normal life, a metonym is based on the contiguity of the elements which it connects. When a realist writer makes reference to a school, for example, the reader will assume that it contains children and that lessons take place there even if these are not explicitly mentioned. Similarly, if we are told that the protagonist lives in a particular area, s/he may be assumed to be

66. Roman Jakobson, 'Two Aspects of Language and Two Types of Aphasic Disturbance', in Roman Jakobson and Morris Halle (eds), *Fundamentals of Language*, The Hague, Mouton, 1956, pp. 55–82. Cf. David Lodge, *The Modes of Modern Writing: Metaphor, Metonymy, and the Typology of Modern Literature*, London, Edward Arnold, 1977, esp. pp. 73–7.

exposed to certain types of experience even if these are not explicitly articulated. His or her personal experiences may in turn be taken to typify those of neighbours or peers. In this way, the description of a particular incident may lead the reader to imagine a more extensive sequence of events than is actually spelt out, and the story of a single individual may be read as the representation in miniature of an entire group or social order. The metonymic mode may therefore render figuratively present to the reader many dimensions of meaning which, at a literal level, are absent from the text.

Les ANI du 'Tassili' illustrates these processes well. There can be no doubt that in writing *Les ANI du 'Tassili'*, Tadjer was fundamentally concerned with exploring his own sense of self. It is hard to believe that a seemingly ordinary 24-hour boat journey could be the single most important event in the author's life, yet the representation of such a voyage occupies most of the text. If Tadjer chooses to omit the great majority of his own life-history from the fictional story of Omar, it is in part because, in the boat journey, the author has found an extremely powerful metonym. The literal meaning of each detail in the story may be read as representative of a much larger whole. The continual movement of the ship, for example, positions the action literally between Algeria and France; it also serves as a simple but constant reminder of the importance of the migratory process in conditioning virtually every aspect of the lives of Omar and his fellow Beurs. Behind the seemingly minor irritations and tensions of this 24-hour journey, we sense the potential for much more enduring conflicts in life ashore; that Omar has suffered in this way is indeed clear from the manner in which he tries to evade Nelly's questions. Having stepped aboard the ship, Omar is compelled to wander among what amounts to a sociological cross-section of the French and Algerian peoples. On a much larger scale, this is exactly the situation of the Beurs from the moment of their birth onwards. Thus the individuals on board the *Tassili* effectively represent in miniature a much wider socio-historical panorama. It would be difficult to imagine a more natural setting in which to bring together such a microcosm. In no other situation would individuals of such diverse types mingle so freely. This ensures the credibility of the story at a literal level, as required by the realist aesthetic, while maximising its metonymic resonance.

Belghoul displays a similar mastery of the metonymic mode in *Georgette!*. The novel concerns less than a year in the life of the protagonist, and most of the action takes places in a single day. However, the specific experience on which the narrative focuses –

that of learning to write at school – serves as a uniquely powerful metonym for the whole process of socialisation, and in particular for the cross-cultural conflicts which characterise a large part of that process where the children of immigrants are concerned. The girl's father has a rudimentary understanding of how Arabic is written, but is totally ignorant of the system of writing taught in French schools. When she has homework to do, he opens his daughter's exercise book at what for him is its first page (and which is, of course, the last page by French conventions). Modelling herself upon him, the girl writes her homework there only to be scolded by her schoolmistress who, on opening the exercise book at the normal place, finds nothing and concludes that her pupil has failed to do what was required of her. Unable to reconcile the contradictory cultural systems of home and school, the girl flees her classroom and wanders the streets. She meets an elderly French lady who, by writing letters to fake addresses, has been trying to conceal from her neighbours the fact that her three sons have abandoned her without a trace. The illusion of continuing contacts between the old lady and her sons cannot be sustained unless someone writes back to her. The woman invites the little girl to take on this role as soon as she has learned to write, signing her letters Pierre, Paul, and Jean. This provokes the following thoughts in the mind of the protagonist:

> C'est terminé: je veux plus jamais un jour d'école. Sinon, j'apprends et elle me sort un porte-plume tout de suite. Et j'écris 'chère maman' à une vieille toute nouvelle dans ma vie. Et je signe Pierre, Paul, ou Jean. Et si mon père l'apprend, il me tue immédiatement. Il ne m'enterre même pas: il ne creusera jamais la terre pour des inconnus pareils. Surtout, il gueule: 'j' t'envoye à l'école pour signer ton nom. A la finale, tu m' sors d'autres noms catastrophiques. J' croyais pas ça d' ma fille. J' croyais elle est intelligente comme son père. J' croyais elle est fière. Et r'garde-moi ça: elle s'appelle Georgette!'[67]

The grotesqueness of the false identity which her French would-be mother wants the girl to assume is underlined by the fact that the latter would have to sign herself in a series of male names. Far from this appearing as an aberration dreamed up by an eccentric old lady, it is seen as simply a logical extension of the violence to which the girl's identity is subjected by the demands of the schoolteacher.

At one point we see the teacher rummaging through the girl's

---

67. Belghoul, *Georgette!*, pp. 147–8.

schoolbag in search of her missing homework. Among the objects in the bag is a small pouch containing extracts from the Koran. Similar pouches are often given to their children by illiterate immigrants who purchase their Koranic messages from educated Muslims as a kind of protective emblem. The girl is deeply attached to the Islamic beliefs of her father, and is horrified when the schoolmistress, who is interested only in the missing homework, suggests that they might as well throw the pouch away. In this little incident, we see the true magnitude of what is at stake in the girl's education: the destruction of Islamic culture by the inculcation of Western norms.

The corrosive effects of the girl's schooling are summed up in the imaginary name Georgette. Proper names are often among the most emotionally charged elements in a language. The name by which an individual is known serves in part to mark his or her engagement in the cultural system from which it springs. When, in the passage quoted above, the girl imagines her father accusing her of taking a false name, Georgette, the name serves as a metonym for all that is alien about French culture in Arab eyes and ears. Behind it, we can imagine arguments over hair-styles and boy-friends, sexual independence and religious restrictions if and when the girl reaches adolescence (she in fact dies before the day is out).

Begag depicts precisely such an argument in *Béni ou le Paradis Privé*, except that here the youngsters being pressurised are boys. The narrator-protagonist, Béni, is twice the age of the girl in *Georgette!*, and consequently very much interested in relations with the opposite sex (a matter largely absent from Belghoul's novel). With his passion for his blonde dream-girl, France, Béni becomes the target of his father's anger along with his older brother Nordine when the latter refuses to accept an arranged marriage to an Algerian:

C'est à ce moment qu'Abboué [i.e. the father] s'est laissé aller.
– Quoi? Quoi? C'est des Françaises que vous voulez, bandes de chiens! Vous voulez salir notre nom, notre race! Vous voulez faire des enfants que vous appellerez Jacques . . . Allez, allez épouser des Françaises: quand vous pleurerez parce qu'elles vous auront traité de 'bicou', vous reviendrez chez votre vieux qui comprend rien.
Debout sur ses deux jambes d'Algérien, de musulman, de paysan sétifien, de maçon acharné et fatigué, il a insulté pendant encore long-temps toute sa vie, sa famille et la France. J'en avais marre. J'ai pris le coran de ma chaîne entre mes doigts et je l'ai posé sur la table.[68]

68. Begag, *Béni*, p. 109.

The terms in which the father insults his sons are very similar in spirit to the imagined remonstrations of his counterpart in *Georgette!*. In each case, the taking of a French proper name is seen as fundamentally incompatible with pride in the cultural traditions of North Africa. The projected adoption of the name Jacques, like that of Georgette in Belghoul's novel, is for the protagonist's father the thin end of a French wedge. The cultural roots which induce this reaction are signalled in the final paragraph of the passage quoted above, where we are reminded of the father's Islamic origins. The challenge to those traditions seen in Béni's attraction for France, a girl he has met at school, is forcefully dramatised in the boy's removal from his neck of a Koran-shaped pendant. The personal relations between the different characters represented here are inseparable from the socio-historical context in which this heated confrontation occurs. Beyond its immediate function in the story, each detail in this little scene serves in effect as a metonym for the historical collision of whole cultures engendered by the migratory process.

To maximise the resonance of their narratives, writers such as Begag filter their autobiographical experiences through extensive processes of selection and compression. We can see these processes at work in successive manuscript revisions. As noted in Section 2.3, characters such as the schoolteacher M. Grand are composite creations. Near the end of *Le Gone du Chaâba*, considerable licence seems also to have been taken in the depiction of the relationship between Azouz and a new teacher, M. Loubon. Loubon, a pied-noir with fond memories of Algeria, gives the boy a new sense of respect for the cultural heritage of North Africa. They meet after Azouz's family have moved from Le Chaâba to a run-down apartment block in the city centre. The original manuscript shows how, among a range of teachers at the Lycée Saint-Exupéry, Loubon is the one with whom, after a period of several months, Azouz eventually gets on best. The book deals solely with Loubon, with whom Azouz establishes an extremely close relationship right from his very first day at the lycée. These and other deletions (many minor incidents and characters represented in the original text are eliminated in the finished version) enable the author to focus the story more sharply around key moments in the development of Azouz's bi-cultural condition.

A more radical telescoping of time seems to have been at work in the composition of *Béni ou le Paradis Privé*. It will be recalled that *Le Gone du Chaâba* ends with the family about to move from the city centre to the La Duchère housing estate, and that the early pages of

Béni ou le Paradis Privé find them freshly installed there. In *Le Gone du Chaâba*, the move to La Duchère comes after Azouz has spent no more than two years at the Lycée Saint-Exupéry. The final version of *Béni ou le Paradis Privé* opens with the protagonist in the fifth form of a different lycée after having passed his BEPC at a Collège d'Enseignement Secondaire the previous year. There is therefore a jump of several years between the two narratives, despite their apparent dovetailing through the family's removal to La Duchère. Just as the final pages of *Le Gone du Chaâba* seem to have telescoped the chronology of the relationship between Azouz and M. Loubon, so the early section of *Béni ou le Paradis Privé* appears to compress what was originally a period of several years into a few months. Béni's initial difficulties in finding new friends on arrival in La Duchère enable the author to lay the groundwork for the theme of social exclusion; the dénouement brings this into climactic focus in the nightclub incident, which could only happen to someone several years older than Azouz had been at the end of *Le Gone du Chaâba*. Again, the dramatic intensity of the narrative is sharpened by the compression of events.

If the diegetic omissions which we have so far considered serve in effect to highlight within Beur narratives key areas of autobiographical experience, certain elements appear to be excluded for very different reasons. The most important issue here is Islam. Bearing in mind the centrality of Islam in the cultural traditions transmitted by first-generation immigrants, its often marginal role in the writings of their children is remarkable indeed. Arriz Tamza's short stories, reminiscent of *A Thousand and One Nights*, are virtually unique in their elaborate displays of Islamic belief. There are occasional moments of religious commitment in other Beur narratives, as when Mustapha Raïth solemnly observes Ramadan in his prison cell.[69] *Béni ou le Paradis Privé* is unusual in that it both begins and ends with allusions to Islam. The opening pages show how, as part of a Muslim family, Béni feels excluded from the fun of Christmas. Despite the dream of a Mohammed-like figure with which the story concludes, in the main body of the text Béni basically sees the Muslim beliefs of his parents as a handicap of which he is impatient to divest himself. This is seen most evidently in the row with his father over the choice of marriage partners. In many other Beur narratives we find no more than passing references to Islam.

The muted role of their parents' religion in the works of Beur

---

69. Raïth, *Palpitations*, pp. 111–12.

writers appears to have its origins in a paradoxical blend of anguish and indifference. For most of these writers, Islam is a relic of their past rather than a current preoccupation; they are in this sense indifferent to it. Divesting themselves of its influence has, however, often been a more painful process than they care to recall; moreover, they remain subject on this issue to uncomfortable pressures of a personal and sometimes political nature.

There could be no clearer illustration of the marginalisation of Islam than Lallaoui's 'La Colline aux oliviers'. The Beur protagonist's account of his quest for information about a long lost ancestor is preceded by a shorter narrative in which his grandfather, Baba Mous, describes his own attempts at solving the mystery. The combined narratives are used as a peg on which to hang a portrait of the Algerian people in its dealings with France during the last hundred years. Indeed, through the character of Cheikh Iskandar, who acts as a mentor for Baba Mous, we are presented with a distillation of all the wisdom accumulated by the inhabitants of Algeria in the centuries preceding French rule. Yet almost totally absent from this portrait of the protagonist's forbears is Islam. Throughout the text, we are presented with an almost wholly secularised version of Algeria's cultural heritage. A striking example of this is Baba Mous's summary of Iskandar's teachings:

> Il se révéla que Cheikh Iskandar possédait cette richesse que connaissent les savants après une vie d'étude. Mon maître, Cheikh Iskandar, m'apprit tout ou presque des choses du ciel et de la terre . . . 'La terre effectue une révolution autour du soleil en trois cent soixante-cinq jours un quart, que nous appelons une année. Cette année se divise en saisons qui rythment les semailles et les cultures, les migrations des hommes du désert et les transhumances des troupeaux. Autour de nous, la lune qui souvent nous éclaire se promène. Elle fait le tour de la terre en vingt-sept jours virgule trois et effectue pendant cette période une rotation sur son axe . . .' Il m'apprit les secrets des lettres et des chiffres, me révéla les pays lointains, me parla beaucoup des hommes, de leurs œuvres et de leurs excès.[70]

Iskandar's account of '[les] choses du ciel et de la terre' contains no heavenly teachings at all, beyond those of a purely astronomical nature. This undoubtedly reflects the secular nature of the author's own world view. It seems likely, too, that in constructing this

70. Lallaoui, 'La Colline aux oliviers'.

passage Lallaoui wished to impress upon his French readers the sophisticated body of scientific knowledge accumulated by the Arab world prior to the French conquest. We shall return in Section 3.4 to the implicit role of the predominantly French audience anticipated by Beur writers in shaping their narratives.

In *Le Sourire de Brahim*, an important part of Chapter 4, 'Ces chants qui viennent de très loin', is devoted to Brahim's awe-struck discovery of the richness of the cultural heritage of Algeria, particularly Kabylia. This comes to him initially when he attends a concert by Taos Amrouche, a singer of traditional Algerian songs. Later he begins to read a number of francophone Algerian writers and takes optional classes in the Berber language. Brahim is deeply impressed by the oral transmission of pre-literate cultures, exemplified in the songs of Taos Amrouche, which have been transmitted across countless generations. A friend sums up the cultural importance of oral traditions throughout Africa: 'Tout y est consigné, l'apparition de l'homme, l'évolution des techniques, l'esclavage, la colonisation et bien d'autres choses encore . . . En Algérie, c'est pareil, l'histoire et la culture, c'est le peuple qui la possède vraiment.'[71] At no point in these panegyric pages does either Brahim or his friend, or for that matter the narrator, mention Islam. The novel engages in a kind of folklorisation of Algerian culture, which, in this chapter, provides a colourful but ultimately harmless backdrop to the story; the idea that Islam, the core of Algerian culture for over a thousand years, might be relevant to the personal itinerary of the protagonist is never entertained.

The same chapter in which he makes his acquaintance with Taos Amrouche covers Brahim's successful completion of the baccalauréat and university enrolment as a medical student. Brahim may have studied Berber as an optional extra for a few weeks, but his many years of full-time education have served essentially to inculcate within him the language and culture of France. He believes in the virtues of 'une démocratie laïque et libérale'.[72] These are the classic values instilled in generations of children through the system of compulsory schooling instituted under the Third Republic by Jules Ferry. They are, Brahim observes, values 'dont peu de pays arabes pouvaient se targuer',[73] and are wholly incompatible with the constitutional bonding of Islam and the state in countries such as Algeria. 'L'Orient et ses rois', the second of two chapters

71. Kettane, *Le Sourire*, p. 71.
72. Ibid., p. 77.
73. Ibid., p. 77.

describing the summer he later spends in Algeria as a volunteer medic, shows Brahim to be quite out of sympathy with the authoritarian attitudes of officials there, and he is unwilling even to go through the outward motions of observing Ramadan, despite the public opprobrium which his attitude attracts.

Despite Brahim's evident lack of interest in the religion of his forbears, neither he nor the narrator makes any explicit criticisms of Islam. References to Islam are even more guarded in *Les ANI du 'Tassili'*. The only incident of any substance occupies no more than a page. It does, however, suggest a second reason (in addition to simple lack of interest or forgetfulness) for the reticence of Beur writers where Islam is concerned. During the crossing to Marseilles, Omar is invited by an old man to join him in prayers:

> – Tu viens à la prière, mon fils? insiste-t-il.
> Blocage net. C'est certainement la question la plus embarrassante qu'on m'ait jamais posée. Si je lui dis que mon savoir théologique se limite à 'Allah ou Akbar' et 'Inch Allah', je vais passer pour le dernier des connards. Si je lui réponds que ça ne m'intéresse pas, je vais passer pour le fils du diable en personne, et qui peut deviner la suite . . .?[74]

Omar finally resorts to a delaying tactic (he promises to come to prayers later) so as to avoid slipping into the old man's clutches while at the same time averting an argument. While Omar's ignorance about Islam is fundamental to its perfunctory role in the novel, there is also a sense in which he (and, we may assume, the author) finds the religious question too hot to handle. If the protagonist were to articulate his true feelings, what, he wonders, would the consequences be?

Salman Rushdie discovered to his cost just how devastating those consequences could be after publishing *The Satanic Verses* in 1988. Islamic fundamentalists can make life very unpleasant indeed for those who question the teachings of the Koran, particularly if, having been raised in the faith, their criticisms have the appearance of apostasy. Just a couple of months before the Ayotollah Khomeiny issued his death sentence on Rushdie, I witnessed a small but significant incident at a conference in Brussels.[75] During a talk on his work Rachid Khimoun, a Beur painter and sculptor, explained how, in

---

74. Tadjer, *Les ANI*, p. 63. The two Arabic phrases mean respectively 'God is Great' and 'God willing'.
75. 'Territoires de la mémoire', conference organised by the Commission Française de la Culture, Brussels, 9–10 December 1988.

composing some of his early collages, he had torn fragments of pages from a copy of the Koran and mixed them with miscellaneous papers which he had found lying around here and there in Paris. When he finished his talk, Khimoun was subjected to a sustained verbal assault by a handful of Islamic militants dotted around the packed lecture theatre. It was an ugly and strangely menacing confrontation, quite unlike the normal question-and-answer sessions heard at the end of a lecture. For the militants, the Koran was not to be subjected to that kind of questioning, and still less to the artistic liberties which Khimoun had taken with it.

Khimoun had been careful to explain that in ripping pages out of the Koran, he had not been inspired by any feelings of disrespect. The Arabic in which they were written had struck him as visually beautiful, but at the same time he had been conscious of his inability to read what it said. His main concern was to use the fragments, mixed in which secular objects, as images of the peculiar cultural condition which was his by virtue of his origins as the son of an Algerian immigrant. This was of no interest to Khimoun's critics, for whom the Koran was a holy book which existed for the sole purpose of guiding believers in the faith; it was under no circumstances to be adapted to the creative purposes of individual artists.

Beur writers have undoubtedly been aware of the sensitivity attaching to Islam among militants of this kind, even if few can have anticipated the virulence of the response to Rushdie's novel. It is difficult to quantify the importance of this awareness in inhibiting the depiction of matters relating to Islam, but it would not be surprising if, like Omar, many preferred to keep off the subject rather than expose themselves to ideological harassment.

The incident aboard the *Tassili* indicates, too, that this discretion may not be inspired solely by self-protective instincts. The old man who invites Omar to join him in prayers seems a perfectly pleasant fellow, and Omar evidently has no desire to upset him. Bearing in mind that all Beur writers come from Muslim families, it is impossible for them to criticise or condemn Islamic beliefs without running the risk of hurting their parents' feelings. As noted in Section 1.2, compromises between the older and younger generations often involve an element of subterfuge or mendacity. Certain subjects are avoided or white lies are told because those involved know that this is the only way to avoid open conflict. It will be recalled that Begag told a seminar in England that he was not a Muslim, while adding that he would never say that to his father. Along with Boukhedenna in her *Journal* and to a lesser extent Houari in *Zeida de nulle part*, Begag is one of the few Beur authors to have written candidly about the conflicts which have sometimes opposed younger and older members of the immigrant community where Islam is concerned. The author could make that statement in England and depict in his novels only slightly fiction-alised family arguments like the one in *Béni ou le Paradis Privé* quoted earlier in this chapter only because his illiterate father could neither hear nor read his words.

When Begag appeared on 'Apostrophes', Bernard Pivot quoted a sentence from *Béni ou le Paradis Privé* beginning: 'Entre France et mon père, j'ai choisi . . .'[76] Jokingly, the author cut in with the words: '. . . le père, je l'espère'. Pivot reminded him that in fact, the sentence ends: '. . . j'ai choisi la blonde'. Continuing in hu-moristic vein, Begag retorted with mock surprise: 'Oh! Il a choisi la blonde? Oh là là, il y a mon père qui écoute, je suis obligé de dire . . .'[77] Here again, the territorial demarcation of separate cultural zones, discussed in Section 2.2, breaks down. Begag's remarks may be made in a television studio to which his illiterate father will never have access (the *sine qua non* for entry into the select company of Pivot is to have written something of note), but the ubiquity of television is such that his remarks are, like the passionate kiss witnessed in *Le Gone du Chaâba*, carried directly into the family home.

Beneath the light-heartedness of this little interchange, the underlying issue is a serious one. Many of the most painful mo-ments in the lives of Beur authors have involved conflicts with their parents. The flashpoint where Islam is concerned has often taken precisely this form. Yet strong bonds of affection generally persist despite these disagreements, and these bonds have almost certainly inhibited Beur authors in their depiction of Islam. If the illiteracy of the older generation gives these writers a greater margin of free-dom than they might otherwise enjoy,[78] there are still many things which they find just too sensitive to say publicly. In their face-to-face dealings with their parents, many Beurs have gone to great lengths to avoid giving personal offence while at the same time

---

76. Begag, *Béni*, p. 110.
77. Begag speaking on 'Apostrophes', Antenne 2, 24 Feb. 1989.
78. Begag specifically states that he would never have dared to write as frankly as he has done in *Le Gone du Chaâba* and *Béni ou le Paradis Privé* if his parents had been able to read. See Begag's interviews with Michel Cressole, 'Le Gone de Chaâba réédite ses exploits', and with Florence Assouline, 'Azouz Begag, écrivain: "Khomeiny et Rushdie ont blessé mon père"', *L'Evénement du jeudi*, 2 Mar. 1989, p. 14.

insisting on their right to independence in matters of conscience. If, in their published works, Beur authors have written comparatively little about Islam, this may in some measure be explained by a reluctance on their part to say anything which could be interpreted as an open disavowal of their parents.[79]

Islam is not the only area of sensitivity in relations between Beur writers and their parents, nor are those relations the only area in which significant elements have been filtered out in the process of literary composition. Practically nothing in *Le Thé au harem d'Archi Ahmed* is invented. Its graphic depiction of life in a poverty-ridden HLM estate makes it one of the toughest of Beur novels. Yet in all kinds of ways, Charef has attenuated the raw edges of the original experiences on which the novel is based. Commenting on the film adaptation of the novel, Charef remarked: 'Madjid, c'est moi [. . .] Quand il dit à sa mère qui lui parle en arabe: "Je ne comprends *pas* ce que tu dis". J'ai failli mettre *plus*. Mais ça aurait été trop dur.'[80] Charef, like Madjid, did once understand Arabic, but the sense of betrayal implicit in the forgetting of his parents' language, as against his never having known it, is something stronger than the writer–director cares to depict in his screen *alter ego*.

As a teenager, Charef and his friends committed various petty crimes. Some of these are depicted in both the novel and the film, but out of loyalty to his friends, whom he had no wish to cast in a bad light, Charef left out many of their deeds.[81] The prison sentence to which his own wrong-doings led (the counterpart of the one we see Madjid about to begin at the end of the story) was too painful to talk about at all.[82] One of the most gripping moments in the novel, as in the film, is the attempted suicide of a young woman who is saved at the last minute by Madjid's mother. In the actual events witnessed by Charef, the woman died.[83] Asked

79. A survey of opinions carried out among youths of North African origin in the Paris area found that while most knew little about Islam and showed scant interest in its teachings, they retained a sentimental attachment to it out of respect for their parents. See Yves Gonzalez-Quijano, 'Les "Nouvelles" Générations issues de l'immigration maghrébine et la question de l'Islam', *Revue française de science politique*, vol. 37, no. 6, Dec. 1987, pp. 820–31.

80. Interview with Claude-Marie Trémois, '*Le Thé au harem d'Archimède*: Un espoir en béton', *Télérama*, 1 May 1985, p. 8; punctuation and italics as in original. This scene in the film is based on a similar incident in Charef's novel, *Le Thé*, p. 13. It will be observed that the title of the film, *Le Thé au harem d'Archimède*, is a slightly modified version of that used for the novel.

81. This aspect of his work was discussed by Charef in an interview with Richard Vieille, '*Le Thé au harem d'Archimède*', *Lire*, June 1985, p. 153.

82. Charef stated this in his interview with Salim Jay, 'Mehdi Charef', p. 107.

83. This was revealed by Charef in his interview with Olivier Dazat, 'Mehdi

to explain why he had toned things down in this way, Charef replied: 'On aurait dit que j'en faisais trop. Et surtout, je n'ai pas voulu faire un drame social et misérabiliste. J'avais très peur de cet adjectif: misérabiliste. J'ai préféré une chronique allègre plutôt qu'un film accusateur conçu pour choquer systématiquement le spectateur.'[84] Here again, we see the anticipated reactions of the French audience as an important constraint on Beur writers. We shall return to this in Section 3.4.

Charef's comments also point up one final area in which Beur writers are relatively taciturn, that of politics. When Charef rejects any idea of creating 'un drame social', he has in mind a didactic approach to art intended to influence more or less directly the organisation of society. Beur novelists are far more concerned with basic problems in the construction of a sense of personal identity than with the mechanics of collective organisations. Belghoul led an extremely active political life for a brief period in the mid-1980s, but there is no trace of this in *Georgette!*. The novel was in fact written as a kind of retreat from the manipulative forces which, the author had become convinced, were at work everywhere in the political arena; literary expression alone seemed to offer the possibility of personal authenticity. Kenzi's *La Menthe sauvage*, Boukhedenna's *Journal*, Lallaoui's *Les Beurs de Seine* and Raïth's *Palpitations intra-muros* are unusual among Beur narratives in including relatively sustained passages of ideological analysis. Some of the earliest childhood memories of Beur authors date back to the politically explosive years of the Algerian war. The personal impact of those events is depicted in heavily autobiographical novels such as Zemouri's *Le Jardin de l'intrus*, Imache's *Une Fille sans histoire*, Kettane's *Le Sourire de Brahim* and Yacine's 'Les Années de brume'. Apart from Kettane and Lallaoui, however, few Beur writers dwell at any length on the forms of collective organisation initiated by the immigrant community.

Even Bouzid's account of the Marche des Beurs is largely devoid of political analysis, and the organisational mechanics of the march take second place to its personal meaning for the author. Bouzid's narrative recounts above all a journey of self-discovery. Before the march arrived in Aix-en-Provence, he had been thinking about leaving France because of the racism rampant there. He had hopes of trying his luck in Algeria, despite his unhappy experiences in that country in 1977. The hostility which surrounded him in France

---

Charef', *Cinématographe*, July 1985, p. 11.
84. Ibid., p. 11.

made life intolerable: 'Je ne pouvais plus rester dans ce pays sans être mal à l'aise devant l'image que me renvoyait mon miroir.'[85] The march convinced him that instead of leaving the country, he should, to put it at its simplest, find a way of being himself in France. That, fundamentally, is the problematic which conditions most Beur fiction.

85. Bouzid, *La Marche*, p. 26.

-3-

I, We, You, They

3.1 Viewpoint

A work of fiction is far more than mere diegetic 'content'. The story is necessarily mediated through a variety of mechanisms which contribute significantly to the overall meaning of the text. None of these mechanisms can function except through the master medium of a particular language. Within such a language, events have to be recounted by one or more narrators, and the whole of the text is of course guided by the hand of the author. S/he must in turn write with a certain audience in mind, and the text cannot be said to engender any meaning at all until it is decoded and interpreted by a reader. More prosaic but none the less important are the economic and material relations which condition the physical dissemination of the printed word. Through each of these mechanisms the narrator and/or author is positioned in relation to diverse individuals and groups. This positioning is the subject of the present chapter.

Every story has at least one narrator, though not all narrators signal their presence explicitly. The narrator's representation of events is inevitably conditioned by his or her position in time and space, as well as by the affective and ideological prism through which s/he views the world. This combination of spatio-temporal and psycho-social positioning marks what, in the following discussion, will be called a viewpoint. Defined thus, each viewpoint is the manifestation of a personal or, in certain circumstances, group identity.

Few if any narratives confine us to a single viewpoint. Narrators often focus on the way in which characters experience events recounted in the text. Indeed, through focalisation of this kind the affective and ideological viewpoint of a particular character may interpose itself between the reader and the story more overtly than that of the narrator. By the hierarchical ordering of the different viewpoints represented through narration and focalisation, the author presents the reader with an interpretative framework for the story. To grasp that framework the reader must infer the spatio-temporal and psycho-social position of each narrator and focalising consciousness. The eventual direction in which the reader's own sympathies run will depend to a very large extent on how the author orchestrates the interplay between these different perspectives. This interplay is the subject of Section 3.2. The present section is concerned with some of the key markers of individual viewpoints.

In categorising the spatio-temporal positions of narrators, we may usefully draw on the conceptual framework developed by Gérard Genette.[1] Genette distinguishes between homodiegetic and heterodiegetic narrators: while the former feature as characters in the stories which they narrate, the latter do not. In spatial terms, we may speak of a heterodiegetic narrator as standing outside the story, whereas a homodiegetic narrator is an insider. Genette also distinguishes between intradiegetic and extradiegetic narrators: the former speak or write simultaneously with events, whereas the latter are removed in time, and generally recount the story retrospectively. A homodiegetic narrator speaking from an extradiegetic position stands both inside and the outside the story, for while featuring as a character in the flow of events, s/he describes them from a separate point in time. Grammatical persons offer the most explicit markers of narratorial presence. When the narrator says 'I' or uses the plural form 'we', s/he signals his or her position as the subject speaking or writing the words in the text. In the case of a homodiegetic narrator, the first person may also signal his or her presence as a character within the story. As heterodiegetic narrators are absent from the story, they generally recount events in the third person ('he'/'she'/'they'), except when commenting on them from their external vantage point. While texts featuring heterodiegetic narrators may, in traditional parlance, be labelled third-person narratives (in the sense that the third person predominates in them), it is technically misleading to speak of third-person narrators. Every narrator by definition has the role of first person in his or her narrative; what varies from one text to another is the extent to which that role is explicitly enunciated.

Some narrators articulate their psycho-social position very explicitly, spelling out their beliefs and allegiances in seemingly

---

1. See Gérard Genette, *Figures III*, Paris, Seuil, 1972, and idem, *Nouveau discours du récit*, Paris, Seuil, 1983.

unequivocal terms. There are many other cases, however, in which the ground is far less clear. Moreover, explicit statements of ideological commitments may present more complex problems than at first meet the eye. Sakinna Boukhedenna's *Journal. 'Nationalité: immigré(e)'* offers particularly clear examples of this. The method of narration here is among the simplest to be found in any Beur narrative. Other works often involve more than one narrator and/or changes of focalisation, but Boukhedenna's has a single narrator-protagonist, Sakinna, through whom the whole of the story, such as it is, is focalised. In fact, specific events occupy a secondary role in the text compared with Sakinna's reflections upon them, together with her wider thoughts on the condition of the immigrant community. This is probably the most ideologically explicit of all Beur narratives. Much of Sakinna's discourse is categorical to the point of being dogmatic. Yet it is extremely difficult to define her position, for at different points in the narrative she aligns herself with seemingly contradictory ideas. These contradictions are summed up in an introductory note, where she states:

C'est en France que j'ai appris à être Arabe,
C'est en Algérie que j'ai appris à être l'Immigrée.[2]

Spurned in France as a second-class citizen, Sakinna seeks a sense of dignity in her Arab roots. She takes to wearing Algerian dress and enrolls for classes in the Arabic language: 'Je suis Algérienne, colonisée culturellement, mais je ferai tout pour retrouver mes racines.'[3] At the same time, she develops a fiercely feminist stance, and latter embraces Marxist ideology. When, in her early twenties, she travels to Algeria for the first time, it becomes impossible to square these ideological circles. She tries to convince herself that her secular values can be accommodated in an Islamic country ('Tu peux être Arabe sans croire à Dieu'[4]). But the sexist attitudes of Algerian men make her life a misery: 'Si la culture arabe, c'est de réduire la femme à l'état où elle est, je ne veux pas de cette arabité.'[5] Derided as an ignorant foreigner in Algeria, Sakinna concludes that

---

2. Sakinna Boukhedenna, *Journal. 'Nationalité: immigré(e)'*, Paris, L'Harmattan, 1987, p. 5.
3. Ibid., p. 71.
4. Ibid., p. 82.
5. Ibid., p. 100.

she must return to France: 'La France est raciste, mais en France je peux vivre seule sans mari, sans père, mère, et la police ne m'épie pas tous les jours. Je peux crier, "non" au racisme, "non" à l'exploitation de la femme, je me sens un peu plus libre que sur ma terre.'[6] Despite Sakinna's apparent dogmatism, hers is not a firmly anchored viewpoint. On the contrary, she is, in her own words, 'victime d'un manque: mon identité culturelle.'[7] Consequently, the terms in which she makes even the simplest declaration of allegiance must be interpreted with great care. It is moreover impossible to define Sakinna's viewpoint without reference to its position in time, for it is constantly evolving. The handling of time is in fact such a fundamental element in the fabric of any narrative that the whole of Chapter 4 will be devoted to this.

At the opposite extreme from large-scale ideological analyses, grammatical persons often serve as small but revealing indicators of narratorial identity. Emile Benveniste was the first theorist seriously to explore the affective power attaching to grammatical persons.[8] He observed that the use of the third person generally implies a greater affective distance between the speaker and the referent than is suggested when the first or second person is employed. Of particular interest in the present context are the plural forms, which may serve to place differential affective marks on the groups thus designated. The emotive charge associated with the demarcation between 'us' and 'them' is a familiar one. In saying 'we', I include myself among the group thus designated; when I say 'they', I place myself outside the group. The plural forms of grammatical persons may serve therefore as a kind of short-hand for the affective ties binding an individual to different collectivities.

Boukhedenna's *Journal* provides a wealth of examples. Sakinna's use of the 'nous' form consistently carries a positive affective charge, but its referent varies enormously. Sometimes it articulates a bond between Sakinna and Arabs in general, in contrast with the French: 'Oh! Si seulement les Français pouvaient prendre conscience que notre culture n'est pas une culture inférieure. Nous sommes Arabes noyés dans l'interdit français.'[9] Elsewhere, the referent of 'nous' narrows to the immigrant community, who are seen as victims of both the French and Algerian authorities. This is

6. Ibid., pp. 100–1.
7. Ibid., pp. 74–5.
8. See Emile Benveniste, *Problèmes de linguistique générale*, vol. 1, Paris, Gallimard, 1966, esp. ch. 18.
9. Boukhedenna, *Journal*, p. 67.

the case, for example, in Sakinna's account of a conversation with an elderly lady in Algeria, whose views she endorses:

> Fouzia [. . .] était pour moi, le reflet de la femme telle que je l'aime. [. . .] Nous, les immigrés, nous étions, à ses yeux, juste des victimes non seulement du colonialisme, mais d'un système à double face. Celui du colonialisme français et celui du néo-colonialisme de l'Algérie, qui en rien ne veut de nous.[10]

Sakinna articulates a similar divide between the immigrant community and Arab students in France: 'Souvent, ils viennent de la bourgeoisie arabe. Ils jouissent de privilèges que nous, les immigrés, on ne reçoit pas.'[11] On many occasions, Sakinna restricts the referent of 'nous' to women. Sometimes it situates her in the female camp in a global split between men and women. In the following example, 'they' are male Arab intellectuals who argue that the emancipation of women is incompatible with Islamic civilisation: 'Pour moi, ce n'est pas un argument valable: ils veulent nous diviser. N'avons-nous pas, après tout, le même sexe, que nous soyons occidentales ou orientales?'[12] More commonly, Sakinna identifies herself specifically with Arab women against their menfolk: 'Je pense que ce sont les hommes arabes qui assument beaucoup moins leur sexualité que les femmes arabes. [. . .] C'est parce qu'ils ne nous connaissent pas, nous femmes arabes, qu'ils se méfient de nous.'[13]

On occasions, the gender split is overlaid with the politico-cultural divide between France and Algeria: 'Je suis Arabe, bougnoule d'Algérie, née en France en 59, quand les Français violaient nos sœurs en Algérie.'[14] Elsewhere, the dividing line is between women members of the immigrant community and their husbands, as in the following prose poem by Sakinna:

> Ils ont les yeux fermés, prient le grand!
> Pas de beaux jours, c'est nos hommes:
> Notre vie, c'est se taire, se soumettre, accepter toute cette souffrance, nous sommes femmes![15]

10. Ibid., pp. 94–5.
11. Ibid., p. 72.
12. Ibid., p. 54.
13. Ibid., p. 114.
14. Ibid., p. 52.
15. Ibid., p. 57.

Most commonly of all, however, 'nous' refers to the female part of the younger generation among the immigrant community:

> Nos hommes disent que nous, les femmes immigrées de la deuxième génération, nous ne sommes plus des vraies Arabes car nous sommes comme les Européennes. Nous nous dévergondons, nous traînons dans les bars, nous buvons et nous baisons. Comme si femme arabe, à leurs yeux, voulait dire: maison, chiffon, enfant et ferme ta gueule.[16]

At times, the field of reference narrows still further to include only the most militant of these young women:

> Rares sont les Arabes qui pensent comme nous. Dans le quartier, la plupart des filles sont mariées ou ont été mariées. Les familles arabes nous regardent d'un mauvais œil. Nous ne sommes pas honorables et respectables à leurs yeux car ils pensent que nous, les filles, on n'est plus vierges. C'est tout ce qui compte quand on est une bonne musulmane. C'est ce qu'ils veulent les hommes arabes. Nous ligaturer notre sexualité, nous convaincre que nous sommes inférieures. Le malheur, c'est que beaucoup de femmes arabes-musulmanes, croient à cette bêtise. Alors elles font tout pour garder la virginité, qui est l'honneur du cousin, du frère, du père et pas le leur.[17]

The instability in Sakinna's affective ties, manifest in these variations in her use of the 'nous' form, is a direct reflection of her uncertain sense of identity. In all the examples quoted above, 'they' (whoever they may be) are consistently cast in a negative role. The alienating effect of the 'ils' form is deliberately played upon by Sakinna when she describes how, every time she and a girl friend left a house where they were staying, they had to be accompanied by one of the menfolk, as they had been everywhere else in Algeria. On one occasion, they were bought ice-creams by their escort:

> Il nous acheta des glaces. Il jouait les durs. Nous reprîmes, les glaces dans la main, le chemin de cette maudite prison, qui était la maison quotidienne où ils nous obligeaient, tous ces 'Ils', à survivre jours et nuits. Ah! Ces glaces aussi glacées que le glacis qu'était ce type dont je ne me souviens plus du prénom tant je le haïssais.[18]

16. Ibid., p. 55.
17. Ibid., p. 51.
18. Ibid., p. 80.

Though she hates the sexism and ostracism which she experiences in Algeria as a young woman from an immigrant family in France, Sakinna tells herself that she must master the language of her homeland:

> Quand tu auras appris la langue qui est la tienne, tu pourras apprendre à te confronter avec ces 'ils' arabes qui te considèrent comme ne faisant point partie de la nation arabe, ceux qui pensent que 'femme immigrée' veut dire: put inquahba [i.e. prostitute]. Tu pourras dans leur langage leur apprendre quelle force nous sommes, nous les 'putains' immigrées de la deuxième [génération] comme disent les Français. Ne tombe point dans leur piège, ne les traite pas d'arriérés, tourne ta langue, apprends, immigrée, quelle est ta vraie société.[19]

The intellectual logic of this passage, arguing that Sakinna belongs in Algeria, is consistently undercut by the affective charge generated by the distribution of grammatical persons. These tensions are indicated not only by the negative charge attaching to the third person plural, but also by the self-designating use of the second person singular ('tu'). This 'tu' is being addressed by an implicit 'je'; both are, of course, Sakinna. The attitudinal divide in which this pronominal separation is grounded and the rhetorical appeal which it provokes here reflect the fact that one part of Sakinna feels differently from another.[20]

Even the consistent use of the first person singular is no guarantee of a unified viewpoint. This is not simply because the narrator may display conflicting attitudes at one point in time compared with another or even (as in the passage above) at one and the same moment. Equally important may be the temporal divide between the experiencing self and the narrating self. In the case of a homodiegetic narrator, both may be designated by the same grammatical person, but if events are recounted extradiegetically, i.e. from a vantage point outside the story (most commonly, at a later point in time), the narrating 'I' may take a very different view of things from the experiencing 'I'. The tenses of verbs are in this regard important grammatical markers. These issues will be taken up again in Section 4.2.

19. Ibid., p. 82.
20. For a similar passage, in which the self-critical narrator-protagonist is designated at various points in the first, second and third persons, see Bouzid, *La Marche*, Paris, Sindbad, 1984, p. 132.

It follows from this that the scale of intimacy suggested by Benveniste in his analysis of grammatical persons cannot on its own suffice to gauge the affective rapport between narrators and protagonists in literary texts. Heterodiegetic narrators, who customarily use the third person, are not necessarily more emotionally distanced than homodiegetic ones, who normally designate themselves in the first person. The narrator's position in time may be as significant as his position in space, and this ontological positioning is inevitably overlaid by the ideological baggage carried by a perceiving consciousness at any particular moment. The affective relationship between the narrator and the protagonist is at least as close in Nacer Kettane's *Le Sourire de Brahim*, whose heterodiegetic narrator confines himself almost entirely to the use of the third person, as it is in Kamal Zemouri's *Le Jardin de l'intrus*, where the homodiegetic narrator makes heavy use of the first person; in both cases, the life-histories of the protagonists are recounted with obvious sympathy.

Homodiegetic narrators sometimes take the unusual step of speaking of themselves in the third person in order to emphasise the gap between the narrating self and the experiencing self. At the beginning and end of Tassadit Imache's *Une Fille sans histoire* the narrator-protagonist, Lil, speaks of her grown-up self in the first person, but in the main body of the text, which is devoted to her childhood and adolescence, she designates herself in the third person. The split between these grammatical persons reflects the narrator's sense of perplexity concerning the relationship between her past and present selves. There can, however, be no doubt as to the intimacy of the affective bonds between them. The third person serves to erect a more deliberate affective barrier in Mustapha Raïth's *Palpitations intra-muros*. The earliest extant draft of Raïth's novel, an unpublished typescript entitled 'Et le bonheur en prison? . . .', is narrated almost entirely in the first person; the narrator-protagonist designates himself in the third person in just one or two experimental passages. In the final version of the novel, the relative weightings of the first and third persons are reversed. In this way the narrator attempts to put firmly behind him the wrongdoings which, in his role as protagonist, led to his imprisonment.

A reverse effect is achieved when the narrator of Mehdi Charef's *Le Thé au harem d'Archi Ahmed*, who confines himself almost entirely to the third person, momentarily slips into the first person plural at several points in the text. The third person is customarily used by heterodiegetic narrators, but the referent of the 'nous' form, where it appears in *Le Thé au harem d'Archi Ahmed*, is clearly the band of youths at the centre of the story,[21] or, in its final appearance, those present in the home of one of them.[22] As the 'je' implicit in this 'nous', the narrator must be present at these points in the story (making him a homodiegetic narrator), and the references are sufficiently extensive to make it clear that he and the main characters grew up together, but we never see him individualised in any way. The third person never interposes any barriers between the narrator and the protagonists, and these fleeting uses of the first person plural confirm the affective bond between them. In a more discreet way, this bond is sometimes suggested by the narrator's use of the indefinite pronoun 'on', by which he implies his own presence alongside the characters.[23] Asked about these uses of 'nous' and 'on' when I interviewed him, the author told me that, through the narrator, he had wanted to indicate his solidarity with the characters, who are closely based on his own past and that of his friends, but felt it would have sounded too self-important if he had used the first person throughout the text.

We have seen that the affective and ideological coloration of the viewpoint from which a text is narrated or focalised is signalled through a complex and often subtle range of mechanisms. As the next section will show, the reading experience is liable to be rendered still more complex by the interplay of multiple viewpoints.

3.2 Dialogism

Few if any Beur narratives present a single viewpoint, though in a number of cases one obviously predominates over all the others. More commonly, the reader encounters a range of perspectives, and the relationship between them is complex. Changes of narrator always carry shifts of perspective, but these do not necessarily mark the most significant divergencies of viewpoint, in the sense in which I am using that term. The first of the two Parts into which Leïla Houari's *Zeida de nulle part* is divided alternates between stretches of first-person and third-person narrative. All are focalised primarily around the eponymous protagonist, that is to say

---

21. Mehdi Charef, *Le Thé au harem d'Archi Ahmed*, Paris, Mercure de France, 1983, pp. 57, 84, 135.
22. Ibid., p. 156.
23. Ibid., esp. pp. 25, 31, 39, 58, 135.

that the ideas and emotions which she experiences in the story are given prime attention, even when she is not the narrator. We can glean very little information from the text about the psycho-social make-up of the heterodiegetic narrator with whom she shares the narration of Part I, and who takes over from her completely in Part II. The representation of Zeida's consciousness continues to dominate throughout the text, even when it is reported in the third person. The almost total anonymity of the main narrator is such that his or her viewpoint is scarcely perceptible at all except for its spatio-temporal position (outside the protagonist and situated at some point in time later than the events in the story). In this sense, the dominant viewpoint (i.e. the main centre of consciousness represented in the text) is consistently that of the protagonist. When I discussed these twin narrators with the author, it became clear that Houari had initially adopted a homodiegetic approach because she wanted to recreate as vividly as possible the emotional turmoil which she herself had experienced as an adolescent. The switch to a less emotive heterodiegetic narrator was a token of the increased psychological control enjoyed by the more mature Houari and, eventually, by the protagonist herself.

Other viewpoints do make themselves felt in the novel, but they are those of other characters, rather than that of the shadowy figure who narrates most of the text. The most obvious way in which they intervene is in patches of dialogue. Part I includes an important discussion between Zeida and her mother, while in Part II there are many conversations between the protagonist and people she meets on a return visit to Morocco. Early in Part II, for example, Zeida enjoys going off for a walk in the countryside, but is scolded on her return by the aunt with whom she is staying in a remote Moroccan village:

– Zeida! s'exclama sa tante, je t'ai déjà dit de ne pas t'éloigner, si tu veux partir te promener demande à l'un de nous de t'accompagner.
– Les chiens? . . . ah! oui . . . amti [i.e. auntie] il ne faut pas avoir peur, ce n'est rien.
– Fais attention quand même, tu as eu de la chance: en général, ils sentent très vite les étrangers.
Zeida regarda sa tante bizarrement, étranger, qui est étranger? c'est mon village ici, elle était triste maintenant.[24]

24. Leïla Houari, *Zeida de nulle part*, Paris, L'Harmattan, 1985, p. 43.

Two completely different viewpoints are articulated in this dia-logue. The protagonist feels she belongs where she is; her aunt, while affectionately disposed towards Zeida, sees her as an out-sider. The validity of the aunt's viewpoint is implicitly confirmed by the incomprehension with which the protagonist greets her remarks. Zeida assumes that when the old lady reprimands her for wandering around on her own, she is worried about the dangers of local dogs; although her aunt responds to this suggestion, it is far more likely that her original comment concerned the unseemliness, from a Muslim point of view, of a young woman walking alone in public.

Strictly speaking, when dialogue of this kind is represented in the form of direct discourse, each speaker is a secondary or embedded narrator,[25] though by convention only those who speak with few or no interruptions over a sustained period are referred to as such. Zeida's mother does exactly this when she recounts her own childhood and marriage,[26] and in this sense clearly ranks as a secondary narrator. Hearing the mother speak in her own words (or at any rate apparently in her own words – we shall return to this point shortly) is important for a number of reasons. Her temporary displacement of Zeida as both narrator and focaliser establishes an affective bond between the mother and the reader. While the reader's main allegiance is to Zeida, around whom most of the novel is focalised, this secondary affective strand helps us to partici-pate more fully in the protagonist's own divided emotions. Despite her determination to break away from her mother, Zeida feels a very deep affection for her. The main part of the mother's narrative is devoted to her arranged marriage as a young woman in Morocco. Thinking back on her mother's words, Zeida reflects:

Tu parlais, je t'écoutais, j'aurais tellement voulu être comme toi, accep-ter les choses telles qu'elles sont, tu n'as pas été très heureuse et un rien te fait sourire. J'ai honte de moi, à force de me révolter j'en arrive à ne plus savoir ce que je veux. Tu me racontes ta nuit de noces, simplement, parce que c'est comme cela et moi je me fâche, pourtant je ne trouve rien à répondre.[27]

25. Each meets the criterion by which Genette, for example, tests for a narrator ('Qui parle?') as against a focaliser ('Qui voit?'): see Genette, *Nouveau discours*, pp. 43–4.
26. Houari, *Zeida*, pp. 32–9.
27. Ibid., p. 38.

The mother's submissive attitude, which Zeida refuses to share, is imbued with a real sense of dignity by allowing the older woman to speak directly in her own words, and the reader cannot but share the protagonist's own divided emotions.

Yet can these really be the mother's words? Most of her story is recounted in very elaborate French, making heavy use of the past historic (a tense normally reserved for written, as against oral, discourse). The use of the past historic is in itself sufficient reason for doubting that the words in the text can have been exactly those uttered by the mother in conversation with her daughter. When we recall that Zeida's mother is an illiterate Moroccan, for whom French is a foreign language, it seems quite impossible that she can have spoken the words attributed to her in the novel. Her speech, though presented in the form of direct discourse, has clearly been at the very least amended by the primary narrator who appears to be transcribing it; it may indeed be more plausibly regarded as a wholesale translation of words originally uttered in the woman's mother-tongue. The primary narrator (in this case, Zeida) may well intend to achieve in such a translation an exactly equivalent meaning to that of the original discourse, but this is a notoriously elusive (and, some would say, ultimately impossible) objective.

The underlying issues raised here may be usefully illuminated with the aid of Mikhail Bakhtin's ideas on the interaction of different discourses within works of fiction. Bakhtin argues that whereas poetry aims to be single-voiced, the novel is essentially double- or multi-voiced.[28] In Bakhtin's writings, a voice corresponds roughly to the articulated form of what I have called a viewpoint. At times Bakhtin uses a number of related and overlapping concepts such as speech types and social languages, denoting the types of discourse characteristic of broad social groups, and suggests that it is the interaction of these (rather than of the articulated consciousnesses of particular individuals) which characterises the novel form. The two levels distinguished here are not necessarily incompatible with each other. As Bakhtin rightly notes, language always comes to us in the form of discourse. We learn a tongue through hearing it used, not out of a dictionary or through abstract generalisations. The learning of what is conventionally (though not altogether accurately) called a national language, such as French or Arabic, is inseparable from exposure to the particular

28. See M.M. Bakhtin, *The Dialogic Imagination*, trans. Caryl Emerson and Michael Holquist, Austin, University of Texas Press, 1981, esp. the essay 'Discourse in the Novel' (pp. 259–422).

types of language use, i.e. discourse, practised by certain speakers of this or that tongue. Similarly, the speech types or social languages associated with different sub-groups of those who share a given tongue become familiar to us through their articulation by particular individuals. Conversely, therefore, the voice of an individual is inseparable from the speech types which he or she has internalised.

One of Bakhtin's most important contentions is that any individual utterance is always in some degree overlaid by the discourse of others. The words we utter always bear the imprint of those from whom we borrow them, and are coloured in turn by those to whom they are addressed. As each of us interacts with a variety of others, and through them with a diversity of speech types or social languages, the words we use are in a constant condition of heteroglossia, i.e. suffused with meanings which vary according to the context in which they are placed. The novel form, according to Bakhtin, is grounded in the recognition and orchestration of heteroglossia through a process which he calls dialogism. In dialogism, discourse is constantly relativised through the more or less open confrontation of contrasting speech types.

When, in an early draft of Raïth's *Palpitations intra-muros*, the narrator states that 'les mœurs de notre "civilisation" ont toujours été décalés, retardés par la bêtise',[29] the quotation marks which he places around the word 'civilisation' demarcate it off as part of some one else's discourse.[30] Through the commentary with which he surrounds it, the narrator dissociates himself from the ideas of social progress and sound morality which this word normally connotes. The word and its connotations are not attributed to any particular individual, but clearly emanate from a viewpoint other than that of the narrator. They are, in Bakhtin's terms, part of a speech type or social language, and as such represent a type of consciousness, i.e. a way of thinking common to many individuals. Thus viewpoints (i.e. centres of consciousness), as defined for our

29. Mustapha Raïth, 'Et le bonheur en prison? . . .'.
30. An interesting reverse phenomenon may be observed in a second version of the typescript, entitled 'Douleur ensemencée', which a Catholic nun circulated in a small photocopied edition in 1984. Evidently shocked by much of the strong language used in the original draft, Raïth's amateur publisher deleted many of the seemingly cruder passages. At one point, she changed the typescript to read: 'l'immense "merdier" du monde'. While each word in this phrase was present in the original typescript, the quotation marks around 'merdier' were not. Through their insertion, the narrator is made to apparently disown a word which was originally his.

purposes here, do not necessarily correspond to the minds of individualised characters.

At several points in Arriz Tamza's *Ombres*, whole sentences are punctuated to indicate direct discourse, but without the speakers being named. The following passage, for example, describes the reactions to which the female French protagonist is exposed after her relationship with an Arab lover becomes public knowledge:

Au travail. Regards – chuchotements. Sur la place. Regards – chuchotements – attroupements. On sortait des magasins.
– Tè, vè! C'est celle qui est avec l'Arabe. Pute – vicieuse – mal baisée. Les voisins. Regards – chuchotements – portes claquées. La boîte aux lettres.
– C'est honteux – salope – traître . . .[31]

None of the speakers here is personalised in any way. We know neither their sex nor their age nor their names. Yet it is clear from their discourse that they think in certain ways, and that these are essentially racist in character. Attitudes of this kind are not, of course, confined to the woman's workmates or neighbours. These disembodied voices represent a type of discourse (in Bakhtin's terms, a single voice) which can be found among a disturbingly large number of men and women in many parts of France. Because they are depersonalised, the individual acts of verbal hostility to which the protagonist is exposed are to be seen as part of a wider socio–attitudinal malaise.

In all the examples which we have looked at so far in this section, shifts of viewpoint or voice have been signalled by punctuation marks (generally quotation marks or, as in the passage from *Ombres*, dashes at the beginning of lines of dialogue indicating changes of speaker). Marks of this kind signal pieces of direct discourse, i.e. words emanating from a source other than the narrator, reproduced as nearly as possible in their original form. By no means every change of viewpoint is handled in this way. In indirect discourse the conjunction 'que' replaces quotation marks, and tenses, grammatical persons and other deictics used by the original speaker are modified in ways which reflect the interposed consciousness of the narrator. The rules governing the use of these

31. Arriz Tamza, *Ombres*, Paris, L'Harmattan, 1989, p. 85. For a very similar passage see Tassadit Imache, *Une Fille sans histoire*, Paris, Calmann-Lévy, 1989, p. 19.

markers are applied in a much more loose fashion in free indirect discourse, where it is often extremely difficult to distinguish precisely between the voice of the narrator and that of the other consciousness represented in the text. This blurring effect is compounded when, instead of quoting directly or indirectly particular speech acts, the narrator incorporates into sentences of his or her own making, imprecisely marked phrases mimicking the general style of another speech type.[32]

Let us consider, for example, a seemingly simple remark made by Omar, the narrator-protagonist in Akli Tadjer's *Les ANI du 'Tassili'*. In conversation with another Beur on board the *Tassili*, Omar recalls having felt sadly out of place during his visit to Algeria, despite his having prepared as meticulously as possible in the hope of feeling at home there: 'C'est con, j'm'étais super bien préparé. J'avais toute la panoplie, sandales, saroual, quelques mots d'arabe, la crème solaire, enfin tout, quoi!'[33] A key distinction here, signalled by the use of tenses, is between Omar before and Omar after his visit to Algeria. The naïve expectations of the former are being gently mocked here by the latter. It is by no means easy to establish a precise demarcation line between the two, however. Omar may well have thought of each item mentioned here before setting out for Algeria, but no matter how naïve he was, can he really have imagined them forming a coherent whole when listed in this way? On its own, practically every item has a certain credibility in relation to Omar's original project. The wearing of traditional Algerian dress (sandals and a 'saroual', a type of baggy trousers traditionally worn in North Africa) is by no means absurd in itself, and the Arabic language was clearly a vital tool if Omar's project was to succeed. Yet placed at the head of this list, footwear seems a strange starting point for induction into another culture: can Omar really have prioritised it thus? And while he was right to see that knowledge of the local language would be indispensable, can Omar have imagined that 'quelques mots' would suffice? These deflationary touches seem to be added with hindsight. The crowning touch in this list, a supply of sun-tan lotion, surely belongs to Omar's retrospective self: it is quite external to traditional Arab

---

32. The complexities of free indirect discourse are discussed by Bakhtin, writing under the pseudonym V.N. Volosinov, *Marxism and the Philosophy of Language* trans. Ladislav Matejka and I.R. Titunik, New York/London, Seminar Press, 1973, pp. 141–60. For a wider survey, see Brian McHale, 'Free Indirect Discourse: A Survey of Recent Accounts', *PTL*, vol. 3, 1978, pp. 249–87.
33. Akli Tadjer, *Les ANI du 'Tassili'*, Paris, Seuil, 1984, p. 65.

culture and is evidently placed here in order to strip what precedes of any remaining credibility. In retrospect, Omar's serendipity approach is shown to have been that of a tourist, someone who picks up odd items of clothing along with a few words of a foreign language without ever achieving more than a skin-deep acquaintance with the local culture.

Besides those of the before- and after-selves of Omar, a third voice is fitfully present in this list: that of traditional Arab culture. The key word here is 'saroual'. Preceded by the reference to sandals, this Algerian locution fits into a pattern of associations that makes sense within the traditional life-style of the country; followed by a few words of Arabic and a dash of sun-tan lotion, it is reduced to a mere token of superficial exoticism. The discourse of authentic Algerians is the least fully developed of the three viewpoints represented here, but without it neither of the other two could be understood for what they are. In a very real sense, Omar torpedoes his own self by incorporating into his speech traces of a discourse that is not his own and that he will never fully master.

There are no quotation marks, and no indication that specific speech acts are being reported indirectly, yet there is clearly a meeting of different discourses within Omar's remarks. In Bakhtin's eyes, dialogism is at its most intense in seamless robes of this kind. Consequently, the most multi-voiced works are not necessarily those with the largest range of characters. Multi-voicedness is rather a function of the distance originally separating different discourses and the intimacy of their textual interplay. The orchestration of that interplay requires sophisticated literary skills. If we approach Beur fiction with these considerations in mind, we may distinguish three broad categories of works. At one extreme are a number of narratives which display relatively limited technical skills, wherein we may discern an underlying tendency to become single-voiced; at the other are what may be seen as the most multi-voiced texts. Between these two poles stand a group of works characterised by an intermediary level of complexity.

The rationale behind this categorisation may be illustrated in more detail by considering first this intermediary group. It includes a number of narratives with multiple narrators, and some with only a single narrator; all, however, present a variety of focalisations. At the same time, these works present less marked differences and/or less intimate forms of interplay between the various viewpoints than are to be found in the most multi-voiced narratives.

Houari consciously adopted different types of narration and

focalisation for each of the short stories in *Quand tu verras la mer . . .*: 'C'est comme un carrefour. C'est chaque fois une nouvelle perspective, une nouvelle écriture.'[34] The untitled opening text is cast in the form of an interior monologue, with simultaneous narration by the homodiegetic narrator, a young woman of Moroccan origin now living in Brussels. The second story, 'La Vieille et l'enfant', is recounted retrospectively by a heterodiegetic narrator, but is focalised alternately around the two main characters, an old Belgian lady and a small boy of immigrant origin. 'La Mer dans tes yeux . . .' features two homodiegetic narrators, a Belgian woman and her Arab lover; their thoughts are in each case framed briefly by a heterodiegetic narrator. 'Rencontre' is recounted by a heterodiegetic narrator, but features extensive dialogue between the two principal characters, a middle-aged European intellectual and a girl of Moroccan origin whom he encounters in Brussels; a substantial part of her remarks is given over to the narration of a number of stories. The final story, 'Mimouna', is again recounted by a heterodiegetic narrator, but it is focalised around a young Moroccan woman who eventually ends up emigrating to Paris. It will be observed that, with the exception of the opening text, all the stories are framed by a heterodiegetic narrator. There is in fact a strong hint at the end of the introductory text that the young woman featured in it is the narrator of all the subsequent stories.[35] There is certainly no significant difference from one story to another in the affective or ideological tone in which the heterodiegetic narrator speaks. Moreover, although each of the three middle texts is focalised around alternate sides of an inter-ethnic relationship, the two main characters are in each case linked to each other by affective bonds. We are certainly presented with a range of voices, but this underlying unity sets fairly tangible limits on those variations.

Most of Ahmed Kalouaz's *Point kilométrique 190* is divided between two principal narrators: the thoughts of Sabine, a newspaper photographer investigating the racist killing of Habib Grimzi, alternate with the imagined voice of the dead man. Parts of the text are focalised around a number of secondary characters, notably Grimzi's mother as well as his girlfriend Hélène, and a mutual friend of her and Sabine, Alix. In places they speak in direct discourse, and there are also extensive quotations from television and newspaper reports of the murder and subsequent legal

---

34. Interview with Leïla Houari, 10 June 1988.
35. Leïla Houari, *Quand tu verras la mer . . .*, Paris, L'Harmattan, 1988, p. 25.

proceedings. Through this diversity of narrators and focalisers, Kalouaz builds up an intricate network of affective relations. The range of perspectives opened up for us nevertheless has limits. Almost all the narrators and focalised consciousnesses are bound together by a chain of personal sympathy. The only real exceptions are the media reports (which adopt a relatively neutral tone) and some of the eye-witnesses quoted in them (who are generally concerned to explain that they thought it too dangerous to intervene on behalf of Grimzi). The minds of Grimzi's killers remain almost entirely closed to us. There are occasional hints as to their account of things, as in the following reference to a remark made by one of them during the police investigation into the murder: 'Ainsi les meurtriers du Bordeaux-Vintimille [Grimzi was killed on a train travelling between these two towns] disent que leur victime leur avait lancé "un regard insolent".'[36] The impersonality of this disembodied voice (we are not told which of the three assailants made the remark) may act as a subtle form of revenge against those responsible for Grimzi's death, but it also leaves the attitudes which inspired the attack beyond our reckoning. Those attitudes are named in the discourse of others (as in an early part of Grimzi's narrative: 'Je parlerai contre le mutisme des évidences, pour nommer le règne de *la barbarie*'[37]) but they are never confronted as a voice in their own right.

Mehdi Lallaoui's *Les Beurs de Seine* features a trio of protagonists. Kaci, Mourad and Belka have grown up together in the Parisian suburb of Argenteuil, where their immigrant fathers settled after leaving Algeria. Although most of the story is recounted by an anonymous heterodiegetic narrator, it is evident that he has his roots in the same neighbourhood as the protagonists, whom he presents throughout in a sympathetic light. This is not to say that the three of them agree about everything. Kaci is determined to integrate as far as possible into the society where finds himself, while Mourad is generally hostile towards the French; Belka is indecisive. There is a good deal of dialogue, enabling each of them to articulate his position clearly. In several places, they effectively take over as secondary narrators. We are thus exposed to a genuine variety of viewpoints. As in *Point kilométrique 190*, however, there are limits to that variety. Without exception, all the main characters, together with the heterodiegetic narrator, stand within and on the side of the immigrant community, even if they differ as to the

36. Ahmed Kalouaz, *Point kilométrique 190*, Paris, L'Harmattan, 1986, p. 109.
37. Ibid., pp. 12–13; my emphasis.

best means of securing its interests.

Shifts of viewpoint in Mehdi Charef's *Le Thé au harem d'Archi Ahmed* carry us repeatedly across the ethnic divide, yet their effect is ultimately to suggest that all the main characters share similar values. The two most prominent characters, Madjid and Pat, are of Algerian and French origin respectively. Their close friendship, like that which binds together the multi-ethnic gang of which they are part, is rooted in the material and social deprivation which they share by virtue of the working-class milieu in which they have been raised. Similarly, Josette, an unemployed single parent of French stock saved from a suicide attempt by Malika, Madjid's mother, shares the same maternal and material anxieties as her rescuer. The focalisation of the narrative moves repeatedly from one to another of these and other characters, but these shifts seldom suggest that ethnic differences count for much.

Conflicting attitudes are certainly represented in the novel, but Charef orchestrates them in such a way as to suggest that the dividing lines in society are not where racially prejudiced observers think they are. Madjid and Pat turn the shortsightedness of these misconceptions to their advantage in the tactics they employ as pickpockets in the metro. As soon as Madjid has stolen a wallet he passes it secretly to Pat, and then deliberately remains in the victim's field of vision. On noticing his loss, the victim immediately suspects Madjid because of his Arab appearance. Madjid delights in displaying his apparent innocence by allowing himself to be searched, at the same time reprimanding the man for his racial prejudice. Although Pat is standing close by, it never occurs to the victim that this French youth might have been involved in the theft. The man was right to suspect Madjid, but he did so for the wrong reason. The life of petty crime which Madjid shares with Pat has nothing to do with his ethnic origins. As the narrator observes, the motivation of both youths lies in the material deprivation which they share: 'Quand on est chômeur et pas aidé, on ne regarde pas aux moyens de se payer un sandwich et un paquet de cigarettes.'[38] In incidents like this, racist attitudes are represented in the text, but they are marginalised in the overall economy of the novel.

Back on the HLM estate where Pat and Madjid live, we certainly see evidence of racial prejudice, particularly among the older generation, but in the eyes of the multi-ethnic gang to which the two youths belong, the real source of conflict is age rather than ethnicity: 'Comme dit Pat, un jour ce sera la guerre entre les parents

38. Charef, *Le Thé*, p. 100.

et les jeunes de la cité, une guerre à mort.'[39] Worried by his dissolute ways, Malika tries in vain on a number of occasions to persuade Madjid of the need to return to the Islamic values of Algeria. Most of the time, he claims simply not to understand her when his mother speaks to him in Arabic, and her Islamic beliefs are represented in the text in no more than a fragmentary and marginal way. Moreover, despite this gap between Madjid and his mother, we are shown that when it comes down to basics – such as life or death for Josette – they are both on the same side: while Malika pleads with the would-be suicide, Madjid runs to find Josette's small son, the sight of whom finally persuades her of the need to live despite her unemployment and poverty. Thus even the generation gap fades away compared with the underlying solidarity among all the main characters in the face of material deprivation.

Narration by and/or focalisation around a range of different personae is not in itself any guarantee of a real diversity of viewpoints. Some of the most single-voiced of Beur narratives feature quite a wide range of characters. A central protagonist tends to overshadow all the others, however, and his voice is generally difficult to distinguish from that of the narrator, even when they are formally distinct from each other. Typical of this category is Nacer Kettane's *Le Sourire de Brahim*. In the early pages of the novel, the retrospective heterodiegetic narrator often knows things of which the eponymous protagonist is ignorant. This gap reflects the fact that Brahim is no more than a child at the beginning of the narrative. Despite this spatio-temporal distance, the viewpoints of the narrator and protagonist are marked by no significant affective or ideological differences: as Brahim advances in years, the political and cultural ideas which he develops are entirely in line with those of the narrator. The cultural diversity to which he is exposed by virtue of his immigrant origins seems to present no problems for Brahim. He devours the literary heritage of France as eagerly as he does the oral culture of Algeria. All this is apparently digested with ease; in the final chapter, Brahim dismisses journalistic clichés about youths from immigrant families being torn between two cultures: 'Ils [i.e. journalists] ne comprennent pas que, nous, on n'a pas le cul entre deux chaises et qu'il est assez gros pour s'asseoir sur les deux.'[40]

Genuine conflicts of viewpoint might potentially have been presented through Brahim's conversations with various political

39. Ibid., p. 23.
40. Nacer Kettane, *Le Sourire de Brahim*, Paris, Denoël, 1985, p. 166.

activists and ideologues. In practice, the narrator so loads the dice against the middle-class French Maoists and Algerian party hacks with whom Brahim clashes that it is impossible for the reader to take their position seriously.[41] While training to be a doctor in Paris, the protagonist decides to spend the summer as a volunteer medic in Algeria. The low standards of hygiene which he finds there provoke some sharp verbal clashes between Brahim and members of the Algerian medical profession. In these clashes, Brahim is very obviously right and his interlocutors wrong.[42] His critical comments are, however, omitted from the final report drawn up by the authorities on the basis of the impressions recorded by the group of volunteers with whom Brahim has served: 'Pour la direction, il ne devait pas y avoir de fausse note.'[43] Unwittingly, the narrator provides us here with an image of his own handiwork. In the final chapter, we witness a long discussion between Brahim and some Beur friends about the best way forward for the immigrant community in France. In this supposedly spontaneous debate, represented in the form of direct discourse, all the speakers mouth virtually identical positions. Eventually, the evening draws to a close:

> C'est Tahar qui mit un point final à la discussion.
> – Allez, arrêtez de vous égosiller, sinon vous serez encore là demain matin. Je vous propose *Blowing in the wind*.
> Tous reprirent en choeur et la cité tout entière retentit d'un chant d'espoir.[44]

Were it not for the fact that we are evidently meant to take this seriously, it could almost be taken for a parody of Bakhtin's idea of dialogism as the orchestration of different voices. Many different characters speak in the dialogue closed here by Tahar, but we effectively hear only one voice, and it is identical to that of both Brahim and the narrator. By failing to incorporate into the text genuinely conflicting voices, the author produces a one-dimensional narrative. As such, *Le Sourire de Brahim* is, in technical terms, one of the least arresting of Beur novels.

Far from implying harmonisation and closure, dialogism, as

41. Ibid., esp. pp. 64–5, 102–3.
42. Ibid., esp. pp. 113–14.
43. Ibid., p. 123.
44. Ibid., p. 170.

conceived by Bakhtin, hinges on the unresolved competition between different types of discourse. The most multi-voiced of Beur narratives do not necessarily have multiple narrators. They tend in fact to have a single homodiegetic narrator. Yet his or her discourse carries within itself the orchestrated heteroglossia which is characteristic of dialogism. What distinguishes these works from those in our intermediary group is the locus of this heteroglossia. On the whole, in the works discussed so far it arises from the gap between different narrators or focalised consciousnesses, each of which remains relatively stable internally. However, in the most multi-voiced narratives – defined here as those which present the most extended and at the same time the most intimate forms of interplay between different discourses – heteroglossia invades the narrating or focalised consciousness itself.

Les ANI du 'Tassili' is teeming with a great diversity of characters, and as the narrator-protagonist, Omar, often seems averse to talking about himself, this may seem an unlikely narrative to place in this category. Yet as we shall see, Omar's discourse is among the most multi-voiced in the whole corpus of Beur fiction. As noted in Section 2.4, behind the apparent simplicity of the main part of the story (a sea-crossing between Algiers and Marseilles) lies a much more tangled social and historical web. Similarly, the seemingly light-hearted and at times even simple-minded Omar is in reality one of the most complex protagonists created by a Beur author. Most of the text takes the form of dialogue, cast as direct discourse, woven together with connecting commentary by Omar. Although seemingly side-lined for much of the time (while others speak), Omar is constantly present as both narrator and protagonist. The other characters are by no means without interest in their own right, but everything they say is seen within the context of Omar's expectations and reactions, even when these are not explicitly articulated. In this sense, Omar's consciousness subtly pervades the reader's perception of every other character's discourse. Sometimes, this additive takes the form of a brief comment or aside; on occasions, the simple fact of entering or breaking off a conversation is sufficient to indicate something of Omar's feelings.

Within the space of a little over a dozen pages,[45] we see Omar deciding to step firmly into or out of conversations with half a dozen different interlocutors. When a devout Muslim invites Omar to join him in prayers, the protagonist cannot get away fast enough. He considers going down to the bar, but has had enough

45. Tadjer, *Les ANI*, pp. 63–76.

for the time being of his conversations with immigrant workers there. Bored with his own company, Omar asks the nearest passenger, a young middle-class Algerian, what time it is. Irritated by the pretentiousness of the answer he receives, the protagonist is relieved when Féfer, a fellow-Beur, interrupts and opens a conversation of his own. Although Omar seems genuinely happy to prolong this talk, he cannot resist opening another conversation when Féfer absents himself momentarily. He positively forces his way into conversation with Nelly, an attractive French blonde, but is aghast when she falls asleep, leaving Omar feverishly looking for an exit from the confrontation forced upon him by her feminist friend, Francine.

From these comings and goings, we can infer a certain amount about Omar. He clearly feels little attachment to Islam, and dislikes middle-class snobbery, but there are also limits to what he has in common with first-generation working-class immigrants, despite coming from such a family himself. He is generally more at ease with fellow-Beurs such as Féfer, and very much attracted by certain types of young women, be they French like Nelly or Algerian like Safia, a hotel courier whom he met shortly before boarding the ship back to Marseilles, and whose image returns to him constantly during the voyage.

Yet it is impossible to pin down a stable picture of Omar simply from his outward movements. Inwardly, he remarks in an aside, he would hate to be stuck with Féfer's company indefinitely. The more he learns about Nelly, who turns out to be a social worker, the less he is attracted by her, though he allows her to sleep the night away with her head on his shoulder. This emotional let-down seems to be connected with unhappy memories of an earlier generation of French social workers during Omar's impoverished childhood. We need to look inside Omar's mind if we are to understand him properly, but this is more easily said than done. As is the way in casual encounters among travellers, Omar's interlocutors expect him to talk about himself, but he is often resistant to their questions. In his role as protagonist, Omar is very reluctant to share his true feelings with his fellow-passengers, and even as narrator, despite his numerous asides to the reader, Omar remains in many ways enigmatic.

The nearest he comes to making programmatic statements about himself is when Omar and Nelly spin a coin to determine which one of them should answer the questions of the other. Having lost, Omar has to submit to interrogation by Nelly. The ready-made list of questions which she reels off – typified by the fourth of them:

'culturellement, tu te sens plus d'affinités avec la France ou avec l'Algérie?'[46] – invite precisely the kind of analytical closure denied to us in the novel. As Nelly falls asleep before Omar gets as far as responding to even half her questions, most of them remain unanswered.

There seem to be at least three reasons for Omar's reluctance to talk about himself. As he admits to Nelly, one is the painfulness associated with many aspects of his immigrant background, of which he prefers not to be reminded; another is the conviction that an outsider like her can never really understand what he has been through. We shall return to this second point in Section 3.4. A final reason is that Omar has no clear-cut answers to match Nelly's neatly-defined questions. When asked by another passenger what he does for a living, Omar replies enigmatically that he is a 'vendeur de vent, à temps complet'.[47] Returning to this phrase in his role as narrator after Nelly has fallen asleep, Omar comments: 'Elle ne saura jamais [. . .] que vendeur de vent à temps complet, c'est un métier fascinant. Elle ne saura pas qu'il n'est pas permis à tout le monde de passer sa vie à s'inventer des pays, des histoires, des cauchemars, des rêves, la vie et moi-même.'[48] Omar cannot truthfully answer Nelly's questions by saying that he 'is' this or that. The mixture of cultures to which he is heir is such that Omar is for ever obliged to find new ways of holding them together; in making his way through life, Omar must constantly reinvent himself.

The twenty-four hours spent in the company of his fellow-passengers aboard the *Tassili* typifies this process. Those on board this ship serve as a microcosm of all the main social groups involved in the Franco-Algerian relationship. As he moves among them, Omar must constantly adjust to changes of roles, and these are reflected in his own discourse. Some of these adjustments are quite small. When he observes that the hard-pressed bartender seems to like being addressed as 'chef', Omar falls in line with this to be sure of getting served when ordering drinks. Having noticed than an ill-tempered Algerian passenger takes pleasure in being called 'Monsieur' Omar responds accordingly: 'Apparemment papa a l'air d'apprécier que je lui donne du monsieur à tout bout de champ; moi, ça ne me gêne pas.'[49] There are, however, limits to his flexibility. His initial conversation with Francine, for example,

46. Ibid., p. 163.
47. Ibid., p. 69.
48. Ibid., p. 175.
49. Ibid., pp. 92–3.

becomes insufferable not only because she strikes an aggressive posture which irritates him, but above all because she attempts to foist upon Omar a role which he refuses to play. For Francine's militant feminism to be displayed to maximum effect, she needs Omar to defend the traditional male domination of Algerian society. After trying to joke his way out of the proffered role, Omar is eventually forced to trade some straight-talking insults.

Because he is not attracted to Francine, Omar sees no point in playing along with her. It is a different story where her friend Nelly is concerned. Attracted by her good looks, Omar treats her much more seriously, and is even prepared to submit to Nelly's questions when the spinning of the coin goes against him. Yet his answers are far from convincing. They are loaded with so much self-mockery and cliché-ridden theorising that Nelly feels cheated of her victory. Self-mockery is a recurring feature of Omar in his role as narrator, and it leaves the reader, like Nelly, uncertain as to the narrator-protagonist's position on many issues. Much of the irony deployed against himself is ultimately self-protective, as is the manifest insincerity of much of what he tells Nelly. Omar makes her and the reader laugh by adopting transparently false postures while at the same time keeping his innermost feelings to himself. Beneath all this light-heartedness there is a real seriousness of purpose: in many situations, humour serves Omar's underlying interests better than any other weapon.

To negotiate his passage through the multi-cultural waters into which he has been cast by virtue of his Algerian parentage and upbringing in France, Omar takes on and casts off the roles proferred by others in such a way as to further his own self-interests. When the old Muslim calls him to prayers, the protagonist 'souri[t] et acquiesce hypocritement',[50] and eventually bluffs his way out of the man's grasp by promising to join him later. Earlier, the sight of a pied-noir couple reminds Omar that he has forgotten to visit the shop which his concierge and her husband, M. and Mme Vergeli, left behind when they fled Algeria in 1962. He decides to lie to them, and projects a long description of how he purportedly found the shop, based on what the Vergeli family has told him and miscellaneous clichés culled from pied-noir folklore.

Out of cigarettes and hard currency, Omar later runs through all the people he has met on board the *Tassili*, imagining the kinds of posture he would have to adopt in relation to each of them in order to secure a donation of money or tobacco. Addressing himself

50. Ibid., p. 63.

directly to the reader, the narrator declares: 'Eh oui, je peux sans scrupule jouer de l'hypocrisie . . . Attention . . . Attention . . . Mon hypocrisie à moi ne peut être que momentanée et circonstanciée. Donc rien à voir avec la définition qu'en ont donnée certains encyclopédistes.'[51] To explain his point, Omar cites the often abstruse definitions of hypocrisy given in dictionaries such as the *Petit Robert* and the *Grand Larousse*, as well as in some of the quotations which they reproduce from well-known French authors, and then gives his own definition:

> L'hypocrisie serait le jeu qui consiste à séduire femmes et hommes, toutes tendances confondues, afin d'en tirer de substantiels bénéfices. Le Grand Omar illustré cite pour exemple: 'Il aimait à faire illusion auprès de son entourage, mais, à force d'abuser, il ne savait plus s'il jouait ou s'il s'en amusait' (Omar de la Garenne-Colombes).[52]

The playful form in which these lines are cast does not alter the underlying seriousness of their message. Its form is in fact an exemplification of the message, for this little spoof of dictionary-style discourse is just one among a whole range of pastiches presented by the narrator of *Les ANI du 'Tassili'*. In his explanation of the mock-acronym ANI, for example, he adopts the tone of a news magazine journalist, whose copy is in turn heavily laden with the traces of various types of scientific discourse.[53] The very letters ANI (signifying 'Arabe Non Identifié') are a play on those of the pseudo-scientific OVNI ('Objet Volant Non Identifié'). The discursive complexity of his constant role-playing as both narrator and protagonist reflects the uncertain sense of personal identity jokingly alluded to in Omar's self-designating acronym. While some of those roles may be masks worn in a spirit of calculated self-interest, others appear to be reluctantly donned under various types of emotional pressure; some again may be flaunted for the sheer fun of it. As Omar acknowledges in his mock dictionary entry, the truth or falsity of this or that role may finally escape even him. So deeply ingrained are the discourses of others in Omar's own words that it often seems impossible to tell where their voices end and his begins.

---

51. Ibid., p. 97.
52. Ibid., p. 98. La Garenne-Colombes is the Paris suburb where Omar was born and brought up.
53. Ibid., pp. 23–7.

Socialisation is inescapable from role-playing. As children grow
up, they learn what is expected of them if they are to win acceptance from the individuals and groups with whom they come into
contact. At the age of twenty-three Omar is relatively adept at
managing the various personae which he finds it expedient or
pleasurable to display in different circumstances. For children half
his age or less, the learning process can be much more hit and miss.
By focusing on the minds of growing children, writers such as
Azouz Begag and Farida Belghoul have produced some of the most
multi-voiced of Beur narratives. Like *Les ANI du 'Tassili'*, these
works derive a good deal of humour from the interplay between
different discourses. They also contain a substantial amount of
dialogue. What makes these narratives so intensely multi-voiced is
not, however, the presence of many different speakers. Rather, it is
the internalisation within the narrator-protagonist of the highly
divergent discourses to which s/he is exposed.

In Begag's novels there is a complex interplay between the
discourse of the mature, retrospective narrator and the evolving
voice of his childhood self as it switches between the different
role-models which surround him. In a passage deleted from the
initial draft of *Le Gone du Chaâba*, the narrator sums things up as
follows: 'J'étais ambigu et faux, jamais moi-même et toujours ce
que les autres voulaient que je sois. C'était le prix de la réussite.'
The finished text deals far less in retrospective generalisations of
this kind, focusing instead on particular moments of ambiguity and
conflict. The depiction of the young Azouz's response to the police
raid on the bidonville and of the later incident in which he disowns
his mother outside school, discussed in Section 2.2, typify these
complex cross-currents, in which the multi-voiced mind of the
narrator-protagonist repeatedly traverses the ethnic divide between
France and North Africa. Azouz's slightly older incarnation, Béni,
is so prone to role-playing his way across that divide that he fancies
he will make a career for himself as a professional actor.

Belghoul's *Georgette!* is cast in the form of an interior monologue
narrated simultaneously with her experiences by the seven-year-old
protagonist. It will be recalled that the central thread of the story
concerns her instruction in the skill of writing. If manual dexterity
is an essential part of this learning process, it is also inseparable
from certain ways of thinking. In her narration of the story, the
little girl switches back and forth between passages based on French
notions of normality and a framework of ideas derived from her
Algerian parents. The battle between these two viewpoints is made
visually tangible in the tussle over the 'correct' way of looking at

the girl's exercise book. Having written her homework at what her father regards as the beginning of the exercise book, the protagonist at first assumes that her teacher is looking at it back-to-front. When the girl accepts the teacher's viewpoint, she reverses her visualisation of the exercise book. As long as she adheres to the guidance offered by her father (based on the writing of Arabic) it seems to the girl that her schoolmistress is crazy for criticising her. When the protagonist realises that her teacher practises a perfectly coherent form of writing that is utterly beyond her father's grasp, it is he who appears insane. Yet as we saw in Section 2.4, even after accepting the validity of the teacher's instructions the girl remains haunted by the fear that in learning to write she is becoming, in her father's eyes, inhabited by a foreign discourse.[54]

Thus although the novels of Begag and Belghoul focus consistently on a single narrator-protagonist, in the representation of his or her consciousness we witness the co-habitation of voices which are almost literally worlds apart. In Bakhtin's terms, the intimacy of this interplay makes these works among the most multi-voiced in Beur fiction. By the same token, they are also among the most subtle and intriguing narratives to have been written by Beur authors.

3.3 Intertextuality

After making what he feels to have been the most spontaneous speech of his life, the narrator-protagonist in Ralph Ellison's *Invisible Man* is seized by doubts as to the authenticity of his achievement. Perhaps, unknown to himself, he had been mouthing the words of others. Had he, he wonders, been reiterating the discourse of a previous speaker at the political rally he had been

---

54. Begag makes similar point in an early draft of *Le Gone du Chaâba*, where he recalls the strategy which he adopted when writing French compositions at school: 'Je choisissais des thèmes en fonction de la manière selon laquelle l'enseignant allait les percevoir. Jamais en fonction de ce que je voulais vraiment dire.' Asked to write about what he did in the holidays, the young Azouz regurgitates cliché-ridden tales of holidays in France, pretending that he has participated in activities which in reality his parents have never had sufficient money to take him on. Research among a sample of children from immigrant homes suggests that the fabrication of similar 'compliant' fictions is a widespread practice at school: see Hélène Milet, 'L'Identité culturelle en constitution dans les écrits scolaires d'enfants d'immigrés maghrébins', in Georges Abou-Sada and Hélène Milet (eds), *Générations issues de l'immigration: 'Mémoires et devenirs'*, Paris, Arcantère, 1986, pp. 53–61.

attending? Was his speech an echo of words uttered long ago by his grandfather, a former slave in the American South, or maybe by Woodridge, a literature teacher at the all-black college which he attended in his youth? The protagonist recalls the teacher

> half-drunk on words and full of contempt and exaltation, pacing before the blackboard chalked with quotations from Joyce and Yeats and Sean O'Casey [. . .]. I could hear him: 'Stephen's problem, like ours, was not actually one of creating the uncreated conscience of his race, but of creating the *uncreated features of his face*. Our task is that of making ourselves individuals.'[55]

The protagonist's anxieties over this particular speech are emblematic of those which obsess him throughout the length of the narrative. The central theme of the novel is the fear that whenever African-Americans speak, they are being manipulated by others, particularly powerful whites, and are consequently prevented from accomplishing the task prescribed by Woodridge.

Ellison's novel was the original inspiration behind an unpublished short story by Farida Belghoul entitled 'L'Enigme', which eventually expanded to become *Georgette!*. The thematic parallels between the two novels are not difficult to see. *Georgette!*, like *Invisible Man*, suggests that ethnic minorities are in constant danger of being brainwashed by those in the cultural mainstream who hold the levers of social power. Both works present a bleak picture of the relationship between an individual consciousness and the socio-cultural forces surrounding it. At the end of *Invisible Man*, the narrator-protagonist suggests that at root, his findings hold good not simply for members of ethnic minorities, but for most people: their consciousness is to a very large extent a plaything of forces beyond their control.

Bakhtin's ideas, conceived in the very midst of Stalinist totalitarianism, offer both support for and relief from this gloomy diagnosis. As we have seen, Bakhtin emphasises that the discourse of every individual is fashioned out of borrowings from others. This is not to say, however, that we all internalise exactly the same discourse. Each individual interacts with a unique range of others and is free to combine and adapt their discourses in his or her own particular way. The Irish mentors recommended by Woodridge

---

55. Ralph Ellison, *Invisible Man* [1952], Harmondsworth, Penguin, 1965, p. 286; Ellison's emphasis.

show that African-Americans are free to look to other continents for lessons in handling cultural colonialism; Belghoul's borrowings from Ellison contain a similar message for the Beurs.

France's immigrant community has available to it a variety of discursive models, and each writer has drawn on and refashioned what has been to hand as s/he has seen fit. It is true that the Beurs are constrained within certain limits, but it would be a mistake to see any of these writers as simply regurgitating existing patterns of discourse. Some, of course, are more inventive than others, but all have made choices from among the range of models open to them, and these choices are important indicators of how Beur authors see their position in relation to the different strands of their socio-cultural heritage.

So far in this chapter we have been concerned primarily with intra-textual matters, i.e. with relations between different elements in the internal fabric of Beur narratives. The present section examines the ways in which these works draw on external models. As an integral part of their daily lives, the Beurs, like all human beings, are exposed to and influenced by representations of the experiences of others. Sometimes it is the experiences themselves, and sometimes it is the manner of their representation which leaves the deepest imprint on the Beurs. Some borrowings of this kind were discussed in Chapter 2, where the main focus was on gauging the diegetic significance of autobiographical experiences. In only a minority of Beur narratives – the works of Ahmed Kalouaz being the clearest examples – do images of others outweigh autobiographical elements at the level of diegesis. Yet all Beur authors borrow from others both at that level and in the manner of narration adopted in their works. Indeed, so extensive are these borrowings that it would be impossible to catalogue them all.

While dialogism denotes the interplay between different discourses within a given work, relations between such a work and discursive practices outside it constitute the field known as intertextuality. Usage of this term varies considerably,[56] so it is as well to be clear about its meaning in the present context. The field of intertextuality may embrace both the antecedents and the after-comers of a particular text. As most Beur fiction is of too recent vintage to have spawned a significant network of relations with later works, I am concerned here only with the intercourse between

---

56. See Marc Angenot, 'L'"Intertextualité": enquête sur l'émergence et la diffusion d'un champ notionnel', *Revue des sciences humaines*, vol. 60, no. 189, Jan.–Mar. 1983, pp. 121–35.

Beur authors and their discursive predecessors. Some students of intertextuality limit their investigations to specifically textual sources, and in particular to those of a literary nature. This would, I think, be unduly constraining where Beur writing is concerned. Oral influences of various types have been of major importance in shaping the textual practices of Beur authors. In addition, visual images have often combined with aural stimuli through the modern electronic media to exert a powerful hold on the minds of young people. If we wish to gauge the influence of different cultural traditions on Beur authors, we must take into account the full range of representational forms to which they have been exposed.

In *Les ANI du 'Tassili'*, the first two in Nelly's list of questions concern Omar's favourite television programme and greatest film hero when he was a child. Although she is not entirely convinced as to the truthfulness of Omar's answers, Nelly is right in principle to regard these questions as potentially revealing indicators of personal identity. In the late twentieth century, the audio-visual media are for many children far more powerful sources of role-models than are works of literature. Recorded music, films and television are able to circumvent language barriers relatively easily. In so doing, they throw the Beurs wide open to the influences of cultural communities beyond those of the French- and Arabic-speaking worlds. The most obvious of these is American popular culture, with its near-stranglehold on the audio-visual media. The combined answer which Nelly receives to her first two questions is 'Zorro', an American film series screened in the early years of French television whose eponymous hero fascinated the young Omar. While some of the details of Omar's comments seem to be deliberately self-mocking, it would not be surprising if, like many of his peers in France, he had fallen under the spell of an American celluloid image such as this.

It remains true that the single most important representational medium is language. Their mother tongue, as practised in its spoken forms by their parents, is the earliest system of signification to be internalised by children. Where the Beurs are concerned, however, a second language rapidly rivals the mother tongue, and soon displaces it as the primary vehicle of communication. The dominance of French arises from a combination of quantitative and qualitative factors. As they advance in age, the children of immigrants spend ever larger amounts of time outside the family home. French is the language of instruction at school and the language of most of their peers at play. It is also firmly seen as the language of social advancement. To succeed in France, it is essential to master the national language; the generally low level of prestige attaching to their mother tongue is apt to downgrade this part of their cultural heritage in the eyes of the Beurs themselves.

This lack of prestige is intimately bound up with the illiteracy of most of their parents and the low socio-economic status to which this has condemned them. Although a rich Arabic literature is widely read in other countries, the illiteracy of most Arabic-speakers in France means that their language tends to be equated with economic poverty and cultural deprivation. A large number of immigrants in any case speak Berber, rather than Arabic, and until recently their language had almost no written tradition. The low level of esteem in which their mother tongue is held, combined with the central importance of written French in the achievement of educational (and thereby social) success has encouraged the Beurs to draw an equation between culture and literacy.

There is, however, an appreciation among Beur authors of the superficiality of this view. In Kettane's *Le Sourire de Brahim*, the protagonist realises how short-sighted he has been when he attends a concert by Taos Amrouche, a leading singer of traditional Algerian songs; the power of those songs enables Brahim to see that oral culture is in fact a rich repository of historical and artistic achievements.[57] Story-telling is an important oral tradition among the North African population, and the Beurs have been exposed to this as part of their upbringing. Mehdi Charef has recalled how, before coming to France, his mother would tell him stories to send him to sleep when there were disturbances in their home area during the Algerian war.[58] In Raïth's *Palpitations intra-muros*, the narrator-protagonist recounts one of the many folktales told to him and brothers and sisters during their childhood. Their mother's repertoire included tales from *A Thousand and One Nights* along with stories peculiar to her native region of Algeria.[59] Some Beurs have now begun to collect these tales,[60] while others have written

---

57. Kettane, *Le Sourire*, pp. 68–71. Farida Belghoul has described a similar experience. In her case, the key factor was seeing traditional Algerian songs performed on French television; the prestige attaching to that medium seemed to validate cultural practices which had previously appeared marginal. See Belghoul's remarks in 'Quand nos parents nous ont perdus: un déjeuner-débat au FIC', *Cahiers FIC*, [no. 1], Mar. 1984, p. 40.
58. Interview with Olivier Schmitt, 'L'Homme qui marche', *Le Monde*, 29 Dec. 1987.
59. Mustapha Raïth, *Palpitations intra-muros*, Paris, L'Harmattan, 1986, pp. 186–7.
60. Mohamed El Boubsi Hamadi who, like Leïla Houari, was brought up by Moroccan parents in Belgium, plans to publish an extensive collection of tales recorded on tape by first-generation immigrants. A book of this kind was

stories of their own in a similar style.[61]

These are of course relatively marginal compared with the main body of Beur narratives. The never-never land of myth and legend to which we are transported by folktales and similar stories is far removed from the world of autobiographical actuality in which most Beur fiction is grounded. This does not, however mark the end of oral influences. On the contrary, the French in which many Beur narratives are cast often seems more characteristic of the spoken word than of formal written discourse.

The works of Begag, Belghoul, Boukhedenna, Charef, Lallaoui, Tadjer and Touabti are all liberally dosed with slang and other types of colloquialisms. For foreigners these are a notoriously difficult part of any language, since they cannot be fully mastered at a distance. Regional variations and constant innovations carried essentially by word of mouth are such that only someone born or long resident in a particular locality can hope to become wholly proficient in its linguistic peculiarities. The generally working-class milieux in which the Beurs have been raised have ensured that much of their French has been learned from practitioners of popular, rather than élite, forms of discourse. Consequently, their familiarity with various forms of slang often outstrips that of regional or social outsiders. As noted in Section 1.3, a form of slang in which Beurs brought up in the Paris area have shown themselves to be particularly adept is verlan. Narratives such as *Le Thé au harem d'Archi Ahmed* and *Les ANI du 'Tassili'* are liberally spiced with verlan expressions. Begag's narratives make conspicuous use of Lyonnais slang words, one of which is incorporated into the very title of *Le Gone du Chaâba*.

As a researcher with the CNRS, Begag engages as an everyday part of his professional life in the writing and reading of formal academic discourse. If he has chosen to adopt a colloquial tone in his autobiographical narratives, it is not because of any lack of competence in formal French. It is rather a mark of the depth of his linguistic roots in the city of his birth. He knows its dialect better than those of 'pure' French stock who have never lived in Lyons. By displaying that familiarity in the title of *Le Gone du Chaâba*,

---

published with the assistance of a group of French social workers by a collective known as S.A.H.Y.K.O.D., *Lundja: contes du Maghreb*, Paris, L'Harmattan, 1987. See also Marie Féraud (ed.), *Histoires maghrébines, rue de France*, Paris, Karthala, 1985.

61. See especially Arriz Tamza, *Lune et Orian: conte oriental*, Paris, Publisud, 1987 and idem, *Zaïd le conquérant*, Paris, Publisud, 1989; cf. Houari, *Quand tu verras*, pp. 79–84.

Begag makes foreigners of the French in the face of their language, and turns the tables on those for whom the immigrant community remains unalterably alien to French culture.

The obvious danger in all this is that, in emphasising their deep-rootedness in the French language, the Beurs inevitably distance themselves from their Algerian heritage. Begag attempts to guard against this by balancing the Lyonnais element in *Le Gone du Chaâba* with an equal dose of Arabic. This is done not only in the title of the novel, but also in the main body of the text, where Arabic locutions stand cheek by jowl with pieces of Lyonnais slang, and in the set of glossaries supplied at the back of the book. Yet this balancing trick is something of an optical illusion. The overwhelming majority of the narrative is in French, for the simple reason that this is the only language in which the author is able to write. The related inability of Beur authors to read anything more than a few words in their mother tongue is a subject to which we shall return shortly.

While the retrospective narrators of *Le Gone du Chaâba* and *Béni ou le Paradis Privé* have no desire to denigrate their mother tongue, they show us that in their younger incarnations as the protagonists of these works, they were apt to become impatient of the social stigma attaching to the Arabic language in France. Béni in particular attempts to use his nickname in such a way as to mask his Arab origins from those at school. While his father can regard it as a contraction of the family name, Ben Abdallah, Béni encourages his friends to invest his nickname with French and English connotations. The fake English mother whom he invents in order to impress France, the girl with whom he has fallen in love at school, is a revealing indicator of Béni's alienation from the culture of his parents.

This little subterfuge is also symptomatic of a much wider interest among the Beurs in the cultural practices of the English-speaking world. Far more Beurs learn English at school than learn Arabic, and in general a much more positive image attaches to this language in France. This has less to do with England than with the United States, though the French themselves tend to blur the distinction. The dominance of English in the world of commerce is intimately bound up with the political and economic leadership of the United States during the twentieth century. Whereas Arabic is apt to be linked with poverty and social exclusion, English is associated with wealth and economic success. Of particular importance where young people are concerned is the related connection between the English language and modernity. The United States has long been the trend-setter in virtually every field of popular culture. For fashion-conscious youths, modernity is inseparable from an understanding of English, or at any rate from the brandishing of at least a few words of 'franglais'. The forms of wordplay by which the Beurs demonstrate their linguistic prowess often include a sprinkling of English. In *Les ANI du 'Tassili'*, for example, Omar consistently refers to the pieds-noirs as 'blackpannards', combining in this neologism a French slang word for 'pieds' with an English translation of 'noirs'.

The positive image associated with the English language is sometimes more important to young people in France than a detailed understanding of it. Anglo-Saxon popular culture frequently serves as a badge of identification with their peers against the older generation. The Beur protagonists in Lallaoui's *Les Beurs de Seine* signal exactly this by turning up the volume on their Pink Floyd records when the noise made by their middle-aged French neighbours becomes irritating; this is also Madjid's message to his mother in *Le Thé au harem d'Archi Ahmed* when he drowns out the appeals she makes to him in Arabic with the sounds of another British rock group, The Sex Pistols. In each case, the modernity and loudness of the music is more important than the precise meaning of the lyrics.

The visual images of films and television can be strong enough to stand without any direct linguistic support. We see this, for instance, in the film version of *Le Thé au harem d'Archimède*, when Madjid lingers in front of a picture of Humphrey Bogart, whose tough-guy image makes him an appealing role-model. In *Béni ou le Paradis Privé*, the protagonist attempts to woo France and other girls by walking and smiling like Robert Redford. Béni's creator, Azouz Begag, read widely in the social sciences as part of his professional training, but until the publication of his first novel, he read very little for pleasure: 'J'étais de ces gens qui ne consomment qu'un livre ou deux par an, ceux qui s'engourdissent de jour en jour par la facilité des images de la télévision.'[62]

While Begag is not alone in having adopted such a casual attitude to the written word (Mustapha Raïth also read very little for pleasure during his youth) many Beur writers are genuine bookworms. Belghoul, Houari, Kalouaz, Touabti and Yacine are among those with extremely wide habits of reading. Moreover,

---

62. Azouz Begag, 'Le Souvenir d'un homme torturé', in Abdelkader Djeghloul (ed.), *Kateb Yacine: le provocateur . . . provoqué!*, Paris, Actualité de l'émigration, 1987, p. 112.

even the least enthusiastic schoolchild is exposed to the literary tradition of France during his or her passage through the education system, which inevitably leaves an imprint on all of them, even if only at an unconscious level. In *Le Gone du Chaâba*, when Azouz changes schools he is shocked to find himself accused of plagiarism because of a French composition written for his new teacher. He had drawn on a tale told to him by a teacher at his old school; unknown to the boy, it came from a volume of Guy de Maupassant's short stories.[63] One of the most widely cited French authors in Beur fiction is Emile Zola, whose works are a permanent and often popular fixture in school syllabi. Jean-Luc Yacine read *Germinal* during his school days and does not recall having reopened the book, but it made a sufficiently profound impression on him to leave unmistakable echoes in both the opening and the closing pages of his first novel, *L'Escargot*.[64]

Until very recently, practically no Third World authors were included in official school syllabi. The acquaintance of Beur writers with the literary output of North African authors has therefore involved more of a deliberate choice on their part. Their inability to read Arabic has, however, confined them to the works of francophone North Africans; as very few works originally published in Arabic are translated into French, most literature written in that language remains closed to them. It is true that the colonial experience and its aftermath, which provides the basic frame of reference for francophone North African writers, presents a number of parallels with the condition of the Beurs. Both groups write in a language which is marked by images of dependence and exploitation. The reactions of the younger generation to their more established predecessors are nevertheless mixed.

Kateb Yacine is the Algerian author mentioned most frequently by Beur writers. Most have read Kateb's novel *Nedjma*, which, after its publication in 1956, rapidly established itself as one of the key founding texts of francophone North African literature. Six Beur authors were among those who contributed to a book on Kateb brought out in 1987, two years before his death, by the magazine *Actualité de l'émigration*, a semi-official publication of the Algerian authorities in France. Mehdi Lallaoui had no hesitation in

---

63. Azouz Begag, *Le Gone du Chaâba*, Paris, Seuil, 1986, pp. 220-1.
64. The beginning and concluding sections of both novels contain references to monstrous mechanical beasts consuming human victims; both works also close with the suggestion that new hope for the future may arise from the depths of apparent death and defeat. Zola is actually mentioned by name at the end of the opening paragraph in *L'Escargot*.

stating: 'Nous, issus de l'immigration et Kateb Yacine, écrivain algérien d'Algérie, appartenons à la même communauté.' A dithyrambic poem contributed by Nacer Kettane presented a similar assessment. Farida Belghoul and Mustapha Raïth wrote in more measured, indeed ambivalent, terms, though Raïth's unpublished second novel, 'Houria', is undoubtedly modelled in part on *Nedjma*. Ahmed Kalouaz expressed a frank preference for other North African authors: 'Sans aller jusqu'à dire que l'œuvre de Yacine[65] m'est totalement indifférente, force est de constater qu'elle m'est moins proche que celle de Boudjedra, de Haddad, ou de Ben Jelloun. Question de génération sans doute.' Azouz Begag preferred the writings of fellow-Beurs to those of the older generation; he also admitted to being unable to cope with the complicated formal aspects of *Nedjma*. Hocine Touabti made a similar comment when I interviewed him, while in her *Journal*, Sakinna Boukhedenna offers a much more enthusiastic appraisal of Kateb.[66]

In their choice of reading and in some cases of mentors, Beur writers have clearly not opted *en bloc* for one particular part of the varied literary heritage which is open to them. Nor has their attention been confined solely to French or North African authors. Through French translations, they have been able to sample many other literatures. Belghoul cites Japan's Mishima Yukio and the African-American writer Chester Himes in the same breath as Kateb Yacine and Louis-Ferdinand Céline.[67] The reading matter of the male narrator in Arriz Tamza's *Ombres* includes the Bible and the Koran, together with classical Greek and Hindu writings, as well as Nietzsche and Kant.[68] Hocine Touabti stated in an interview that he regarded Jorge Luis Borges as the finest writer in the world, while the two authors of whom Mehdi Charef has spoken most frequently with admiration are Henry Miller and Fyodor Dostoevsky.[69] Jean-Luc Yacine (who is no relation to Kateb) is a

65. Kateb Yacine's family name was in fact Kateb; he customarily placed it before the other part of his name.
66. The comments of Begag, Belghoul, Kalouaz, Kettane, Lallaoui and Raïth appear in Djeghloul (ed.), *Kateb Yacine*, pp. 112–13, 115, 118, 119, 121, 123. Touabti spoke of Kateb in his interview with me on 17 Sept. 1987. For Boukhedenna's appraisal, see *Journal*, pp. 95–7.
67. Belghoul in Djeghloul (ed.), *Kateb Yacine*, p. 115.
68. Tamza, *Ombres*, pp. 17–18.
69. Touabti made this comment when I interviewed him on 17 Sept. 1987. For Charef's comments see his interview with Salim Jay, 'Mehdi Charef: *Thé au harem d'Archi Ahmed*', *L'Afrique littéraire*, no. 70, Oct.–Dec. 1983, p. 107; Charef, 'J'ai écrit mon premier roman pour eux', *Migrants Formation*, no. 56, Mar. 1984, p. 53; interview with Olivier Dazat, 'Mehdi Charef', *Cinématographe*, July 1985, p. 12.

great admirer of the French surrealists, most notably Philippe Soupault, whose influence can be discerned in several dream-like sequences in *L'Escargot*, but the author also speaks with enthusiasm of Dostoevsky, Peter Handke, William Faulkner, Frantz Fanon and many other writers. The sources drawn on in Ahmed Kalouaz's works, discussed in Section 2.3, range from the French press to a Polish-born poet, a Moroccan dramatist and an African-American essayist.

A great deal more research would be necessary before attempting anything approaching a definitive assessment of the significance of these and many other sources in helping to shape the fabric of Beur writings. A number of tentative generalisations may, however, be hazarded. Firstly, in their basic conception of their purpose as writers, the Beurs are profoundly influenced by Western models. Their preoccupation with the exploration of personal identity and the related importance of autobiographical elements in their works reflect a tradition of individualism which is long-established in the literatures of Europe and America, but which until recently was quite foreign to other cultures, such as those of the Arab world. This is closely related to the secular values predominant in the West, which are heavily felt in Beur fiction. Perhaps the clearest illustration of this is Lallaoui's second and as yet unpublished novel, 'La Colline aux oliviers'. The first quarter of the text is narrated by an elderly Algerian sage in the manner of *A Thousand and One Nights*. As noted in Section 2.4, however, there is really no Islamic dimension to his tale. The remaining three-quarters of the text are narrated by his Beur grandson, who is entirely secular in outlook. Moreover, the central thread of the whole novel is the quest for information about a particular human being, whose fate is eventually learned via a number of eye-witness accounts. The genre on which this novel is most closely based is in fact the 'whodunnit', where the reader is constantly teased by a range of tantalising clues and finally presented with a neatly rational solution to a seemingly baffling mystery. It would be difficult to imagine a more secular genre than this, or a view of history more distant from the mythical world of *A Thousand and One Nights*.

As a second generalisation, it is safe to say that all Beur authors have learned from a variety of French writers, and in some cases we may speak of particular and heavy debts. Leïla Houari, for instance, is an *aficionado* of Marguerite Duras, whose elliptical style is echoed in *Zeida de nulle part*, and more particularly in *Quand tu verras la mer*. . . . Kamal Zemouri greatly admires Balzac, whose influence we may well suspect in some of the descriptive *longueurs* in *Le Jardin de L'Intrus.* Other examples of French models have already been mentioned.

Yet if French sources are, as it were, the air in which all Beur writers have learned to breathe, many have chosen to spread their wings in other skies. We may suggest, as a third generalisation, that the most important of these external horizons lie in places other than North Africa. Although most Beur authors speak with respect of older North African writers, the textual influence of the latter seems to have been relatively weak. Encounters with American authors in particular appear to have played a much more tangible role in launching a number of Beur authors into flight.

Mustapha Raïth had read very little literature before he began his prison sentence. In jail he was introduced to the works of Henry Miller, with whom he immediately identified. Having fallen under the spell of Miller, Raïth resolved to begin writing about himself, and the end result, after many revisions, was his first novel, *Palpitations intra-muros.* Charef, as already noted, has also acknowledged Miller as a major influence. Like Miller, Charef and Raïth (a convicted rapist) write with considerable frankness about sexual matters, and the twilight world of poverty and insecurity which features in their narratives has many parallels with the autobiographical elements in Miller's best-known works.

The writings of African-American militants such as Angela Davis and the Soledad brothers were of fundamental importance to the intellectual awakening of Sakinna Boukhedenna during the 1970s; reading them, she felt able to understand for the first time her condition as an Arab in France. In purely technical terms, Boukhedenna's adoption of an ideologically committed journal form may also reflect this influence. Farida Belghoul's encounter with Ellison's *Invisible Man* was, as noted earlier, the starting point for her career as a writer. Belghoul was so gripped by the notion of personal invisibility that she got together a group of Beur friends, each of whom agreed to write a short story based on that idea. In expanded form, Belghoul's own story became her first novel, *Georgette!.* Although the concept of invisibility does not feature explicitly in *Georgette!,* the field of ideas which it embraces in Ellison's novel is at the heart of Belghoul's narrative. Basically, Ellison suggests that members of the African-American community in the United States are subjected to socio-cultural pressures which efface or even render impossible an authentic sense of personal identity. Caught between her Arab family and her French school, the little girl in *Georgette!* faces an exactly parallel situation.

Belghoul and Boukhedenna have been inspired by the writings

of African-Americans because their condition more closely matches that of the Beurs than does the situation of francophone North African authors. Unlike the latter, who have had to grapple with the political domination and cultural legacy of a now departed colonial élite in territories where Europeans were never in the majority, the Beurs, like the African-American community, constitute an ethnic minority within a society which is accustomed to viewing those of non-European descent as second-class citizens. Although that of a white American, Miller's view of life in the margins of society strikes a similar chord with Charef and Raïth.

Resonances of this kind enable Beur writers to learn from and in some degree model themselves on others without having to choose to ally themselves specifically with either the French or the North African side of their heritage. There remains, however, an important area in which their room for manoeuvre appears much more limited. Are not the Beurs condemned to write primarily for a French audience? It is to this question that we now turn.

3.4 Audience

'Yasmine', c'est le nom que l'on donne au jasmin, en Algérie. Son parfum suave s'y répand partout, dans les ruelles étroites comme dans les maisons.
J'en possède un plant que j'essaye d'acclimater en France.[70]

The above are the opening words of Kamal Zemouri's *Le Jardin de l'intrus*. They are presented as part of a short prologue spoken by the father of the protagonist and principal narrator, Lamine. Before he begins his own story, Lamine explains: 'Ce qui précède constitue ce que mon père Mouloud, aujourd'hui disparu, ressassait de son vivant.'[71] Among Beur narratives, *Le Jardin de l'intrus* is by far the most insistent in its championing of Algerian nationalism. With the exception of Kalouaz's *Celui qui regarde le soleil en face . . .*, it is also the only narrative work by a Beur to have been published in North Africa, rather than in France. Its author is moreover alone among Beur writers in having opted to reside on the southern side of the Mediterranean. Yet from the very first sentence onwards, his narrative is tailored to meet the needs of a French audience. The

70. Kamal Zemouri, *Le Jardin de l'intrus*, Algiers, Entreprise Nationale du Livre, 1986, p. 5.
71. Ibid., p. 9.

explanation with which it begins would be quite unnecessary for an Algerian. Mouloud may possibly have furnished such an explanation to his son, who was born and brought up in France, but it seems unlikely to have been phrased in such a formal way. The pair of them were in any case in the custom of conversing in the father's dialect, rather than in French. The likelihood is that Lamine is here inventing or at the very least rephrasing Mouloud's words for the convenience of French readers.

Before independence, the works of leading francophone Algerian writers were generally published in France, and this practice continued in many cases after 1962. Within Algeria, a sizeable share of the domestic publishing industry continues to function in French, despite the government's official policy of Arabisation, i.e. the systematic replacement of French by Arabic in the country's educational system and, as far as possible, in every other sphere of life. Regardless of which side of the Mediterranean they have been published on, it has been difficult for francophone authors to avoid the supposition that a significant number of their readers will be French, and this assumption has undoubtedly influenced the way in which they have written.[72] Unable to write in any language other than French, and unused to the idea of speaking to an audience on the other side of the Mediterranean, the Beurs must almost inevitably assume that the bulk of their readers will be situated in France. More specifically, the low levels of literacy prevalent among North African immigrants mean that commercially viable works will be bought in the main by the French reading public rather than by members of the immigrant community.

The assumption that most of their readers will be French rather than of North African origin is reflected in the pattern of terminological and other explanations provided by Beur writers. Translations of Arabic and Berber terms are supplied in a variety of ways. Texts such as Houari's *Zeida de nulle part*, and to a lesser extent Tadjer's *Les ANI du 'Tassili'* are punctuated by footnotes. Begag supplies a glossary of Arabic terms at the end of *Le Gone du Chaâba*. In many Beur narratives, translations are incorporated into the main body of the text, as in the example from *Le Jardin de l'intrus* quoted above. None of these aids would be needed by readers of North African origin; they are there essentially for the benefit of the French.

72. On this issue, see Charles Bonn, *La Littérature algérienne de langue française et ses lectures*, Ottawa, Naaman, 1974, esp. Part III; idem, *Le Roman algérien de langue française*, Paris, L'Harmattan/Montreal, Presses de l'Université de Montréal, 1985.

There are, by contrast, few if any explanations aimed at non-French readers. When, in *Les ANI du 'Tassili'*, Omar converses with first-generation immigrants, he finds himself having to explain French slang words to them. There can be little doubt that the highly colloquial tone in which this and many other texts are narrated will present those outside France with a significant number of comprehension problems. Yet with only occasional exceptions (as in *Les ANI du 'Tassili'*), none of this slang – some of it extremely modern, and as yet confined in usage to France – is explained. The regional basis of certain terms means that explanations are required for the majority of readers in France; the glossary of Lyonnais slang words included in *Le Gone du Chaâba* is the most obvious example of this. Most French slang passes without explanation, however, and the implication of this is that the needs of potential readers in North Africa are of, at most, marginal concern to Beur writers.

A similar situation obtains where the pattern of assumed knowledge is concerned. Socio-historical explanations are often furnished of events or customs unfamiliar to the non-immigrant population in France. No comparable effort is made to assist potential readers across the Mediterranean who may lack the detailed knowledge of France assumed by the narrator.[73]

While all Beur authors are, I believe, aware that the bulk of their readers will be French, there are very few explicit references to this in their works. A rare instance occurs in the extract from Kalouaz's 'La Mémoire du couteau' quoted in Section 2.3, where the narrator-protagonist distinguishes between 'moi le Français fictif, [et] vous les authentiques'.[74] It is normal practice for the addressee of a piece of discourse to be designated, as here, in the second person. We should note that in its published version, this text is specifically tailored for the stage. It is described as a monologue, and comes complete with stage-directions for the narrator-protagonist. In a live dramatic performance the audience, addressed here as 'vous', is a body of people physically present to the speaker, whereas in the reception of a printed text the reader is physically separate from the narrator and author. Interestingly, this particular remark in 'La Mémoire du couteau' is taken almost word for word from the original text of the unpublished novel, 'Le Pluriel d'espoir n'est-ce pas désespoir . . .' on which this scenario is based. Clearly,

---

73. There are, perhaps, occasional exceptions to this in Zemouri's novel. See, for instance, the description of Saint-Denis in *Le Jardin*, pp. 10–11.
74. Ahmed Kalouaz, *Celui qui regarde le soleil en face . . .*, Algiers, Laphomic, 1987, p. 92.

the harki narrator of the original narrative, which is couched in the form of a journal, already anticipated a French audience.

References of this kind are, however, extremely rare in Kalouaz's works. Far more frequently in both the original novel and the published scenario the narrator uses the 'tu' form to address, in his own mind, one or other of the characters to whom he is emotionally close, and sometimes himself. The narrator of the novel occasionally uses 'vous' with an indefinite singular referent whom we may take to be the reader. On just one occasion in the novel, and never in the scenario, the audience is individualised through the 'tu' form. Describing the medical treatment of his terminally ill lover, the narrator states: 'Lecteur indélicat, tu sais dès à présent la suite des calmants.' The reader, who is cast here in the role of an intruder, is denied any explicit presence at all in the two full-length novels published by Kalouaz. *L'Encre d'un fait divers* takes the form of a journal addressed by the imprisoned narrator, Naïma, to her friend Céline. Occasionally, Céline takes over as a secondary narrator in postcards sent to Naïma. Each addresses the other as 'tu'. A similar reciprocal use of the 'tu' form applies to the two principal narrators of *Point kilométrique 190*, the journalist Sabine and the imagined voice of Habib Grimzi. With each serving as the addressee of the other, the act of narration appears to be motivated quite independently of the reader, to whom no direct reference is made.

Gerald Prince, developing ideas originally formulated by Gérard Genette, has helped to popularise the term 'narratee' to denote the addressee of a narrative.[75] Two important points should be noted. Firstly, as both Genette and Prince have shown, narratees may be individualised or addressed as a group, and they may vary from one part to another of the same text. Secondly, the narratee ostensibly addressed by the narrator cannot necessarily be equated with the real audience anticipated by the author. Just as *Point kilométrique 190* is narrated through the voices of characters who must be distinguished from the author himself, so their intradiegetic narratees are distinct from the actual reader of the novel, who is by definition situated outside the story. Even narratees personified in the text as extradiegetic readers may not necessarily be the actual readers anticipated by the narrator and/or author.

In 'Et le bonheur en prison? . . .', the earliest extant version of

75. See Genette, *Figures III*, pp. 265–7; Gerald Prince, 'Introduction à l'étude du narrataire', *Poétique*, no. 14, Apr. 1973, pp. 177–96; Prince, *Narratology*, Berlin/New York/Amsterdam, Mouton, 1982, pp. 16–26; Genette, *Nouveau discours*, pp. 90–3.

the text eventually published by Mustapha Raïth under the title
Palpitations intra-muros, the homodiegetic narrator repeatedly addresses himself directly to those who stand in the mainstream of
French society. He assumes that they look upon him – a youth of
immigrant origin and a convicted rapist to boot – with hostility,
and generally reciprocates these sentiments. Most of the time he
uses the 'vous' form, often with a plural referent, but on occasions
the 'tu' form is employed. Sometimes the narrator mixes the
different forms of the second person, as in the following rejoinder
to those who say that he should get back to his country of origin:

> Tartelette, je suis né ici! Fier d'être d'origine arabe, et de t'emmerder
> avec ma carte de résidence.
> Oui on sait qu'on est bousculé, méprisé, rejeté par 'notre' société,
> refoulé par les bordels administratifs, maltraité par les flics, massacré par
> la justice. Putain de merde on peut bien parler d'un problème de société,
> et je vous en prie, arrêtez de jouer les éberlués quand une pulsion de rage
> et de violence explose.[76]

In the opening section of this passage, the narrator addresses
himself in his imagination to an individual racist, who is personified in the 'tu' form; at the end, the plural referent of 'vous' is a
mass of people who, in the opinion of the narrator, take a hypo-
critical view of him. Although the text contains many parallel
representations of mutual hostility, it is nevertheless clear that one
of the narrator's primary motivations for writing is to convince at
least some readers that he deserves more sympathy than he is
accustomed to receiving:

> Malgré tout, si j'écris tout ça, c'est que je crois en l'homme. Me disant
> que peut-être quelque part, quelqu'un au bras long lira mes mots . . .
> sinon un autre quelqu'un au bras court mais au cœur gros, me lira avec le
> sentiment (l'intime conviction) que je suis innocent même si je reconnais
> avoir violé.[77]

It may be that the hostile narratees apparently addressed in most of
the text are a rhetorical device, rather than a representation of the

76. Raïth, 'Et le bonheur'; I have corrected a number of typing mistakes in the
manuscript.
77. Ibid.

actual readers anticipated by the narrator. Hypocrites and out-and-out racists are unlikely to be interested in a prison narrative of this kind, and are less likely still to respond sympathetically to such an apparently hostile narrator. The representation of their heartlessness may therefore be set up to encourage actual readers of the text to divorce themselves from such unpleasant company, and thereby to align themselves more closely with the narrator.

It seems clear that in their limited, more sympathetic incarnation, the readers anticipated by the narrator of 'Et le bonheur en prison? . . .' are predominantly French (they would have to be to wield the influence he hopes they might exercise in his favour). In *Palpitations intra-muros*, practically all direct references to the narratee are eliminated, and the narrator gives us virtually no explicit information about his anticipated readership. The few explicit references which remain, and more particularly the handful which are added, contain no trace of hostility on the part of the narrator. In the prefatory note discussed in Section 2.1, the text is said to be 'avant tout destiné à ces milliers d'enfants d'immigrés nés en France qui, un jour ou l'autre, se retrouvent en prison, victimes de la mal-vie'.[78] While the narrator may wish to express his solidarity with others in a similar situation to himself, there is no suggestion anywhere else in the text that he regards them as his primary audience. The prefatory note in fact concludes by describing the narrative as a 'bip-bip de détresse',[79] and those from whom the narrator hopes to receive help are clearly other than his fellow inmates. In the main body of the text, the narratee is cast simply as someone to whom the narrator wishes to demonstrate the truth, and from whom he hopes to receive a sympathetic hearing. The most important of these references are in passages which did not form part of the original text. They occur in poems which the narrator quotes from his prison diary.[80] Although one of them is graphically entitled 'Sauvez-moi', it is as if the narrator cannot bring himself to appeal directly to the reader; self-quotation appears to be a means of attenuating even the most respectful posture. The narrator's criminal record clearly places him at a disadvantage in relation to most of his anticipated readers, no matter how sympathetic, and this may perhaps explain the elimination of references which, if misunderstood, might have proved counterproductive.

It is a striking feature of Beur fiction that where the narratee is

78. Raïth, *Palpitations*, p. 7.
79. Ibid., p. 8.
80. Ibid., esp. pp. 215, 222, 224, 227–8.

explicitly described as French, a tangible affective distance is almost always to be felt between him or her and the narrator. In 'Le Pluriel d'espoir n'est-ce pas désespoir . . .', the French reader appears as an intrusive presence. A similar impression of the evidently European narratee is created by the young Arab woman who serves as the principal narrator in Houari's *Quand tu verras la mer. . . .* On several occasions, she gently but firmly belittles the narratee as an ignorant outsider where the immigrant districts of Brussels are concerned.[81] When, in describing the condition of melancholy to which her truthfulness often exposes her, the narrator addresses the reader as 'mon frère',[82] we sense here an unmistakeable allusion to the 'hypocrite lecteur' featured in the famous opening poem in Baudelaire's *Les Fleurs du mal.* The narrator of *Palpitations intra-muros* clearly feels victimised by French society, and is ill at ease in his dependence on the hoped-for goodwill of the better-natured among his French readers.

So used are the immigrant community to being talked at rather than listened to that reversing the communicative flow may seem an impossible task. A large part of Bouzid's account of the 1983 Marche des Beurs describes the protagonist's nervous preparations for and eventual engagement in the public debates organised at each overnight halt. The central purpose of the march, in Bouzid's eyes, was to enable a previously silent or repressed minority to speak its mind at last. His book was clearly conceived in a similar spirit. In a note written before the march began, Bouzid had dreamed of writing a book that would persuade racists of the error of their ways, but despaired of ever succeeding.[83] After joining the demonstration, he engages in imaginary arguments with xenophobic interlocutors so as to be ready when his turn comes to act as a spokesman. Yet when he takes the microphone for the first time, he addresses himself to the immigrant community. They seem perhaps a less daunting audience than the French. In fact it transpires that there is not a single racist in the hall. Bouzid soon becomes aware that most of the French onlookers attracted by the march see themselves as on its side, and this becomes exasperating in its own way: almost nowhere does he encounter people willing to pay attention to a point of view which is genuinely different from their own.

There are sufficient indirect markers in the text to indicate that

81. Houari, *Quand tu verras*, pp. 22–3, 43.
82. Ibid., p. 16.
83. Bouzid, *La Marche*, pp. 9–10.

the homodiegetic narrator anticipates a mainly non-immigrant readership. Yet he never addresses his readers directly. There is a curious gap between the argumentative self depicted at the level of diegesis and the absence of any direct appeal to the reader at the level of narration. It is possible that the narrator, profiting from what he has learned during the march, anticipates another self-selecting audience, and discounts in advance any idea of preaching to the converted. More fundamentally, however, he probably has serious doubts as to the potential for genuine communication across the ethnic divide. Even the most sympathetic French audience, Bouzid muses at one point during the march, could not cope with a wholly frank account of the immigrant community's woes: 'Est-ce que ça n'allait pas effrayer les salles? Faire mensonger? Parano? Exagéré? Misérabiliste? [. . .] Il faut éclipser une partie de la réalité pour éviter de faire pauvre peuple, pour ne pas donner mauvaise conscience.'[84] As the narrator includes in the text some of the facts withheld during the marchers' speeches, there is an implicit appeal to the reader to treat these disclosures with more credence and respect than they might otherwise be accorded.[85] Overall, however, Bouzid takes at best a diffident view of his French audience, both potential and real. In his eyes, it apparently consists of racists who will not listen and cannot be persuaded and well-wishers who are at root incapable of really understanding the immigrant condition.[86]

Charef was aware of similar dangers and difficulties when writing *Le Thé au harem d'Archi Ahmed*, but was determined to confront them constructively. In an interview, the author told me: 'J'ai voulu que le lecteur soit impliqué. J'avais toujours l'impression qu'ils nous regardaient de loin. C'est comme si je disais aux gars de l'extérieur, aux Français: "On n'est pas des bêtes, nous aussi on cherche quelque chose, on veut vivre." '[87] While Charef's projected audience is essentially French, the 'us' and 'them' distinction which he draws here is based less on ethnicity than on class: 'they' are the materially secure; 'we' are the urban poor. If the former are overwhelmingly French, the latter are a mixture of French and immi-

---

84. Ibid., p. 111.
85. An exactly parallel passage features in Tadjer's *Les ANI du 'Tassili'*, pp. 170–2, where the homodiegetic narrator describes a whole series of personal humiliations which, in his role as protagonist, he refuses to recount to Nelly.
86. Perhaps a similar point is implied when Nelly falls asleep during Omar's replies to her questions.
87. Interview with Mehdi Charef, 17 Sept. 1987.

grant alike. By taking Pat and Madjid as co-protagonists, Charef aims to dismantle the peculiarly alien image associated with the immigrant community: 'Je voulais tout simplement montrer que dans une famille française et une famille immigrée, on vit toujours la même chose.'[88]

At several points in the text, the reader is alluded to in the 'tu' form, though without being directly addressed. The second person is sometimes used in French with an indefinite referent equivalent to that of 'on'. In such cases, the referent is not technically the addressee, but the narrator's view of his or her relationship with the narratee is implicit in the choice of 'tu' or 'vous'. The heterodiegetic narrators in Houari's *Zeida de nulle part* and Kettane's *Le Sourire de Brahim* employ the relatively formal 'vous' form in this function. Only after the publication of his novel did Charef become aware that he had used the 'tu' form in this indefinite but indirectly revealing way. In retrospect, he realised that it represented a spontaneous leap across the divide between the French and immigrant communities: 'Les Français, à l'époque ils avaient l'impression qu'on fermait la porte et on complotait contre eux; et quand je dis "tu", c'est pour dire: "J'en ai marre; tu nous regardes – mais on est comme vous."'[89] Charef's novel eschews generalisations. It enlists the sympathy of its French readers by focusing on the experiences of a range of specific individuals. Similarly, when he addresses the French, denoted collectively as 'vous' at the end of the remarks just quoted, Charef does so via an imaginary individual, using the familiar 'tu' form, employed not in an insulting or dismissive way, but as a mark of cordiality. The narrator's use of the 'tu' form has exactly the same resonance in the novel.

Such an openly cordial attitude is extremely rare in Beur fiction. While narrators often use the 'tu' form to address themselves or, in their imagination, other characters, the reader is almost always addressed as 'vous'. This distinction is drawn consistently, for example, in *Les ANI du 'Tassili'*, and in Hocine Touabti's *L'Amour quand même*. This is all the more noteworthy in that, in their intradiegetic role as protagonists, the narrator-protagonists of these two works instinctively use 'tu' when addressing almost any one in the story, including complete strangers. Although neither of the narrators appears at all uncomfortable in relation to the narratee, the 'vous' form implies a greater degree of formal respect and a less open affective bond than would have been suggested by the 'tu' form.

88. Ibid.
89. Ibid.

There is, however, at least one occasion when 'vous' carries a more positive charge. It occurs when the narrator of *Le Sourire de Brahim* briefly switches away from the indefinite use of this pronoun, and eventually uses it to address the reader directly. The passage begins with a description of France in which the referent of 'vous', while technically indefinite, is implicitly the immigrant community:

> La France est comme l'hydre. Une tête souriante qui vous invite et l'autre avec une grande gueule qui est prête à vous dévorer. Si la douce mélopée de la déclaration des droits de l'homme vous enivre, c'est pour mieux vous conduire dans le placard où le camembert-beaujolais dicte sa loi.
>
> Il faut alors se défendre, tous les coups sont permis au royaume du rouleau compresseur.[90]

The steam-rollering of their identity by France is by definition a fear which affects only those who do not feel French. A similar observation applies to those for whom the more immediate threat is one of exclusion:

> Vous voulez vous incruster? Mais on ne vous a pas sonné! Excusez-moi, mais j'ai trouvé la porte ouverte.
>
> La fenêtre, vous voulez dire? Pas besoin de pression pour tomber. Seul l'insoutenable regard suffit.[91]

The speakers in this imaginary conversation appear to be a Frenchman and a member of the immigrant community. As there are no quotation marks, the referent of 'vous' is constantly shifting from one side of the ethnic divide to the other, and the reader is obliged to re-adjust to a range of roles with no explicit guidance from the narrator. This seems to be a deliberate tactic on his part:

> C'est quoi la frontière? Ah! c'est ce morceau de papier, vous me rassurez! Mais si je pose le pied dessus, on ne le voit plus. Ah! que c'est bon un monde sans papier! Je suis là, vous êtes là, dans le présent. Vous pourriez être moi, je pourrais être vous. Demain d'autres seront là à notre place.[92]

90. Kettane, *Le Sourire*, p. 170.
91. Ibid., p. 171.
92. Ibid., p. 171.

This is the only point in the novel in which the narrator speaks unequivocally of himself in the 'je' form; the 'vous' to whom he addresses himself is pictured as directly present and artificially separated from him by a national boundary. French readers who may have felt distanced from the referent of 'vous' in the first of the three extracts quoted above, then unsettled by the shifts in its referent in the middle extract, will surely identify themselves here with the narratee. Significantly, the central thrust of this, the only passage containing a quasi-direct reference to the reader of the novel, is to invite him or her to see the futility of ethnic barriers. It is equally significant that this passage is almost unique in Beur fiction in using the 'nous' form openly to unite the narrator with what he surely sees as the French reader.

It will be recalled that in Boukhedenna's *Journal*, the huge instability in the narrator's use of the first person plural reflects her unstable sense of identity. While the referent of 'nous' switches back and forth between immigrants and other Third World groups, and across various age and gender divides, it never includes the French. Sakinna sometimes uses the 'vous' form to address, in her mind, groups ranging from Algerian women to French racists; whenever the referent of 'vous' is French, her tone is hostile.

While these groups feature intermittently as imaginary addressees, at a formal level the text is unique among Beur narratives in having an extradiegetic narratee addressed consistently in the 'tu' form.[93] Sakinna's journal-style narrative is written to an unnamed, indeed unknown, addressee. S/he is referred to in the opening passage as 'cher je ne sais qui,'[94] and frequently thereafter as 'cher X', 'X., à qui j'écris ce journal', or simply 'X'.[95] We know virtually nothing about this narratee, apart from the fact that s/he apparently lives outside Algeria. This is clearly implied when Sakinna makes the following comment about her unhappy experiences there: 'Je te les raconte, cher X., ça vaut la peine, comme ça si tu vas en Algérie et que tu es femme, tu seras sur tes gardes.'[96] The phrasing here implies that Sakinna is not even sure as to the sex of her imaginary addressee. When I asked the author how she envisaged the narratee in her own mind, Boukhedenna replied that she had always seen

---

93. Tamza's *Lune et Orian* concludes by invoking a divine blessing 'sur toi, ami lecteur pour m'avoir écouté' (p. 100). However, the protagonist and principal narrator, Orian, addresses most of the text to an intradiegetic narratee, his lover, Lune.

94. Boukhedenna, *Journal*, p. 9.

95. Ibid., pp. 37, 43, 52, 60, 79, 87, 99, 103, 104, 105.

96. Ibid., pp. 117–18.

him as 'mon homme arabe idéal'.[97] The previous quotation from the text must cast some doubt on the sex of the narratee, however, and the fact that s/he seems to be from outside Algeria could even be taken as a sign of non-Arab origins, though it is perhaps more likely that s/he is a member of the immigrant community. What is certainly clear is that Sakinna feels the need for but lacks a real reader with whom she can hope to sustain a relationship of mutual affection and respect. Her imaginary narratee is a protective device which masks the French audience which inevitably awaits her narrative, but from whom she feels emotionally estranged.

In contrast with Sakinna, the narrator-protagonists in Azouz Begag's novels are openly concerned with achieving success within French society. As protagonists, they are aware that this means playing roles derived from the dominant cultural code. As narrators, they seem to experience no misgivings in recounting their experiences in a way that is calculated both to inform and entertain an essentially French audience. That audience is directly addressed, however, on only one occasion. Towards the end of *Le Gone du Chaâba*, the narrator remarks:

> A la maison, l'arabe que nous parlons ferait certainement rougir de colère un habitant de La Mecque. Savez-vous comment on dit les allumettes chez nous, par exemple? Li zalimite. C'est simple et tout le monde comprend. Et une automobile? La taumobile. Et un chiffon? Le chiffoun. Vous voyez, c'est un dialecte particulier qu'on peut assimiler aisément lorsque l'oreille est suffisamment entraînée.[98]

The narrator clearly enjoys explaining to the reader the verbal peculiarities of his parents, and undoubtedly anticipates that they will be a source of amusement. While this humorous effect is ostensibly derived from a contrast between classical Arabic and the dialect of Azouz's parents, the real gap perceived by the reader (who, like the protagonist, may be assumed to know no classical Arabic) is between standard French and their mispronunciation of it. A similar effect is achieved on many other occasions in both *Le Gone du Chaâba* and *Béni ou le Paradis Privé* by the phonetic representation of the non-standard French spoken by the parents of the protagonist.

At no point does the narrator use this as a device with which to ridicule his parents. The humour derived from this and other

97. Interview with Sakinna Boukhedenna, 21 Apr. 1988.
98. Begag, *Le Gone*, p. 213.

textual strategies is designed to make light of conflicts and short-comings, rather than to grind axes over them. The narrator-protagonist repeatedly makes fun of his own misunderstandings and contradictions, and laughs off the material disadvantages of his immigrant background. In an interview, Begag stated: 'Mon dis-cours consiste à manier la misère avec l'humour. "L'humour est la politesse du désespoir," a dit Paul Valéry. C'est par cette voie que je passe, pas par la voie misérabiliste.'[99] These sentiments are echoed by many Beur writers, for whom humour serves as a bridge across some of the more serious problems and handicaps with which their narratives deal. As we saw in Section 3.2, in his dual role as narrator and protagonist in *Les ANI du 'Tassili'*, Omar prefers to engage in self-mockery rather than dwell on the unhappier aspects of his life in France. In the film version of *Le Thé au harem d'Archimède*, as in the novel, Charef applies liberal doses of humour: 'J'avais très peur de cet adjectif: misérabiliste. J'ai préféré une chronique allègre plutôt qu'un film accusateur conçu pour choquer systématiquement le spectateur.'[100]

The fear of 'misérabilisme' – i.e. appearing to wallow in the disadvantaged background from which they come – leads these writers, like Bouzid, to present their readers with a diluted version of the problems experienced by the North African community in France. As we saw earlier in this section, it is because they are addressing an essentially non-immigrant audience that they feel this constraint. Is this not the same as saying that this audience funda-mentally perverts the integrity of Beur narratives? This is precisely the line which Farida Belghoul has taken in some of the most powerfully argued analyses of Beur culture.

Reviewing *Le Thé au harem d'Archimède* when it was released at the cinema, Belghoul complained that it had smoothed over too many rough edges:

> La caméra de Charef, c'est l'œil de Big Brother. [. . .] Ses personnages ne vivent pas entre eux. Ils se montrent. Au détour de chaque scène, on sent la présence d'un certain public. C'est un public extérieur aux banlieues qui fait la loi dans ce film. [. . .] Tout le film est hanté par le désir d'être aimé de la bonne (au sens de bonté) société. Il en oublie d'être vrai: c'est le prix de cette quête d'amour.[101]

99. Interview with Azouz Begag, 2 Dec. 1987.
100. Remarks made by Charef in his interview with Olivier Dazat, 'Mehdi Charef', p. 11.
101. Farida Belghoul, '*Le Thé au harem d'Archimède* de Mehdi Charef', *Ciné-matographe*, May 1985, pp. 32–3.

In a general discussion of Beur film-makers which spills over into the consideration of literary and other cultural practices, Belghoul went on to situate Beur culture at the intersection of two conflicting systems of signification. One is the dominant culture of France, which Belghoul calls her 'milieu d'adoption', and wherein resides her audience; the other is that of the immigrant community, the 'milieu de contre-référence' from which she speaks:

> L'audience [i.e. the fact of being heard], en soi, est une victoire mais j'ai le sentiment que la définition à l'égard du milieu d'adoption l'emporte et que dans ce rapport à l'extérieur, les choses se perdent. Pas forcément dans l'audience elle-même. Mon problème est de maintenir les relations avec ce milieu d'adoption, tout en lui opposant un milieu de contre-référence. Ce milieu d'adoption est conscient comme nous du 'choix': cédér ou pas. Ça sonne guerrier, puisque le milieu d'adoption exprime le désir de nous digérer et la résistance à cette voracité prend parfois les allures d'une guerre.[102]

If writers such as Tadjer, Charef and Bouzid feel compelled by their audience to attenuate their representation of the lot which has been that of the immigrant community, are they not allowing external pressures to dictate to them? When the narrator of *Zeida de nulle part* transposes into a flowery, literary French the mother's oral account of her childhood and marriage, which we may presume to have been delivered in Arabic, how much of the 'milieu de contre-référence' is lost? When Begag's narrators reproduce phonetically the non-standard French of their parents, do they not, however unintentionally, mark these voices as defective in relation to their 'milieu d'adoption', and detach them from the fluency which is theirs within their 'milieu de contre-référence'?[103]

The power of the Beurs' French audience is perhaps most visible in the novels of Mehdi Lallaoui. Each of the three main characters in *Les Beurs de Seine* serves at times as a secondary narrator, and the

---

102. Remarks made by Farida Belghoul in her interview with Gilles Horvilleur, 'Farida Belghoul', *Cinématographe*, July 1985, p. 19.
103. Similar problems are often faced by authors attempting to articulate the experiences of other marginalised or dissident groups, such as feminists or political radicals. See Gilles Deleuze and Félix Guattari, 'What is a Minor Literature?', *Mississippi Review*, vol. 11, Spring 1983, pp. 13–31. Cf. Abdul R. JanMohamed, 'Humanism and Minority Literature: Toward a Definition of Counter-Hegemonic Discourse', *Boundary 2*, nos 12–13, Spring-Fall 1984, pp. 281–99; Barbara Harlow, *Resistance Literature*, New York, Methuen, 1987.

French listeners to whom we often see them speaking serve as images of the audience addressed by the novel. Mourad, for example, lectures a group of French workers about the handicaps suffered by the immigrant community. In response to sympathetic questioning from his French girlfriend, Kaci gives her a guided tour of his native Argenteuil. In two long passages, Belka talks in detail about his Algerian roots, 's'adressant à un auditoire invisible, poussé par le besoin de dire à d'autres ce qu'il avait été'.[104] The pattern of explanations provided during his narration makes it clear that his imaginary audience is situated in France. The anonymous extra-diegetic narrator who frames the whole text makes the same assumption. He may joke about his role, as for instance when he breaks off in the middle of a description of Argenteuil to say 'n'oubliez pas le guide, merci!'[105] but at root he tailors his narration to hold the attention and win the approval of his French readers.

One of the primary aims of Lallaoui's second novel, 'La Colline aux oliviers', is to impress upon the reader the achievements of the Algerian people and the debt owed to them by the French. We are shown, for example, the contribution of immigrant workers to French industry, and the role played by Muslim soldiers in the First and Second World Wars. As noted in Section 2.4, we are also presented with an entirely secular vision of Arab culture, which is seen as an impressive repository of scientific knowledge, rather than as a tower of Islamic belief. The great danger in all this is that in 'proving' the intelligence and utility of Algerians on a scale of values set by the French, the author undermines the very self-respect and independence of vision which he is concerned to promote. Self-validation by the criteria of others hardly seems to be self-validation at all.

At the end of 1984, Belghoul played a leading role in organising Convergence 84, the follow-up demonstration to the first Marche des Beurs, which had been held the previous year. As the marchers passed from one town to another, she became increasingly disillusioned. Everywhere, she and her fellow-marchers were met by the French representatives of anti-racist organisations who seemed to have no real contact with the local immigrant community. The more she spoke to the former, the less she felt able to speak for the latter.[106] At a national level, she concluded that for all its

---

104. Mehdi Lallaoui, *Les Beurs de Seine*, Paris, Arcantère, 1986, p. 46.
105. Ibid., p. 23.
106. See Eric Favereau, 'Divergence 84 de l'antiracisme, l'autre sens de la marche', *Libération*, 20 Nov. 1984; Farida Belghoul, 'La Gifle', *Im'média magazine*, no. 2, Spring 1985, pp. 15, 16, 39.

sympathetic noises, France's socialist government was, in the final analysis, offering the immigrant community 'une intégration qui signifie la destruction de notre intégrité'.[107]

Soon after Convergence 84, Belghoul dropped out of politics altogether and turned instead to literature. Yet here she faced, albeit in a different form, the same problems which had troubled her in the political arena. How could she write for a French audience without cutting herself off from her Algerian roots? In an interview, she was to express her feelings thus:

> L'écriture c'est la mort de la fille Belghoul. En écrivant, je creuse une tombe, je creuse la tombe de la fille de mon père. Sur le plan purement matériel, mon père ne peut pas lire les livres que j'écris. Si j'écrivais en arabe, il y aurait une espèce de continuité, mais en écrivant en français j'ai l'impression de piétiner sur mon héritage, de donner de l'eau au moulin de mes ennemis.[108]

As we have seen, in a fictionalised form, the representation of these fears lies at the heart of her novel *Georgette!*, which she began writing in 1985.

In the composition of the novel, Belghoul found herself confronted with two distinct but related problems. One of these was the moral and emotional turmoil into which she felt plunged by the very act of writing in French. The other was the technical challenge of having the novel narrated by the seven-year-old daughter of an Algerian immigrant worker. The text takes the form of an interior monologue. Genuinely spontaneous thoughts take many things for granted and are often confused; this is all the more obviously the case where the mind of a small child is concerned. If the transcription of the girl's thoughts is to be intelligible to the reader, how can Belghoul avoid imposing upon them an explanatory framework which subverts their integrity?

Wrestling with these problems was to make the author quite literally ill. After the initial short story from which it grew, the novel went through three separate drafts. Belghoul was dissatisfied

---

107. Eric Favereau, 'Beur-Blanc-Black: "la gauche des rues" et des banlieues a fait surface', *Libération*, 3 Dec. 1984. This is a report of the speech which Belghoul made in Paris on the final day of the demonstration. For the full written text of the speech, the wording of which differs in places from her oral delivery, see 'Lettre ouverte aux gens convaincus', in Nelson Rodrigues et al. (eds), *La Ruée vers l'égalité*, Paris: Mélanges, 1985, pp. 53–8.
108. Interview with Farida Belghoul, 23 Apr. 1988.

with the first of these because she felt it contained too many implausible explanations. As she stripped them all away, she found herself with a second draft that was so bare that it seemed to have lost an essential part of the original impetus behind the novel. It was at this point that Belghoul was hospitalised with a skin condition apparently induced by nervous tension. When she left hospital ten days later, she wrote the third and final version, which strikes a balance between the explanatory excesses of the first and the unacceptably compressed state of the second draft.

These problems so preoccupied Belghoul that when she began drafting her as yet unpublished second novel, 'La Passion de Rémi', the author typed at the top of the first page: 'Une loi: pas de commentaires!' She also decided to cast the whole novel in the form of dialogue. As each character speaks to another, and therefore formulates his or her thoughts with this in mind, Belghoul hoped to avoid some of the technical difficulties associated with the interior monologue of the girl in *Georgette!*.

The child in this first novel is effectively her own narratee; no reference is made to the reader of the text, the formal writing of which is not of her doing. The transcription of the girl's fictional thoughts is the work of Belghoul. Many of the effects at which the author aims depend on the assumption that the reader knows certain things of which the girl and her Algerian parents are ignorant. For instance, the protagonist is told by her teacher that she needs an HB pencil. Neither the girl nor her parents are aware that HB signifies a grade of lead. When her mother buys a supply of 2H pencils, the girl points out that they are not what she requires and is immediately accused of ingratitude by her father. To cover up his ignorance, he tells her that 'Zache' (a mishearing of '2H') is simply a manufacturer's name, and that it does not really matter what make of pencils they buy. The girl senses he must be wrong, but does not know why.[109] A proper understanding of this passage and of the novel as a whole is conditional upon the reader possessing a cultural repertoire (symbolised by a knowledge of the grading system used on pencils) from which the narrator-protagonist and her illiterate parents are excluded. The complicity of the author and reader is, in a very real sense, built behind the back of the immigrant community.

109. Farida Belghoul, *Georgette!*, Paris, Barrault, 1986, pp. 15–19.

–4–

Past, Present and Future

4.1 Beginnings

Personal identity involves a complex mixture of memory and desire, which interface with each other across the present. This intercourse is the subject of the present chapter. In it, we shall re-encounter many of the elements discussed in previous chapters, but in a new light. The dominant axis of analysis in Chapter 3 was built on a spatial trope: the central question was whether the narrating or focalising consciousness was perceived as standing 'within' or 'outside' this or that group. All such groups are, of course, situated in time as well as space. Narratives always involve a more or less overt reworking of diegetic time, and the present chapter examines the affective and ideological significance of this within Beur fiction.

Genette has drawn attention to three main ways in which narrative time may differ from the flow of time at the level of diegesis.[1] In its *speed*, a narrative may linger on events or pass over them relatively quickly, thereby shunning any uniform correlation with the duration of different parts of the story. Narration and diegesis may also differ where *frequency* is concerned: an event may be described once (in what Genette calls 'singulative' narrative) or on several occasions thereby producing 'repetitive' narrative); conversely, when repeated or similar events are described only once, the result is 'iterative' narrative. Finally the *order* in which events are recounted may differ from their diegetic chronology. A number of issues relating to speed and duration were examined in Chapter 2, where omissions, for example, (equivalent to zero time at the level of narration) may in their own way shed considerable light on lengthy events elided in the representation of the story. The

---

1. Gérard Genette, *Figures III*, Paris, Seuil, 1972, pp. 77–182; idem, *Nouveau discours du récit*, Paris, Seuil, 1983, pp. 15–27.

distinction between singulative and iterative stretches of narrative will concern us on occasions in this chapter, but our main area of analysis has to do with order, and the present section concentrates in particular on the significance of beginnings.

Narrators often interrupt the flow of the story in order to describe events situated at an earlier or later point in time. These flashbacks and flashforwards, also known as analepses and prolepses respectively in Genette's terminology, imply a pattern of meaning which overlays and in many cases overrides the original order of events. If a narrator or focalising consciousness breaks up diegetic time in this way it is because this suits his or her present purpose. That purpose may be coolly calculated or spontaneously felt by the narrator or character concerned. Whatever its ideological or affective coloration, a projection towards the future always conditions a person's vision of the past. Conversely, memories of the past are of course a major factor in shaping our expectations and ambitions for the future. The subjective reworking of time is thus an inherently dialectical process, in which each element is subject to constant modification in its interaction with others.

The jumbled chronology in Part I of Leïla Houari's *Zeida de nulle part* reflects the nervous tension of the protagonist as she struggles to construct a coherent life-style that will somehow reconcile her North African roots with her European ideas of personal independence. A similar point applies to the representation of Mouss's troubled adolescence in Mustapha Raïth's *Palpitations intra-muros*. When I interviewed Mehdi Charef, he told me that the fractured chronology in *Le Thé au harem d'Archi Ahmed* mirrored the sense of rupture which had been his as well as that of his fictional counterpart, Madjid, as a consequence of their having been torn away from their childhood home in Algeria and thrust into a French bidonville.

Farida Belghoul's *Georgette!* follows the stream of consciousness of the narrator-protagonist. The main action takes place over a single day, but interwoven with the representation of this are extensive anachronies (a generic term used by Genette to cover both analepses and prolepses). The motivation behind these breaks in chronology is clear. The little girl at the centre of the story is trying to learn to write, and in doing so she is forced to wrestle with the conflicting instructions received from her father and schoolteacher. As the day progresses she thinks back on different parts of her past in search of clues with which to understand the present; mixed in with these memories are increasingly frenzied fantasies about the future, which stem directly from the fears and anxieties generated by the confusing events through which she finds herself living. These fantasies clearly incorporate elements from the past, but it becomes increasingly difficult to distinguish with any precision between what is remembered and what is being invented.

A recognition of the importance of similar processes appears to be implicit in the dedication with which Nacer Kettane prefaces *Le Sourire de Brahim*: 'A mes parents pour que jamais la mémoire ne devienne souvenir.'[2] Expanding on this distinction between 'la mémoire' and 'le souvenir', Kettane has stated:

> Dans la signification du souvenir il y a une notion éphémère. Quand on se souvient ce n'est plus tout à fait la mémoire. Celle-ci est une authenticité, une actualité présente et en même temps un élément de l'avenir. [. . .] Pour notre génération, elle est importante. [. . .] La mémoire ne doit jamais laisser la place au souvenir. On doit sans cesse l'entretenir, non pas à la manière de fleurs que l'on porterait sur une tombe, mais plutôt par un questionnement permanent sur nous-mêmes, sur notre identité.[3]

In contrast with 'le souvenir', a 'dead' recollection of the past devoid of any direct bearing on the present, 'la mémoire' is linked organically with the self-projection of the subject towards the future. Through 'la mémoire', the subject's present sense of identity is interrogated by the past as it moves towards future goals. There is a very literal sense in which a person's parents represent the past. They preceded him or her in time, and provided the environment for the child's earliest memories. As we have seen in earlier chapters, when they grow up, the Beurs often pursue a future which places them at a distance from and sometimes positively at odds with their parents. Kettane refers to this pattern by quoting as an epigraph to his novel some lines from the poetry of the Lebanese-American writer Khalil Gibran:

> Vos enfants ne sont pas vos enfants,
> ....
> Car leurs âmes habitent la maison de demain,
> Que vous ne pouvez visiter, pas même dans vos rêves.[4]

2. Nacer Kettane, *Le Sourire de Brahim*, Paris, Denoël, 1985, p. 5.
3. Nacer Kettane speaking in an interview with Ezzedine Mestiri, 'Une Mémoire vivante et grave de l'immigration', *Tribune immigrée*, nos 24–5 Jan.-Mar. 1988, p. 127.
4. Kettane, *Le Sourire*, p. 7.

The apparent contradiction between this epigraph and the dedication which immediately precedes it is very evident. This tension, combined with the author's lucid distinction between 'la mémoire' and 'le souvenir', might lead one to expect Kettane's novel to engage in the exploration of similar contradictions within the Beur protagonist. Such expectations remain largely unfulfilled, however.

Although Brahim occupies the centre of the stage throughout most of the narrative, we seldom see any significant conflicts within him. He never disagrees with his parents, nor do we ever see him agonising over a future course of action. As noted in Section 3.2, the narrator assures us that Brahim feels as comfortable in relation to his Algerian heritage as he does with regard to the culture of France: 'Pour Brahim il n'y avait pas d'équivoque, il était chez lui partout avec la Méditerranée comme drapeau.'[5] In reality, as we saw in Section 2.4, Brahim shows little interest in Islam: he is far more committed to humanistic ideas derived from his education in France. After hearing a recital of traditional Algerian songs by Taos Amrouche, Brahim listens spell-bound while a friend expounds upon the riches of oral culture: 'Les vieux et les vieilles de chez nous sont comme un trésor qu'il faut protéger.'[6] The respect expressed here for the older generation smacks of precisely the folklorisation decried in Kettane's characterisation of 'le souvenir'. There is never any suggestion that the Islamic traditions of Algeria might be of relevance to the protagonist's life now or in the future. Brahim's sense of attachment to his ancestors – 'Il appartenait à ce peuple, à cette culture; [. . .] les mots défilaient devant lui comme une chaîne ininterrompue; ils le reliaient à ses origines'[7] – is built upon a mechanistic idea of time, represented here by the image of a chain. Each link in the chain may be attached to the next, but each is also quite fixed both in itself and in its position vis-à-vis all the others. While one end of the chain (Brahim's secularised self) may be vastly different from what stands at the other end (the Islamic traditions of the protagonist's parents), there is never any confrontation between them.

The contrasts with *Georgette!* could scarcely be more marked. Time, in *Le Sourire de Brahim*, is narrowly linear. Except for a handful of flashbacks, each occupying no more than a few lines, the text faithfully follows the chronological order of the events which it describes. This closely mirrors the affective and ideological

5. Ibid., p. 114.
6. Ibid., p. 71.
7. Ibid., p. 71.

simplifications which characterise the narrative. The past provides a springboard, never a challenge, to the present; the future beckons without ever inducing real perplexity or fear. Even Brahim's lost smile, a symbol of the distinctive identity ruthlessly suppressed by the French authorities during the events of 17 October 1961, becomes, like the eerily smiling faces of those killed that day, a shrine of remembrance rather than the focal point of a new crusade:

> Hommes noyés, fusillés, torturés, à jamais témoins de la barbarie, vous êtes comme un souffle de vie suspendu qui rafraîchira la mémoire des générations en pèlerinage d'identité. En se promenant, les amoureux des bords de Seine pourraient voir votre sourire, au fond de l'eau, bénir leurs baisers.[8]

Lovers' kisses in such a public place may seem entirely natural to the narrator and protagonist, for they are thoroughly Westernised in their sense of propriety; to the first-generation immigrants whose corpses were flung into the Seine such behaviour would have been, in the fullest sense of the word, outrageous. The narrator glides quite unperturbed over this fissure, inviting members of the younger generation calmly to pocket their 'identity' as if it were some tourist's trinket. The idea of personal identity as an arena of conflicting loyalties and uncomfortable choices is never seriously explored.

Beginnings occupy a special position in the order of things.[9] The first lines of a text must be conceived in part in such a way as to induce in the audience a desire to continue reading. They also lay the foundations for the pattern of meaning which will be generated by the narrative. In Beur fiction, the beginning of the text seldom coincides with the beginning of the story, i.e. the earliest point in its chronology. More commonly, the narrative opens with and then follows through a relatively recent sequence of events. These provide the backbone of the text, with earlier periods being represented through analepses. The divergence of text-time from story-time produces a pattern of meaning ruled by an order of priorities other than mere chronological precedence.

The emigration of part or all of the protagonist's family is generally the earliest event in the chronology of the story, but it is almost never positioned at the beginning of the text. The earliest

8. Ibid., p. 23.
9. For a wide-ranging discussion of this issue, see Edward W. Said, *Beginnings: Intention and Method*, Baltimore, Johns Hopkins University Press, 1975.

drafts of Azouz Begag's *Le Gone du Chaâba* began with such a passage, but it was eliminated in the published version of the text, where we are instead immediately plunged into the Lyonnais bidonville where the narrator-protagonist is brought up. Although most of Charef's *Le Harki de Meriem* deals with events during the Algerian war, it begins by describing the murder of Sélim in contemporary France; the experiences of his harki father more than twenty years earlier are recounted subsequently as a prolonged flashback.

Despite its fundamental importance and chronological anteriority where the whole of the younger generation is concerned, the father's emigration is placed at the beginning of only one Beur narrative, Kamal Zemouri's *Le Jardin de l'Intrus*. Significantly, *Le Jardin de l'intrus* is also the only Beur novel so far published to conclude unequivocally with the protagonist's voluntary 'return' to North Africa. In between, the narrative replicates in strict linear fashion the chronological order of events, in which the narrator–protagonist, Lamine, adopts unquestioningly the nationalist ideas of his father as the Algerian war of independence unfolds around them. Like *Le Sourire de Brahim*, *Le Jardin de l'intrus* lacks dramatic tension. Instead of crises or contradictions, the flow of time brings only a simple, incremental development of the protagonist's experiences and ideas. By 'returning' to Algeria Lamine consciously fulfils the hopes and expectations articulated by his father at the start of the novel: 'Je ne ressentirai pas ce voyage comme un départ. Tout naturellement, j'aurai l'impression de revenir à la place de mon père, et dé prolonger ainsi sa vie.'[10]

Most first-generation immigrants have shared similar hopes for their families, but Lamine is exceptional among the Beurs in making a reality of them. Far more frequently, while intensely aware that their presence in France is a consequence of their parents' emigration, the Beurs have proved unwilling to subordinate their future to the original expectations of the older generation. First-generation immigrants think of themselves essentially as *having come from* North Africa; their children are mainly preoccupied with *being in* France.

As their thinking has a different starting point from that of their parents, it has naturally appeared inappropriate to Beur writers to order their narratives purely on the basis of chronological anteriority. Instead of beginning with the departure of the older generation

---

10. Kamal Zemouri, *Le Jardin de l'intrus*, Algiers, Entreprise Nationale du Livre, 1986, p. 214.

from North Africa, practically all the narratives so far published by Beur writers open with scenes set in France (or, in Houari's case, Belgium). The only exceptions are *Le Jardin de l'intrus*, Mohammed Kenzi's *La Menthe sauvage* (where the narrator-protagonist begins with his childhood memories of Algeria, subsequently describing his emigration to France, where his father was already working as a bricklayer) and Akli Tadjer's *Les ANI du 'Tassili'*. Although *Les ANI du 'Tassili'* opens on Algerian soil, it does so with the protagonist preparing to return home to France following his failure to adjust to life in North Africa, an exactly inverse image of the thinking which characterises first-generation immigrants.

Granted that the protagonists in most Beur novels are born and live practically all their lives in France, it is perhaps hardly surprising that these narratives should open there. More obviously significant is the fact that even narratives featuring protagonists born in North Africa begin with scenes set in Europe. *Le Sourire de Brahim*, one of the most linear of Beur narratives, opens with the young protagonist in Paris; earlier memories of his childhood in Kabylia are not represented until the end of the first chapter. We initially meet the world-weary Madjid, in Charef's *Le Thé au harem d'Archi Ahmed*, as he struggles to mend his motorcycle in the cellar of an HLM block in the suburbs of Paris; it is not until half way through the novel that the narrator presents a flashback to the time when the young boy and his mother arrived in France with their minds still full of their native Algeria. Although the birthplace of the eponymous protagonist in Houari's *Zeida de nulle part* is not entirely clear, it seems likely to have been in Morocco. When the novel opens, however, Zeida is a young woman running away from her parents' home in Brussels; her childhood memories of Morocco (in which images of what appears to be the period prior to the family's emigration mingle with recollections of subsequent holidays there) are withheld until half way through Part I. Most of the tales in the same author's *Quand tu verras la mer . . .* feature first- or second-generation immigrants born in Morocco, but only the final story, 'Mimouna', opens there. The others all begin with scenes set in Europe; only later are there flashbacks to the protagonists' earlier experiences in North Africa.

Each of Ahmed Kalouaz's full-length narratives features a protagonist born and brought up in North Africa, but all of them begin by representing later experiences in France. *Point kilométrique 190* focuses from the outset on Habib Grimzi's death in the south of France; his family roots in Algeria are the subject of later intermittent references. In *L'Encre d'un fait divers*, Naïma's arranged marriage and departure from Algeria are not described until half-way through the narrative. In the unpublished 'Le Pluriel d'espoir n'est-ce pas désespoir . . .' the homodiegetic narrator, Ahmed, opens by describing a sequence of events which began when he was thirty years old. He remarks: 'Je marchais à la rencontre du futur. Mais lui marchait vers moi depuis près de trente ans.' Repeated flashbacks to Ahmed's Algerian past underline its importance in shaping the situation wherein he must build his future, but it is with the challenge of his circumstances in France that the narrative opens, rather than with what precedes them chronologically.

Few if any Beurs wish to dissociate themselves entirely from their North African roots. An idea of where they come from is important to their sense of self. Mehdi Lallaoui's second novel, 'La Colline aux oliviers', is indeed the story of a positive quest for origins. The problematic nature of the relationship between the Beur protagonist and the historical past is emphasised by the constant deferral within the text of what, in chronological terms, precedes and conditions everything else. In the first part of the novel the protagonist's grandfather, Baba Mous, recounts how, during the early decades of the twentieth century, he engaged in an unsuccessful search in France and North Africa for an uncle, Sri-Larbi, who had disappeared without trace many years before. In his old age Baba Mous persuades his grandson to resume the search during the 1980s. The younger man's inquiries occupy the bulk of the text, at the end of which he discovers that the missing ancestor had been among those deported to New Caledonia following the uprising of 1871.

After completing the novel, Lallaoui gave the following account of what had motivated its composition:

On cherche tous à avoir une continuité, d'autant plus les immigrés. Nous, une fois qu'on est en France, on a l'impression d'avoir une coupure. C'est quelque chose qu'il faut récupérer à mon avis. Il faut savoir l'histoire de son grand-père, de notre arrière-grand-père, etc. On est né ici, on a l'impression qu'il n'y avait rien avant. Il y a un mur. Tu es ici et tu pars, et quand tu te retournes tu vois le mur. Mais justement avec l'histoire de Baba Mous – ça a été fait de façon inconsciente d'abord, mais c'est fini maintenant depuis deux mois, et j'ai pu réfléchir à tout ça – ça permet aux immigrés, à moi, de lever ce mur. Derrière ce mur il y a la Méditerranée. Derrière la Méditerranée il y a un pays, c'est-à-dire qu'il y a une vie, une histoire, il y a une continuation qu'il ne faut pas oublier. On vient de l'autre côté, on vient d'Afrique. Avec une mémoire qu'on va cultiver, qu'on doit récupérer. Dans tous les peuples, dans tous les individus, il est important de savoir pourquoi on vient d'ici, pourquoi à un moment donné on est passé là, ça c'est important du point de vue psychologique. Je ne suis pas médecin, je ne suis pas psychanalyste, mais du point de vue psychologique ça nous permet de tomber sur nos pattes. Ça nous permet d'avoir une stabilité psychique, ce qui est très important.[11]

No human being can have a satisfactory sense of personal identity without knowing something of where s/he comes from. Yet this cognitive urge, emphasised in these remarks by Lallaoui, is only part of the driving force behind his novel. Equally important is an ideological motivation conditioned by a vision of the future: in its recapitulation of the historical epoch traversed by the narrative, 'La Colline aux oliviers' repeatedly draws attention to the injustices suffered by the Algerian people at the hands of the French and points out the enormous benefits, both military and economic, derived from the Algerians by their former colonial masters. These reconstructed memories are important in giving the Beurs a sense of justification regarding their presence in France: if the country owes so much to past generations of Algerians, how can it now deny the Beurs a future role in its affairs?

Such a vision of the future is clearly incompatible with any idea of the Beurs as mere replicas of their ancestors. Lallaoui's talk of 'une mémoire qu'on va cultiver' is very reminiscent of Kettane's references to graveside flowers and dutiful pilgrimmages. Lallaoui, like the Beur protagonist in 'La Colline aux oliviers', is highly Westernised in his outlook and aspirations; a committed Marxist, he has no interest in Islam. While certain aspects of the historical record may be used to validate a particular vision of the future, there is no question of blind subordination to the older generation. In the novel, the primary motivation which sustains the grandson in his quest for information about Baba Mous's uncle is in fact an aversion to feelings of guilt. He would much prefer to spend the time building his own life in France instead of running after some long-dead ancestor, but feels he cannot refuse the old man's request: the burden of guilt would be too heavy to bear.

The protagonists in many Beur narratives are dogged by similar feelings of guilt when they diverge from the paths prescribed by their parents. Such feelings form part of the complex affective fabric of Farida Belghoul's *Georgette!* Here competing cultural imperatives mediated through her father on the one hand and her

11. Interview with Mehdi Lallaoui, 17 Apr. 1988.

schoolteacher on the other induce in the seven-year-old narrator–protagonist a profound and unresolved sense of anxiety which often crystallises around the quest for a beginning. This quest, which becomes an emblem of the girl's search for mental coherence, is intimately connected with a recurring spatial trope, that of 'l'envers et l'endroi' ('the wrong and the right way round'). This in turn exploits the double meaning of the expression 'le bon sens',[12] which may denote both a pattern of spatial order and the prevailing social norms known as 'common sense'. At school it appears to the child that her teacher has opened her exercise book back-to-front. This supposition is based on the assumption that her father had shown the girl the right place to begin writing her homework. The interpretative grid which goes with each starting point is incompatible with the other. Each grid is of course a matter of social convention rather than of absolute right or wrong. Other recurring emblems of such conventions are the girl's odd socks (one red, one green): each is both 'right' and 'wrong' in relation to the other, depending on which of them we look at first. When the schoolmistress eventually finds the girl's homework, to prove that it has been written in the wrong place she points out that, unseen by her pupil, she had in fact numbered the pages of the exercise book before originally issuing it. At this point the girl decides that precedence in time must be of supreme importance in imposing a pattern of order: 'C'est le premier écrivain qui donne le sens à mon cahier, c'est pas le deuxième!'[13] Henceforth, she attempts to speak first in any conversation, lest her interlocutor impose an agenda and interpretative framework alien to her own concerns.

In practice, however, the girl constantly finds herself tongue-tied in her dealings with others. In a comment echoed repeatedly elsewhere in the text she remarks: 'Je suis toujours muette. Et si par hasard, j'ouvre ma bouche: je dis n'importe quoi.'[14] The feeling that her own discourse lacks order is again symbolised by the girl's apparent inability to find a convincing starting point. The opening words of her interior monologue involve a malapropism: 'La sonne cloche . . . Non, la cloche sonne.'[15] In correcting her own first words, the girl implicitly gives precedence to linguistic norms already established by others, in relation to which 'la sonne cloche' appears as an inversion. There is also a further double entendre here, for the verb 'clocher' serves to indicate a lop-sided way of

12. Farida Belghoul, *Georgette!*, Paris, Barrault, 1986, pp. 35, 36, 57.
13. Ibid., pp. 57–8.
14. Ibid., p. 108; cf. pp. 64, 121.
15. Ibid., p. 9.

walking or, more generally, a defective or cockeyed condition. The protagonist has what to others seems a strange way of walking, and in a less literal but equally important sense she seems for ever out of step with those around her. This condition is replicated in the apparent disorder of her own discourse: 'Je ne dis rien d'important, juste des bêtises les unes derrière les autres.'[16] The textual form of that disorder (and the paradox implicit in this phrasing is intentional on my part) cannot be fully grasped without considering another major aspect of the temporal structure of Beur narratives. In Chapter 3, we delayed considering the temporal position of the narrator and/or focalising consciousness in relation to the story. It is with this that the next section is concerned.

4.2 Deictics

The spatio-temporal position of a narrator is indicated through markers which linguists call deictics.[17] These include the distribution of grammatical persons (discussed in Chapter 3). Where time is concerned, the main deictic markers are verb tenses and adverbial phrases. Thus the narrator's use of the past tense indicates that s/he is referring to a time earlier than that at which s/he is speaking or writing, while adverbial phrases such as 'yesterday', 'a long time ago', etc., indicate the length of time separating the moment of narration from the period being described.

When narration takes places simultaneously with events (as in a stream-of-consciousness narrative) or nearly simultaneously with them (as in a journal), the present tense comes to the fore. However, the use of the present tense does not necessarily signal simultaneous narration. Used in an iterative way, the present tense may serve to resume habitual actions which have been performed on many occasions in the past. The narrator of *Le Thé au harem d'Archi Ahmed* uses it in this way in the following sentence, for example: 'En Algérie on voit des gens parfois qui se baladent avec une feuille de menthe qu'ils portent souvent à leur nez, ça sent bon et ça rafraîchit.'[18] The adverbs 'parfois' and 'souvent' mark the actions which they describe as repeated events separated from each other in time, rather than contemporaneous with the moment of narration. The present tense may also be used in a singulative way to describe

16. Ibid., p. 35.
17. See John Lyons, *Semantics*, vol. 2, Cambridge University Press, 1977, ch. 15.
18. Mehdi Charef, *Le Thé au harem d'Archi Ahmed*, Paris, Mercure de France, 1983, p. 128.

past events. Narrators often begin to describe events in the past historic and then, without any chronological break, switch to what is known as the historic present. This use of the present tense may lend a more vivid feel to the text, enabling the reader to imagine that s/he is actually witnessing events as they unfold, though the preceding past historics indicate that technically, the moment of narration is situated at some later point in time. *Le Thé au harem d'Archi Ahmed* is just one of many Beur narratives containing passages of this kind.

In their classic realist form, novels represent events in strict chronological order, using the past historic. These procedures have been heavily criticised by many modern writers, who see in such narratives an unacceptably mechanical vision of time. 'Nouveaux romanciers' such as Claude Simon, for instance, have taken as a key theme the subjective reworking of time, in relation to which linear chronology and the use of the past historic have a neatness which is quite inappropriate. It is true that relatively mechanistic Beur narratives such as *Le Sourire de Brahim* and *Le Jardin de l'intrus* largely replicate the classic formula of a linear narrative in the past historic. It would, however, be wrong to suggest that in itself the use of such conventions necessarily indicates a naïve or simplistic form of story-telling.

Jean-Luc Yacine's *L'Escargot* is narrated throughout in the past historic and follows the story in chronological order, but several scenes, particularly those involving the café proprietess Adèle,[19] have a fairy-tale quality which seems to place them outside the strict 'realism' of most of the text. There is also a radical break in chronology when the two main characters suddenly start to talk about the person who is currently writing their story.[20] This involves an ontological impossibility: the narrator cannot at one and the same time be writing about events in the past (as indicated by his use of the past historic) and observed at his desk by characters participating in those events. These surrealistic aspects of *L'Escargot* are apt to unsettle the reader, endowing the text with an enigmatic quality despite its apparently simple narrative flow.

A similar technique features repeatedly in Mustapha Raïth's unpublished novel 'Houria'. When the principal female characters, Nadia and Houria, address the narrator and quote from his narrative, they fracture the temporal hierarchy implied by the use of the past historic in the representation of the story. The reader rapidly

---

19. Jean-Luc Yacine, *L'Escargot*, Paris, L'Harmattan, 1986, pp. 35–8, 103–6.
20. Ibid., p. 86.

realises that far from representing the past, the narrative is in fact a fantasy-image of the future life which the imprisoned narrator dreams of living when the time for his release from jail eventually comes.

It is not always easy to pinpoint the time of narration with certainty. Apart from occasional analepses, events in Hocine Touabti's *L'Amour quand même* are narrated in strict chronological order. There are no prolepses, the presence of which would normally indicate retrospective narration: only someone writing or speaking after subsequent events can know what is to come later. The predominance of the present tense in most of the text therefore seems to indicate that narration takes place simultaneously with the story. Past historics are used occasionally, but until the final quarter of the novel, they consistently indicate flashbacks to periods earlier than the main sequence of events. The first three quarters of the novel span a period of three months. The remainder of the text,[21] covering most of the next two years, is narrated in the past historic, except for the last few paragraphs, which revert to the present tense. The switch to the past historic corresponds to a compression of events in this part of the narrative, with the closing present tenses indicating the narrator's position at the end of the story. It may be that the whole of the text has been narrated from that point, with the first three quarters of the narrative using what we may now consider to have been the historic present. On the other hand, as there are no prolepses it is possible that the first part of the narrative was recounted simultaneously with the events in question and then set aside pending the addition of the remainder of the text, written retrospectively from the end-point of the story.

On occasions, Beur authors seem to be quite simply muddled as to the temporal position of the narrator. The title of Sakinna Boukhedenna's *Journal* implies that the narrative is written more or less simultaneously with the events it describes, and this is apparently confirmed by the use of the present tense at the beginning of the text. In this opening passage, headed '4 juillet 1979',[22] Sakinna gives her age as twenty. As we learn later that she was born in 1959, this seems to indicate that the heading corresponds to the date of narration. After a few pages, the present is superseded by past tenses; but as this part of the narrative represents various episodes in Sakinna's childhood and adolescence, these past tenses

---

21. Hocine Touabti, *L'Amour quand même*, Paris, Belfond, 1981, pp. 170–219.
22. Sakinna Boukhedenna, *Journal. 'Nationalité: immigré(e)'*, Paris, L'Harmattan, 1987, p. 7.

are consistent with the moment of narration suggested by the initial heading. This is broadly true of most of the subsequent headings, until we reach the one dated '2 février 1980.'[23] The third paragraph in the passage which follows this heading describes events on 3 March 1980, which suggests that the earlier reference to 2 February may have been to the date of certain events, rather than to that of their narration. Even more confusingly, the next heading reads: 'Fin janvier!'[24]; a page later we encounter the heading; 'Février 1980!'[25] No explanation for this jumbled chronology is offered.

The headings subsequently revert to a linear chronology, with the predominance of the present tense suggesting that the dates indicate simultaneous narration. However, in the middle of the passage headed '4 mai 1980' Sakinna switches to the past tense as she describes the events leading up to her eventual decision to leave France for Algeria: 'La vie m'ennuyait, la France me dégoûtait; ainsi en 1981, je décidais de prendre la valise, et de laisser la clef de ma chambre au propriétaire. Je voulus mettre un point à ce handicap culturel.'[26] The date of this decision, and the tenses used in describing it, evidently put the time of narration later than 4 May 1980. Whatever that heading indicates, it cannot be the date of narration. The rest of the narrative, describing Sakinna's subsequent experiences in Algeria, is clearly narrated retrospectively. Past tenses predominate; where the present tense appears it has the function of the historic present. Remarks such as the following, describing the purchase of ice-creams by a male escort in Algeria, leave no doubt that there is a significant distance between the time of narration and that of the events represented in the text: 'Ah! Ces glaces aussi glacées que le glacis qu'était ce type dont je ne me souviens plus du prénom tant je le haïssais.'[27] The most likely explanation for these inconsistencies is that, in drafting the narrative, the author drew on a journal originally written more or less simultaneously with events, but became increasingly committed to retrospective narration without developing a coherent technical framework for this change of approach.

There appear to be similar but less glaring inconsistencies in Azouz Begag's second novel, *Béni ou le Paradis Privé*. Much of the text is narrated in the present, but it alternates with past tenses in such a way as to suggest that it has the function of the historic

23. Ibid., p. 50.
24. Ibid., p. 59.
25. Ibid., p. 60.
26. Ibid., p. 75.
27. Ibid., p. 80.

present, with the actual moment of narration lying at some later point in time. Describing the first scene in the main sequence of events, the homodiegetic narrator remarks: 'J'avais un âge où je pouvais faire plein de choses tout seul.'[28] The clear implication of this retrospective comment is that the narrator is significantly more advanced in age than his diegetic alter ego. A few pages later, however, the narrator states: 'Maintenant, je suis en seconde au lycée.'[29] As the main part of the story concerns precisely this school year, we seem here to be dealing with simultaneous narration. The context does not lend itself to the idea of this sentence being narrated in the historic present. This and similar lapses elsewhere in the novel occur particularly when the narrator reverts to the main sequence of events after referring back to earlier times. Having become absorbed in these analepses, he seems to forget that they are twice removed from the time of narration; in moving forward from the distant past, he mistakenly represents the more recent main sequence of events as if it were actually the present. Overall, the most plausible interpretation is to see the whole text as being narrated retrospectively, for there is an underlying maturity in the manner of narration which cannot be that of the teenage Béni depicted in the story. Because the narrator has close affective bonds with his younger incarnation, he seems at times to forget his older self, a process which is of course encouraged by the extensive use of the historic present.

In Section 3.1, we saw that in Mustapha Raïth's *Palpitations intra-muros* Mouss narrates most of his deeds in the third person in order to emphasise the affective distance between his present and past selves. This gap is further underlined by his use of the past historic, which endows past events with a firmer sense of separation from the present than any other tense in the French language. The perfect tense, for example, implies an ongoing connection between the past and the present; Mouss makes very little use of it. In recounting his painful and sometimes shameful past, he also avoids the historic present, which would remove the temporal screen separating him from these events. We are told at the outset and reminded periodically that the whole text is being narrated by Mouss in his prison cell. That cell, the physical locus of narration, constantly interposes itself between the reader and Mouss's past wrongdoings. The obvious unpleasantness of prison life may generate some sympathy for Mouss in the reader's mind, thereby

---

28. Azouz Begag, *Béni ou le Paradis Privé*, Paris, Seuil, 1989, p. 31.
29. Ibid., p. 40.

attenuating the horror inspired by the crime of rape for which he is now paying the price.

Begag, by contrast, provides very little information about the spatio-temporal position of his narrators. In both *Le Gone du Chaâba* and *Béni ou le Paradis Privé* the narrator must be situated at some point after the events which he describes, but we are given no explicit information with which to define that position more precisely. Its virtual invisibility (quite the opposite of Mouss's increasingly visible prison cell), combined with the extensive use of the historic present, is such that the reader is liable to forget all about the narrator. Indeed, we have seen that the narrator, too, appears to forget all about himself from time to time! It is the young protagonist who consistently occupies our attention. This is not to say that his is the only viewpoint represented in the text. A subtle note of irony is often struck by the more mature narrator in representing some of the naïve ideas of his diegetic counterpart. Nevertheless, the main focus of attention lies in the protagonist's attempts to chart a way forward through the perplexing and often painful world in which he finds himself.

Some of the most vigorous criticisms of heavily retrospective narration were formulated by Jean-Paul Sartre.[30] He argued that such an approach stripped the characters of their freedom of choice, a freedom which was central to Sartre's existentialist philosophy. It is of course misleading to suggest that fictional characters can somehow be deprived of their free will. Characters in a novel 'possess' the appearance of no more and no less freedom than is endowed upon them by their creator, and even as we read about their deliberations prior to some choice, 'their' decision, already determined by the author, awaits us on the next page of the printed text. However, the reader is perhaps less conscious of this when scenes are narrated in the present tense, for this normally precludes any explicit prolepses. By contrast, past tenses implicitly interpose the narrator's retrospective viewpoint between the reader and the events being recounted, and this may be felt to weaken the reader's identification with the uncertainties experienced by the characters.

In the representation of the uncomfortable and sometimes agonising choices which are a recurring feature of Beur fiction, the present tense has a particular appeal. Begag gradually realised this in drafting *Le Gone du Chaâba*, and made extensive revisions in the manuscript in order to exploit the present tense more fully. The

---

30. Jean-Paul Sartre, 'M. François Mauriac et la liberté', in *Situations*, I, Paris, Gallimard, 1947, pp. 33–52.

earliest draft of the text began with a long passage describing the arrival in France of Azouz's father, Bouzid, the life which he and his wife had led in colonial Algeria and the development of the bidonville in which they were to raise their family in Lyons. The passage ranges across a wide chronological span, from Bouzid's birth in 1925 to the moment of narration in the early 1980s. The narrator, Azouz, frequently departs from the original order of events, however, in order to highlight certain connections and contrasts. In particular, the poverty and illiteracy which character-ised Bouzid's life are contrasted with 'la réussite de ses enfants', and in particular the educational achievements of Azouz. Thus these opening pages of the manuscript present us with an overview of the entire story. The key themes are immediately identified for us and a clear chronological framework is established, at the end of which we know there is a successful outcome for Azouz. The remainder of the original manuscript is heavily analytical in approach. Most of the text describes the general conditions of the various phases in Azouz's upbringing, with a peppering of anecdotes by way of illustration. In addition, from his vantage point at the moment of narration the mature Azouz often comments upon and attempts to explain his escape from the cycle of deprivation and failure which has been the lot of so many immigrant families.

The published version of the text is radically different in empha-sis. There are no direct references to the moment of narration. The original opening passage is deleted, and we are plunged instead into an early incident witnessed by the young Azouz in the Chaâba bidonville. Thereafter events are recounted in strict chronological order, with just a handful of analepses; there are no prolepses. The main emphasis now falls on Azouz's experiences at the time of their occurrence. The absence of prolepses is particularly significant. The reader may suspect that, in view of the uncomplaining and gently confident tone in which events tend to be recounted, the narrating Azouz speaks from a relatively satisfactory position in life. Yet at no point in the published text are we told in advance the outcome of any particular incident. Most events are described in the historic present, and heavy use is made of dialogue. This represents as closely as possible the 'raw' events themselves, with an apparent minimum of mediation by the retrospective narrator. The text focuses particularly on difficult moments of choice for the young Azouz. As the reader is denied any advance knowledge of the outcome, s/he shares in the uncertainty and anguish experienced by the protagonist. When a particular decision has distressing con-sequences (as when Azouz disowns his mother, for example, in order to conceal his Arab origins), there are no words of reassurance from the narrator to tell us that everything will be alright in the end. The reader feels as anxious and upset as the protagonist at such points; no easy solutions are offered.

The bulk of the manuscript went through two major revisions before reaching its published state. In the first reworking, the present tense was systematically substituted for many past tenses, and a number of incidents originally described in just a few lines were expanded into longer passages. However, the main emphasis still lay on generalities rather than on individual events. Many of the past tenses in the original manuscript had been imperfects, signalling habitual actions rather than singulative narrative. In the revised draft, the present tense still had a mainly iterative function, describing regular, as against individual, events. The published text was the product of a second major revision in which the balance tipped decisively against analytic generalities. Many generalising comments by the narrator were removed altogether from the manuscript. By adding or deleting certain adverbial phrases, many passages which in the earlier draft had used the present tense in an iterative way were turned into singulative narrative. A passage describing Azouz's walk to school, for example,[31] was turned into an account of a specific incident by deleting adverbs such as 'toujours' which, in the earlier draft, had indicated repetition, and placing at the beginning of the published version the adverbial phrase 'le lendemain matin'. Individual incidents were also greatly expanded. For instance, the police raid on an illegal abattoir in Le Chaâba, in the course of which Azouz unwittingly betrays its inhabitants, occupied no more than a page in the first draft. The incident grew to three pages in the next version, and more than doubled in length again in the published text.

While Begag's first novel went through several major revisions before settling clearly on its main focal point (the mixture of curiosity, ambition and confusion experienced by the protagonist), Farida Belghoul knew from the outset where *Georgette!* would be focalised. From its earliest germ, the unpublished short story 'L'Enigme', the narrative was conceived as an interior monologue. Like *Le Gone du Chaâba*, *Georgette!* invites the reader to share the uncertainties of the protagonist as she faces one choice after another in a tug-of-war between home and school. The interior monologue form makes advance knowledge of the outcome impossible, thereby assuring an almost permanent condition of suspense. As

31. Azouz Begag, *Le Gone du Chaâba*, Paris, Seuil, 1986, pp. 56–7.

noted in Section 3.4, however, Belghoul's decision to use simultaneous narration by a confused and frightened seven-year-old girl poses enormous technical problems. The temporal separation of the narrator and protagonist in *Le Gone du Chaâba* allows the former (and through him the author) to organise the narrative discreetly without detracting from the childlike qualities of his younger self. The absence of such a separation in *Georgette!* makes the author's task much more difficult.

Belghoul has to find ways of allowing the text to be read simultaneously on two levels: one of them the naïve level of a childlike mind, the other the more knowing level of adults. We saw in Section 2.4 that the novel functions in a metonymic mode: behind each small incident, the reader can sense whole worlds in collision. Double entendre, examples of which were noted in Section 4.1, is another recurring device. When the schoolmistress asks her pupils to stand in a straight line she tells them: 'Je ne veux voir qu'une seule tête!'[32] The protagonist takes these words literally (the straightness of the line having the effect of hiding one head behind another), but further references to the teacher's remark encourage the reader to see in it a figurative meaning, too: the teacher wants all her pupils to internalise the same ideas, thereby appearing as one single mind.

After running away from school, the girl imagines her teacher scouring the streets in her car in search of the missing pupil:

> Cette femme au volant c'est un boule-d'ogre.
> C'est un gros chien qui adore cuisiner les grenouilles. Il les empile l'une sur l'autre et, avant de les éplucher, il sort son premier commandement. Il en a deux seulement. De sa voix affreuse, il dit très fort: 'Je veux voir qu'une seule tête!' Ensuite, il les coupe en morceaux. Il se garde juste les cuisses et prononce le deuxième: 'Assieds-toi!'[33]

It is difficult to decide whether to read the play on words at the end of the first sentence as deliberate on the part of the girl or as an unintended malapropism. On several occasions earlier in the text she likens the teacher to an ogress attempting to swallow her up. The bloated form resulting from this is alluded to here in 'un boule-d'ogre', wherein the reader can see a pun on 'bouledogue'. We may also see a caricature of French eating habits in the refer-

32. Belghoul, *Georgette!*, p. 12.
33. Ibid., p. 140.

ences to frog's legs, which in a grotesque way echo earlier allusions to this delicacy. How far the girl herself may be considered to be aware of all this is unclear, for by this point she is becoming frantic, mixing all kinds of images and memories in terror rather than in play. The schoolmistress is now metamorphosed into a ferocious dog. We recognise in its bark commands originally issued by the teacher ('Je veux voir qu'une seule tête!' and 'Assieds-toi!'). In this fantasy of what might happen to her, the girl is projecting a nightmare future in which memories of the past are deformed under the pressure of present anxieties.

The feeling that she risks being literally chopped up reflects the girl's inability to link the different cultural imperatives within her in a controlled and orderly way. The fractured chronology of the various elements represented in her discourse mirrors this condition. Yet it cannot be said that the text lacks form. We as readers can see a pattern where the protagonist cannot. Our additional maturity enables us to relate each of the girl's thoughts to her bi-cultural condition and to the underlying chronology of her day at school. These thoughts often wander to other times and places, but their textual duration corresponds uniformly to the flow of that day.

The girl is certainly unable to order time as clearly as most adults, but the author ensures that there are just enough signposts in the text to enable the reader to construct a meaningful pattern. In successive versions of the manuscript, Belghoul pared down deictic markers to a minimum in order to reflect the narrator's limited control over her own discourse. When combined with adverbial phrases, the full system of tenses available in the French language enables the user to delineate a complex temporal hierarchy. Leaving aside pieces of direct discourse quoted in the text, the girl in *Georgette!* seldom uses any tense other than the present. The perfect, imperfect and future appear occasionally, but other tenses such as the past historic, pluperfect, conditional, future perfect and future conditional are almost entirely absent.

Chronological shifts are instead signalled by small markers such as adverbs or conjunctions, but even these are used very sparingly. In formal discourse, a subordinate clause in the present tense introduced by 'si' often accompanies a main clause in the future tense. In *Georgette!*, the expected future tense is generally replaced by the present, but the conjunction 'si' is sufficient to ensure that the reader will interpret the main clause as a reference to the future. One of the author's key *trouvailles* was the adverbial phrase 'un jour'. During an interview, Belghoul recalled that she had suddenly realised while drafting the novel that this little phrase would enable her to signal shifts of chronology without changing tenses. At the same time, by avoiding more precise, sequential adverbs such as 'le lendemain' or 'hier', the phrase enabled the author to leave each day represented in the girl's thoughts undefined in its chronological relationship with the others. There are usually enough signs to indicate that a particular scene takes place prior to the day of narration or at an imagined point in the future, but it is impossible to establish a detailed chronology beyond this. Each scene is suspended as it were in mid-air. We are caught, like the girl, in an endless disconnected present. This condition is vividly communicated by the form of the narrative. Yet just as a clear sense of a beginning eludes her for ever, as does an unequivocal sense of purpose, so we as readers are denied a conclusive sense of order.

4.3 Endings

One of the most striking features of Beur narratives is the frequency with which they end with departures. *Le Gone du Chaâba* concludes with Azouz's family being forced to remove to a new home in an HLM tower block because the landlord wants more money for their city-centre apartment than they can afford to pay. This fresh move and the emotional upheaval which goes with it recapitulates the migratory experience which the father, Bouzid, initiated when he left Algeria many years earlier, and which is still far from complete in its consequences. An even stronger sense of turmoil marks the end of Mohammed Kenzi's *La Menthe sauvage*, where the narrator-protagonist suddenly finds himself expelled from France. In the final paragraph of Begag's second novel, *Béni ou le Paradis Privé*, the protagonist imagines himself flying away into the heavens with a Mohammed-like figure following his exclusion on racist grounds from a French nightclub. At the end of Lallaoui's *Les Beurs de Seine* Mourad is shot dead, the victim of a racist attack, and Belka leaves Paris 'en direction du soleil, de la mer qui le séparait de sa terre natale'.[34] Kaci, too, decides to leave for an unspecified destination, with no idea of when he will return. Zemouri's *Le Jardin de l'intrus* closes with Lamine departing France for a new life in Algeria, and there is a similar conclusion to Kalouaz's unpublished 'Le Pluriel d'espoir n'est-ce pas désespoir . . .'. Tassadit Imache's *Une Fille sans histoire* ends with the protagonist in

---

34. Mehdi Lallaoui, *Les Beurs de Seine*, Paris, Arcantère, 1986, p. 171.

a state of indecision as to whether to embark on a similar journey.

In novels which follow the protagonist across the Mediterranean, s/he is invariably disappointed by North Africa. The core sequence of events in Tadjer's *Les ANI du 'Tassili'* revolves around Omar's return voyage to France following his frustrating experiences in Algeria. The novel concludes with Omar's journey home still incomplete, the overland journey from Marseilles to Paris remaining ahead of him. At the end of *Zeida de nulle part* we see the protagonist awaiting a flight out of Morocco to an unspecified destination; the final words of the narrative read: 'L'hôtesse appela les voyageurs et les pria de se dépêcher, les destinations étaient . . . Bruxelles . . . Amsterdam . . . Hambourg . . . Paris . . .'[35] At the end of Boukhedenna's *Journal* we see the protagonist returning to France. Islamic constraints have made life impossible for her in Algeria; Sakinna's final words are: 'Me voilà immigrée sur le chemin de l'exil, identité de femme non reconnue je cours le monde pour savoir d'où je viens.'[36]

These open-ended conclusions reflect the unsettled conditions in which the children of immigrants live, and the deeply unsettling effects of this on their sense of identity. 'Quand ils sont chez eux, ils sont arabes,' Charef has remarked. 'Quand ils sortent, ils deviennent français. C'est dans cet instant, où ils ouvrent et referment la porte, qu'ils peuvent se construire leur culture.'[37] Because Beur narratives are built in an in-between world, it is natural that many of them should retain an unfinished feel. The fresh departures with which so many Beur protagonists bow out are a measure of their inability to find a settled sense of belonging. They also reflect the relatively young age of those concerned. The Beurs still have most of their lives ahead of them, and it is around decisions about their future that most of these narratives revolve. Except perhaps for Lallaoui's 'La Colline aux oliviers', no Beur novel ends with an unequivocal sense of completion.[38] 'La Colline aux oliviers' concludes with the aged Baba Mous calmly contemplating his own death, content that his grandson has finally found the solution to the mystery of Sri-Larbi's disappearance more than a hundred years earlier. As we saw in Section 4.1, however, the grandson, like the

35. Leïla Houari, *Zeida de nulle part*, Paris, L'Harmattan, 1985, p. 84.
36. Boukhedenna, *Journal*, p. 126.
37. Remarks made by Mehdi Charef in an interview with F. de G., 'Le Dernier des maudits camps', *L'Unité*, 15 Apr. 1983, p. 7.
38. On the notion of completion and related issues see Frank Kermode, *The Sense of an Ending: Studies in the Theory of Fiction*, New York, Oxford University Press, 1967.

rest of the younger generation, is ultimately more preoccupied with the future than with the past.

It is true that several Beur narratives end with the death of the protagonist. Yet in these texts, death is always perceived as the rude interruption of a life in mid-stream, never as a visitor whose time must inevitably come. There could scarcely be a clearer illustration of this than the brutal murder of Habib Grimzi, a young Algerian flung to his death through the door of an express train. Grimzi's death is the starting point rather than the conclusion of *Point kilométrique 190*. The fundamental purpose of the text is in fact to perpetuate Grimzi's voice. As such, the narrative has no natural ending. Commenting on its lyrical tone and indifference to chronological time, Kalouaz has commented: 'C'est un choix volontaire d'écrire de cette manière-là et de ne pas faire un truc linéaire sur une affaire. A la limite, on peut prendre le livre à la page 62 par exemple, lire jusqu' au bout et puis revenir au début; ce n'est pas important. [Je voulais] simplement traduire quelles sont les images de la vie qui font que la vie est importante.'[39] A similar sense of incompletion is powerfully conveyed by the absence of a full stop at the end of *Georgette!* where, after being run over by a car, the little girl lies dying in the road. Death prevents the girl from placing a full stop at the end of her narrative, the incompletion of which is a graphic reflection of her inability to articulate a holistic sense of self.

It would be entirely wrong to suggest that all is doom and gloom in Beur fiction. Despite the stressful and sometimes distressing experiences which they recount, there is a keen sense of humour at work in many of these narratives, and most are anything but defeatist. Hocine Touabti's *L'Amour quand même*, the first Beur novel to appear in print, ends with the unnamed Algerian protagonist playfully arguing with his French girlfriend over what to call the baby she is expecting. Julien-Mohammed seems an impossible compromise; one or other of these names will have to be chosen, but the narrative ends inconclusively. In this little incident we see the ethnic mix, the youthfulness and the uncertainties over the future which are so central to the corpus of writing initiated by Touabti.

---

39. Ahmed Kalouaz speaking in an interview with Frédéric Kocourek, '*Point kilométrique 190*', *Plurielle*, nos 5–6, July 1987, p. 13.

– 5 –

'Beur' Writers in the 1990s

5.1 Naming and Positioning

The first four chapters of this study were based on a corpus of 25 narrative works by 17 authors published up to 1989. Since then, a dozen new authors have entered print, and the total number of narrative volumes published by authors of Maghrebi immigrant origin has risen to almost 70.[1] A vigorous critical debate has also developed among scholars in Europe, the Maghreb and North America around these writings as well as the wider field of what, in the English-speaking world, is now generally known as post-colonial literature. The word 'Beur' has been to a large extent assimilated into anglophone academic discourse, and 'Maghrebi' is now frequently used in place of 'North African'. Concurrently and paradoxically, despite its widespread adoption in popular discourse within France, 'Beur' has been increasingly rejected as a label by those to whom it is applied. The rationale behind this rejection can best be understood within the context of the debate over the positioning of these writers within the conventional topography of literary spaces.

1. A comprehensive list of narrative works by second-generation Maghrebis is given in the bibliography. It incorporates three texts published prior to 1989 which were not included in my original corpus. These are a short story Jean-Luc Yacine, *La Béotie*, Paris, Editions Saint-Germain-des-Prés, 1977, and two autobiographical texts: Adda Boudaoud's *Renaître: j'ai vaincu mon alcoolisme*, Mulhouse, Salvator, 1985, recounting a personal struggle against alcoholism, and Habib Wardan's *La Gloire de Peter Pan ou le récit du moine beur*, Paris, Nouvelle Cité, 1986, tracing the author's conversion to Christianity. In view of the difficulty of establishing personal authorial responsiblity, narratives written with the acknowledged assistance of other parties – for instance, Aïcha Benaïssa and Sophie Ponchelet, *Née en France: histoire d'une jeune beur*, Paris, Payot, 1990, and Salem Kacet and

National or quasi-national boundaries have played a major role in structuring the framework within which literary studies have traditionally been organised. National or regional literatures have been implicitly defined by an assumed or desired coincidence between cultural and political boundaries. This fusion is in many ways symbolised by the idea of 'national' languages, each of which is taken to incarnate a distinctive and unified cultural community bounded by the territory over which sovereignty is exercised by a particular nation-state. In reality few, if any, languages are neatly bounded in that way, and cultural diversity exists within all so-called nation-states. If 'French' literature is habitually distinguished from 'Algerian' or 'Maghrebi' literature written in French, this is because each of the politically bounded spaces with which these literary fields are associated is felt also to be culturally distinctive, despite their shared used of a common language, i.e. French (alongside Arabic and Berber in the Maghreb).

Within this literary topography, where are we to position the writings of second-generation Maghrebis in France? Scholars and critics are deeply divided over this question. Three main schools of thought may be distinguished. According to one line of analysis, the descendants of Maghrebi migrants belong within the national cultures of the home countries. Another approach views them as essentially French, while in a third optic they are seen as standing outside national frameworks altogether.

Typical of the first approach is the following statement by Ahcène Bouchedda, an official in the Amicale des Algériens en Europe (AAE), set up by the authorities in Algeria to monitor and assist the expatriate population in France: 'Il n'y aura jamais de culture "beur" au élaboré du terme. Il y a une culture algérienne en France qu'il faut sans cesse développer.'[2] This is more a normative than a descriptive formulation, reflecting the official line of the AAE, according to which migrants

---

Georges Memmi, *Le Droit à la France*, Paris, Belfond, 1991 – are not included in the bibliography. For more detailed bibliographical guidance, see Alec G. Hargreaves, *La Littérature beur: un guide bio-bibliographique*, New Orleans, CELFAN Edition Monographs, 1992, and Charles Bonn, *Littératures francophones de l'émigration maghrébine: petite bibliographie*, supplement to *Etudes littéraires maghrébines*, no. 9, 1994. On recent socio-political developments, see Alec G. Hargreaves, *Immigration, 'Race' and Ethnicity in Contemporary France*, London/New York, Routledge, 1995.

2. Ahcène Bouchedda, 'Culture, au diapason de l'Algérie', *Actualité de l'émigration*, 29 June 1988, p. 26.

and their descendants should remain within the cultural orbit of the home country. In practice, the decline of the AAE during the 1980s was due in no small measure to its failure to keep pace with the developing interests and activities of second-generation Algerians, for whom the so-called home country was only a distant point of reference. Although extracts from the works of second-generation Maghrebis are included in two recent anthologies of Algerian literature in French,[3] the editor of one of them, Charles Bonn, acknowledges that these authors

> n'ont probablement pas leur place dans une anthologie de la littérature algérienne, car la plupart d'entre eux ne se reconnaissent plus que de très loin dans l'identité culturelle de leurs parents, mais plutôt dans une identité de banlieues de grandes villes européennes où les 'origines' ethniques ou culturelles cèdent souvent la place à une conscience de marginalité qui n'a que peu de points communs avec les définitions identitaires consacrées.[4]

More commonly, writers of immigrant origin are located within the sphere of French literature. Abdallah Mdarhri-Alaoui, for example, contrasts them with francophone authors raised and resident in the Maghreb, who are much more deeply marked by Arabo-Berber culture. In the works of second-generation Maghrebis in France

> la dimension culturelle arabo-berbère est réduite à des traces, d'ailleurs limitées à la 'culture (orale) du pauvre' le plus souvent [...] Il serait plus juste de situer ces écrivains comme 'nouveaux écrivains nationaux de France', si on tient absolument aux étiquettes![5]

Djanet Lachmet takes a similar view, arguing that young Maghrebis occupy a particular position within the cultural sphere of France:

> Jusqu'à présent, l'art beur m'apparaît principalement comme un art de contestation, je dirais même de classe, à l'intérieur d'une culture française

3. Christiane Achour (ed.), *Anthologie de la littérature algérienne de langue française*, Paris/Algiers, Bordas/ENAP, 1990; Charles Bonn (ed.), *Anthologie de la littérature algérienne (1950–1987)*, Paris, Livre de poche, 1990.
4. Bonn, *Anthologie* , p. 227.
5. Abdallah Mdarhri-Alaoui, 'Place de la littérature "beur" dans la production franco-maghrébine', in Charles Bonn (ed.), *Littératures des immigrations*, vol. 1, *Un espace littéraire émergent*, Paris, L'Harmattan, 1995, p. 42.

ou européenne. J'ai le sentiment, pour ma part, que les beurs font partie de ce qu'on pourrait nommer l'*underground* français et, qu'à ce titre, ils ne sont pas porteurs d'une spécificité ou d'une sensibilité qui éclaireraient d'une manière radicalement autre l'espace culturel où ils vivent. Les références qui les règlent appartiennent à la culture française et sont mises en jeu par la volonté de devenir français.[6]

While it would be going to far to suggest that the cultural references of second-generation Maghrebis are purely French, there can be little doubt that Maghrebi influences are much weaker. At the same time, there is an important ambiguity in Lachmet's characterisation of the relationship between young Maghrebis and dominant French norms. In positioning this emerging generation as part of French underground culture, she appears to suggest on the one hand that this is an oppositional movement ('un art de contestation') and on the other hand that it is motivated by a desire for incorporation ('la volonté de devenir français'). The apparently contradictory nature of Lachmet's remarks – Beur artists are said to be part of French culture, yet at the same time are held to be seeking to in some sense 'become' French – points to complex tensions in the relationship between writers of immigrant origin and mainstream French society.

A third approach sees these authors as engaged in a cultural project that is trans- or anti-national in spirit. Thus Mireille Rosello argues that the driving force behind Beur culture is 'rather than a dream of integration[,] of belonging, [...] the assertion of one's right to "désappartenir" (not to belong)'.[7] Similarly, Martine Delvaux has analysed the ways in which second-generation Maghrebis use 'l'ironie comme un procédé stylistique dont l'effet consiste à décentraliser la notion d'identité nationale'.[8] Delvaux argues that humour and irony are used as distancing devices through which second-generation Maghrebis 'cherchent à désappartenir de l'identité qu'on leur impose'; their aim is to 'échapper à la réification du sujet (post-)colonisé – en l'occurence *beur* – par le sujet (post-)colonial – en l'occurence français (et peut-être plus globalement, européen)'.[9] In developing these ideas,

6. Djanet Lachmet, 'Une Composante de l'underground français', *Actualité de l'emigration*, 11 March 1987, p. 26.
7. Mireille Rosello, 'The "Beur Nation": Toward a Theory of "Departenance"', *Research in African Literatures*, vol. 24, no. 3, Fall 1993, p. 23.
8. Martine Delvaux, 'L'Ironie du sort, le tiers espace de la littérature *beure*', *French Review*, vol. 68, no. 4, March 1995, p. 681.
9. Ibid., p. 688.

Delvaux draws on the work of post-colonial theorists such as Homi Bhabha, from whom she borrows the notion of a 'third space' transcending the binary opposites (in this case, France and the Maghreb) to which hybrid cultural practices are too often reduced.[10]

Writers of Maghrebi immigrant origin are undoubtedly post-colonial in the sense that they have their origins in former French colonies and are still grappling in many ways with the unfinished business of decolonisation. They are also profoundly hybrid in their cultural references. But they do not altogether fit into either of the main phases which it has become customary to distinguish within post-colonial literature. The earliest phase was closely connected with the nationalist struggle for independence, a now distant matter of political history in the eyes of today's writers. The newer wave of post-colonial writing is associated primarily with expatriates from Third World countries, who are preoccupied with exploring conditions of exile, migration or nomadism.[11] Neither category maps neatly onto authors of Maghrebi immigrant origin. With only a few exceptions, [12] they show little interest in any form of nationalism. To the extent that they live and write in the country where they were born and raised, they cannot in any literal sense be described as exiles, migrants or nomads.

The exemplary figures of contemporary post-colonial writing, such as Salman Rushdie, Derek Walcott or Tahar Ben Jelloun, produce 'a literature written by élites, and defined and canonized by élites. It is writing which foregrounds and celebrates a national or historical rootlessness.'[13] Very little of this applies to young Maghrebi writers in France. Most are from extremely humble backgrounds. They were brought up in conditions of poverty by poorly educated immigrant

10. Homi Bhabha, 'The Commitment to Theory', *New Formations*, vol. 5, 1988.

11. Cf the title of the special issue of *Yale French Studies*, no. 82, 1993, edited by Françoise Lionnet and Ronnie Scharfman: 'Post/Colonial Conditions: Exiles, Migrations and Nomadisms'.

12. The main instances are Kamal Zemouri, *Le Jardin de l'intrus*, Algiers, Entreprise Nationale du Livre, 1986; Sakinna Boukhedenna, *Journal. 'Nationalité: immigré(e)'*, Paris, L'Harmattan, 1987; Laura Mouzaia, *Illis u meksa (la fille du berger)*, Algiers, Entreprise Nationale du Livre, 1994. It will be noted that two out of the three were published in Algeria by the same state-owned publishing house; both trace a linear sequence of events contemporaneous with the war of independence.

13. Elleke Boehmer, *Colonial and Postcolonial Literature: Migrant Metaphors*, Oxford/New York, Oxford University Press, 1995, pp. 239–40.

parents at the bottom of the social scale. Their writings are still to a large extent ignored by cultural elites in France. Far from celebrating rootlessness, one of the main driving forces behind their work is to stake a place for themselves within French society.

The stereotypical identities from which they distance themselves through humour and irony include, first and foremost, the images of foreignness projected onto them in the neo-colonial gaze of the majority French population.[14] What Lachmet refers to as their wish to become French might more properly be described as their wish to be accepted as members of French society, for they are already largely (though not exclusively) French in their cultural practices. So while it is undoubtedly true that these authors assert the right not to belong to pre-determined categories, this is only one part of a more complex dynamic in which they go on to assert to the right to participate in French society on their own terms.[15]

As shown earlier,[16] the writings of young Maghrebis are, like those of other post-colonial authors, syncretic and polyphonic. While fully acculturated to the dominant norms in France, they also share ancestral connections with the Maghreb and participate in global cultural networks drawing in particular on the diasporic space which Paul Gilroy has called the Black Atlantic[17] as well as white American popular culture. At the same time, their writings are profoundly rooted within particular localities, above all the *banlieues* (literally 'suburbs'), which in the last ten years have become synonymous with areas of low quality social housing (HLM) containing dense concentrations of minority ethnic groups. The writings of second-generation Maghrebis thus exemplify the interaction between local and global cultural spaces which is a central part of the post-colonial condition. Yet their apparent circumvention of a specifically national level of cultural identity is in many ways an optical illusion. Their numerous stories of failed journeys of 'return' to their parents' homeland, followed by resettlement in France, amply demonstrate that these are not nomadic

---

14. Cf Susan Ireland, 'Writing at the Crossroads: Cultural Conflict in the Work of *Beur* Women Writers', *French Review*, vol. 68, no. 6, May 1995, p. 1025.

15. Cf Samia Mehrez, 'Azouz Begag: Un di Zafas di Bidoufile (Azouz Begag: Un des enfants du bidonville)', *Yale French Studies*, no. 82, 1993, pp. 25–42.

16. Supra, pp. 96–127.

17. Paul Gilroy, *The Black Atlantic: Modernity and Double Consciousness*, London/New York, Verso, 1993.

migrant intellectuals, but men and women rooted in particular places which, whether they like it or not, are part of France.[18] One of their key aims in writing is indeed to widen conventional notions of Frenchness to include elements reflecting the diverse ethnic origins of the national population.[19] This is perhaps the single most important reason for their rejection of the label 'Beur'. A term that once served to liberate minority ethnic youths from the stigmatising connotations associated with the word 'Arabe' is now seen as a new ghetto into which second-generation Maghrebis are shunted, preventing them from participating in mainstream French society on an equal footing with the majority population. Labelled as 'Beurs', they feel implicitly designated as somehow less than or other than French. Grounded in the *banlieues*, theirs is certainly 'une parole comme eux décentrée'.[20] Yet although they speak from the margins, it is with 'une voix active, interpellative et revendicative de la place du citoyen dans la société française'.[21]

5.2 Reception and evaluation

Unlike expatriate post-colonial authors, who remain in some sense external to the former colonial metropolis even when residing within it, second-generation Maghrebis write 'à partir de la France'.[22] The main characters in their novels are concerned to find a place for themselves within France, and the audience addressed by these texts is primarily French.[23] In these circumstances, not the least of the

18. Cf Alec G. Hargreaves, 'Perceptions of Place Among Writers of Algerian Immigrant Origin in France', in Russell King, John Connell and Paul White (eds), *Writing Across Worlds: Literature and Migration*, London/New York, Routledge, 1995, pp. 89–100.
19. Cf Alec G. Hargreaves, 'Resistance at the Margins: Writers of Maghrebi Immigrant Origin in France', in Alec G. Hargreaves and Mark McKinney (eds), *Post-Colonial Cultures in France*, London/New York, Routledge, 1997.
20. M'hamed Alaoui Adbalaoui, 'Entraves et libération, le roman maghrébin des années 80', *Notre Librairie*, no. 103, Oct.-Dec. 1990, p. 26.
21. Mdarhri-Alaoui, 'Place de la littérature "beur"', p. 44. Cf Mehrez, 'Azouz Begag'; Hargreaves, 'Resistance at the Margins'.
22. Tahar Djaout, 'Une Ecriture au "Beur" noir', *Notre Librairie*, no. 103, Oct.–Dec. 1990, p. 37.
23. Cf supra, chapter 3.

ironies surrounding their work is that it has so far attracted comparatively little recognition among French intellectual elites. Serious
critical attention has been more forthcoming outside France and
indeed the Maghreb: the earliest full-length studies were published by
researchers based in Britain and the United States.[24] Maghrebi and to
a lesser extent French researchers are beginning to catch up, but the
critical reputation of immigrant-born writers remains generally low
on both sides of the Mediterranean.

At least four factors may be advanced to explain this reticence.
Firstly, as Charles Bonn has pointed out, compared with many of their
North American and European counterparts, scholars in France
remain more attached to the concept of national literatures as the basic
unit of analysis.[25] The foreign origins of second-generation Maghrebis
are judged by many academics to consign them to spaces outside the
national literature of France. Yet 'French' literature has a long history
of absorbing foreign writers: Samuel Beckett (from Ireland), Eugène
Ionesco (from Romania) and Julien Green (from the US) are among
the many writers of foreign origin who have been 'naturalised' into
French literature, as categorised by French academics. The exclusion
of Maghrebi authors born in France cannot be fully explained without
reference to a second factor: the history of French colonisation and
the painful scars left by the dissolution of the overseas empire.

Unlike Europeans or Americans, Maghrebis have their origins in
countries where national identity and independence were defined
antithetically in relation to French domination. The struggle for
Algerian independence in particular was marked by a bitter eight-year
conflict which remains one of the most traumatic periods in post-war
French history. More than thirty years on, memories of the Algerian
war still make it difficult for many people in France to conceive of
young Maghrebis as part of the French nation.[26] To the extent that

---

24. The first edition of the present study was published in 1991. A second
    monograph, *Autour du roman beur: immigration et identité*, Paris, L'Harm-
    attan, 1993, was published by Michel Laronde, a French scholar based
    in the US. Abdelkader Benarab's *Les voix de l'exil*, Paris, L'Harmattan,
    1994, was the first book by a Maghrebi scholar to focus substantially
    (though still not exclusively) on authors of immigrant origin in France.
    A number of French academics have published articles or chapters on
    these authors but none has devoted a full-length study to them.
25. Charles Bonn, 'Lectures croisées d'une littérature en habits de
    médiation', *Hommes et migrations*, no. 1164, April 1993, p. 31.
26. Cf Benjamin Stora, *La Gangrène et l'oubli*, Paris, La Découverte, 1991.

their writings are studied by academics, these are generally located in university departments specialising in francophone, rather than French, literature.[27] The dividing line between these fields corresponds to the geo-political boundary between France and other countries where French is spoken and written, the most important of which are former French colonies. When authors of immigrant origin are classified as francophone rather than French, they are implicitly positioned outside, rather than inside, the French nation.

A third explanatory factor concerns the snobbishness of French intellectuals vis-à-vis textual forms other than those fitting the conventional mould of high-brow literature. While British and American universities have extended traditional areas of literary scholarship into the wider field of cultural studies, embracing popular as well as elite forms of literature, together with audio-visual media, French scholars have tended to look with disdain on the more popular arts. The narratives of second-generation Maghrebis often have a distinctly oral quality, drawing on a mixture of street slang and audio-visual influences derived from the mass media, rather than from classical literary models.[28] As such, they are ill suited to attract the interest, still less the praise, of mainstream French academics.

The resistance of French elites to cultural forms carried by the mass media is no doubt connected with the challenge which they pose to traditional concepts of national identity. Television in particular is so dominated by American influences that it is impossible to cast even a cursory glance at the programmes broadcast to French viewers without immediately acknowledging their steady erosion of a distinctively French national culture. The French state has sought to respond to this by imposing programme quotas designed to protect the nation from what is perceived as American cultural imperialism. Hand-in-glove with this has gone a deep resistance across almost the whole of the political spectrum to policies of multiculturalism. This is a fourth factor militating against the incorporation of minority cultural practices within the nationally defined space of France. Multiculturalism is widely regarded as an Anglo-Saxon (i.e. British or

27. Charles Bonn, Director of the Centre d'Etudes Littéraires Francophones et Comparées at the Université Paris-Nord, has been particularly active in this field. See in particular the important collection edited by Bonn, *Littératures des immigrations*, 2 vols, Paris, L'Harmattan, 1995.

28. Cf Alec G. Hargreaves, 'Oralité, audio-visuel et écriture chez les romanciers issus de l'immigration maghrébine', *Itinéraires et contacts de cultures*, vol. 14, no. 2, 1991, pp. 170–6.

more particularly American) invention quite unsuited to the needs of France. Policies designed to improve the employment opportunities of minorities, known as positive action in Britain and, in a stronger guise, as affirmative action in the US, are almost unanimously condemned as divisive and/or discriminatory. These policies have helped to open up American universities in particular to scholars of diverse ethnic origins, who in turn have broadened the curriculum beyond its traditional Eurocentric parameters. In the absence of a comparable policy, French universities remain more closed in upon themselves.

To the extent that they are read and commented upon, the writings of second-generation Maghrebis are often dismissed on the grounds that they lack literary merit.[29] Two main arguments are advanced to support this view: the reliance of these authors on autobiographical material, and a lack of textual sophistication. Neither criticism is entirely justified. Granted that authors are unlikely to feel motivated by subjects in which they have no personal interest, it is hardly surprising if they often draw on autobiographical materials. If the use of autobiographical material were in itself sufficient to condemn a writer, Marcel Proust is just one of many acknowledged masters of French literature who would be knocked from their pedestals. The autobiographical origins of *A la recherche du temps perdu* are irrelevant to the literary merits of the novel, which are rightly judged by two main criteria: the skill with which the diegectic fabric of the text is constructed and resonance of the narrator's voice, the complexity and originalty of which are built on the author's unique appropriation of the French language. If we apply the same criteria to the novels of second-generation Maghrebis, a more nuanced picture emerges.

Some of these narratives may legitimately be found wanting on both counts. Nacer Kettane's *Le Sourire de Brahim*,[30] like Kamal Zemouri's *Le Jardin de l'intrus* and Brahim Benaïcha's *Vivre au paradis*,[31] presents a simple linear narrative in a voice that lacks complexity, driven more by a wish to document a chain of events than to explore the capacity of language for teasing out subtleties of meaning. At the opposite pole, some of the most successful writings by authors of immigrant origin

29. For a revealing analysis of the critical reception accorded to these authors, see Regina Keil, 'Entre le politique et l'esthétique: littérature "beur" ou littérature "franco-maghrébine?"', *Itinéraires et contacts de cultures*, vol. 14, no. 2, 1991, pp. 159–68.

30. Nacer Kettane, *Le Sourire de Brahim*, Paris, Denoël, 1985.

31. Brahim Benaïcha, *Vivre au paradis: d'une oasis à un bidonville*, Paris, Desclée de Brouwer, 1992.

are also among the most autobiographical. As shown earlier,[32] some of the most polyphonic narratives have deceptively simple stories, based not uncommonly on events in the author's own life. The pleasure derived from reading texts by Azouz Begag and Moussa Lebkiri is directly proportional to their manipulation of language to reflect – often through self-mocking humour and irony – multiple reference points and positions within the single but polyphonic voice of the narrator. In novels such as Akil Tadjer's *Les ANI du 'Tassili'* and Farida Belghoul's *Georgette!*,[33] similar features are reinforced by subtly engineered though seemingly simple diegetic structures.

The charge of over-reliance on autobiographical material nevertheless raises an important question concerning the long-term evolution of this corpus of writing: how far is it capable of renewal? This depends partly on the creative talents of the authors themselves, but also in some degree on the publishing opportunities open to them. These elements are not entirely independent of each other, for in their desire to reach an audience authors may write in ways designed to capture the attention of potential publishers. For most writers of immigrant origin, there is no practical alternative to seeking a publisher in France.[34] Although a few specialist publishing houses, such as L'Harmattan, offer outlets that do not depend primarily on mainstream French audiences, in the eyes of most publishers commercial considerations dictate the need to address a wide general readership. In order to minimise their risks, publishers are inclined to select manuscripts for which they feel confident of finding a market. Since the early 1980s, heavy media coverage of 'immigration', and more recently of violent disorders in the *banlieues*, where minority ethnic groups are concentrated, has generated a market for quasi-ethnographic and in some cases frankly voyeuristic texts portraying these marginalised and disturbing spaces.[35] Commercial calculations

32. Supra, pp. 96–115.
33. Akli Tadjer, *Les ANI du 'Tassili'*, Paris, Seuil, 1984; Farida Belghoul, *Georgette!*, Paris, Barrault, 1986.
34. Rare exceptions are discussed supra, n. 12.
35. The voyeuristic strain is particularly pronounced in a narrative published under the pseudonymn Chimo, *Lila dit ça*, Paris, Plon, 1996. The publisher claims that the text, which often verges on the pornographic, was written by an anonymous youth who describes himself as being 'du type normal-banlieue brun et frisé évidemment et les yeux noirs' (p. 71). This and other indications suggest that the narrator is of African, possibly Maghrebi, origin. In the absence of proof to the contrary, I am sceptical as to the authenticity of the text. A more plausible explanation is that it is a commercially-motivated hoax.

made in this context undoubtedly help to explain the similarities between many of the narratives published in the 1990s and those which appeared in the 1980s.

Benaïcha's *Vivre au paradis*, published in 1993, takes the reader to practically the same Nanterre *bidonvilles* described a decade earlier in Mohamed Kenzi's *La Menthe sauvage*.[36] The HLM blocks in which Mehdi Charef set his first novel, *Le Thé au harem d'Archi Ahmed*, in 1983 are to a large degree replicated by those featured ten years later in Belade's *Et Dieu créa l'ANPE* and Soraya Nini's *Ils disent que suis une beurette...*[37] The very title of Nini's novel is a reflection of the pressures to which young Maghrebi authors are subjected by the French publishing industry. Nini had intended to call the novel *L'entre-deux*, but the publisher wanted to retitle it *La beurette* in the belief that this would increase sales. Rejecting 'Beurette' as an alien label, the author eventually agreed to a compromise: 'J'ai accepté *Ils disent que je suis une beurette* car ce sont les autres qui nous appellent ainsi et non moi qui l'utilise.'[38] Despite this partial resistance to the publisher's demands, the text remains marked at every turn by a demonstrative posture, displaying and explaining the feared world of the *banlieues* to an outsider observer.

Each of the narratives just mentioned was the first to be published by the author concerned. The similarities between them reflect not only the commercial calculations of publishers but also the fact all these authors had shared in very similar formative experiences. It is hardly surprising if these similarities are reflected in their first works. As noted above, the literary merits of individual texts depend more on the author's manipulation of language than on the raw materials from which the story is woven. No less important as an indicator of creative talent is the capacity of the author for renewing his or her writing in the light of new experiences and ideas. So far, a dozen authors of Maghrebi immigrant origin have published more than one work of narrative prose. Some have also published texts in other genres, including poetry, drama and essays. The present study is concerned solely with narrative works.[39] Within them, we can see considerable

36. Mohammed Kenzi, *La Menthe sauvage*, Lutry, Bouchain, 1984.

37. Mehdi Charef, *Le Thé ah harem d'Archi Ahmed*, Paris, Mercure de France, 1983; Belade, *Et Dieu créa l'ANPE*, Paris, IM'média, 1994; Soraya Nini, *Ils disent que je suis une beurette...*, Paris, Fixot, 1993.

38. Letter from Soraya Nina to Alec G. Hargreaves, 1 June 1994.

39. Other works by these authors are, however, listed in a separate section of the bibliography. It should be noted that the dividing line between different genres is not always easy to draw. In view of the difficulties

diversity in the degree to which different authors have expanded their horizons.

The second or third works of some authors show relatively little progression from their first. The minority ethnic youths and tough urban milieux featured in Mounsi's second novel, *La Cendre des villes*, are very similar to those in his first novel, *La Noce des fous*.[40] The predicament of Jasmine, in Tassadit Imache's *Le Dromadaire de Bonaparte*, is not fundamentally different to that of Lil in *Une Fille sans histoire*:[41] in each case, the central character is struggling to come terms with her mixed ethnic origins in an elliptical narrative marked by a poignant affective charge.[42] The feminist autobiography of the Kabyle singer Djura, *Le Voile du silence*, displays little originality in its use of language, and verges on the polemical in places; very similar ingredients are recycled by the author in in *La Saison des narcisses*,[43] which is cast more in the form of an essay.

Other authors such as Moussa Lebkiri, having found a distinctive literary voice in early narratives dealing with childhood or youth, have

---

involved in establishing a clear demarcation between fiction and autobiography, both genres are subsumed in the bibliography within the broader category of narrative prose. While listed elsewhere in the bibliography, essays such as Mounsi's *Territoire d'outre-ville*, Paris, Stock, 1995, and Djura's *La saison des narcisses*, Paris, Michel Lafon, 1993, include significant narrative elements. A number of scripts originally used in stage shows are particularly difficult to classify. Smaïn's sketches and some of Moussa Lebkiri's shows take the form of monologues which have in some cases been adapted or interspersed with original material tailoring them to the needs of readers, rather than of spectators. Although these are classified for practical purposes among the narrative works listed in the bibliography, it should be noted that the generic spread within Smaïn's books is particularly wide, including poems and songs alongside comic narratives and mimes. Scripts by Lebkiri featuring dialogue have been classified among 'other works'.

40. Mounsi, *La Noce des fous*, Paris, Stock, 1990; idem, *La Cendre des villes*, Paris, Stock, 1993. These same milieux, the *banlieues*, are also at the heart of Mousni's autobiographical essay, *Territoire d'outre-ville*.
41. Tassadit Imache, *Une Fille sans histoire,* Paris, Calmann-Lévy, 1989; idem, *Le Dromadaire de Bonaparte*, Arles, Actes Sud, 1995.
42. Imache has also written two children's books: *Le Rouge à lèvres*, Paris, Syros, 1988 and *Algérie: filles et garçons*, Paris, Albin Michel Jeunesse, 1991.
43. Djura, *Le Voile du silence*, Paris, Michel Lafon, 1990; idem, *La Saison des narcisses*, Paris, Michel Lafon, 1993.

gone on to apply this to a wider field of experiences. After *Une Etoile dans l'oeil de mon frère*, based on his childhood in Kabylia, and *Bouz'louf!... tête de mouton*, recounting his adolescence as a schoolboy in France, Lebkiri has applied his enormously inventive use of language to the satirical representation of contemporary social life in *Règlements de contes*.[44]

A growing number of authors have alternated between largely autobiographical and more fictional narratives. After the heavily autobiographical *Le Thé au harem d'Archi Ahmed*, Mehdi Charef stepped beyond the field of direct personal experience to explore the world of the *harkis*, agents and victims of the Algerian war of independence, in *Le Harki de Meriem*.[45] Ahmed Kalouaz has moved in a contrary direction, from early narratives devoid of directly autobiographical elements to more recent works inspired partly by the tragic death of a sister, whose loss has brought family memories and tensions into sharp focus.[46] An early short story published by Jean-Luc Yacine, *La Béotie*,[47] makes no allusion to the author's mixed ethnic origins; by contrast, these provide significant material in the more autobiographical *L'Escargot*. In *La Mauvaise Foi*, Yacine confines himself entirely to majority ethnic characters,[48] whereas in *Amghrar, la vérité voilée*[49] he focuses on childhood memories of the Algerian war. The four volumes of narrative prose published by Maya Arriz Tamza explore very diverse paths. The mythical world of *Lune et Orian (conte oriental)* and *Zaïd le mendiant*, inspired by traditional Arab tales, is far removed from the more autobiographical *Ombres*, which in turn is very different from the recreation of colonial Algeria and its immediate

44. Moussa Lebkiri, *Une Etoile dans l'oeil de mon frère*, Paris, L'Harmattan, 1989; idem, *Bouz'louf!...tête de mouton*, Paris, Lierre et Coudrier, 1991; idem, *Règlements de contes*, Paris, L'Harmattan, 1995.

45. Mehdi Charef, *Le Harki de Meriem*, Paris, Mercure de France, 1989.

46. Ahmed Kalouaz, *Leçons d'absence*, Paris, Blandin, 1991; idem, *De Barcelone au silence...*, Paris, L'Harmattan, 1994.

47. Jean-Luc Yacine, *La Béotie*, Paris, Editions Saint-Germain-des-Prés, 1977.

48. Unlike *L'Escargot*, which was published in 1986 by L'Harmattan in a collection entitled 'Ecritures arabes', *La Mauvaise Foi* was brought out by the same publisher in 1993 in a collection entitled 'Voix d'Europe'. For *La Mauvaise Foi*, the author used the name of both his French mother and Algerian father (Istace-Yacine), whereas his other works bear only his father's name (Yacine).

49. Yacine, *Amghrar, la vérité voilée*, Paris, L'Harmattan, 1995.

aftermath presented in *Quelque part en Barbarie.*[50]

While many authors of Maghrebi immigrant origin have moved well beyond the confines of directly autobiographical material, ethnic parameters linked to ancestral origins continue to inform most of their writings, even if only at the margins. Specifically Maghrebi features are relatively muted in the novels of Ramdane Issaad,[51] but their cosmopolitan ingredients no doubt reflect in a wider sense the author's mixed ethnic origins. Ethnic particularities are also fairly discreet in most, though not all, of the children's stories which have helped to make Azouz Begag's corpus of writing the largest published to date by any author of Maghrebi immigrant origin.[52] Begag also has five full-length novels to his credit which, while dealing largely with children and adolescents, are aimed primarily at adult readers. The main strength of these works lies in the author's playful but gently provocative use of language, which brings a similar but polyphonic narrative voice to most of the texts despite the diversity of their settings. The story lines are ethnically marked in ways that reflect directly or indirectly the author's personal origins. After the heavily autobiographical *Le Gone du Chaâba* and *Béni ou le Paradis Privé*, Begag transposes the difficulties of childhood acculturation and poverty from a migratory context in France to the semi-fictional locale of a Third World island under French administration.[53] In *Les Chiens aussi*, he experiments with mixed results with an allegorical representation of the problems and injustices afflicting young people in the *banlieues*,

---

50. Maya Arriz Tamza, *Lune et Orian: conte oriental*, Paris, Publisud, 1987; idem, *Zaïd le mendiant,* Paris, Publisud, 1989; idem, *Ombres*, Paris, L'Harmattan, 1989; idem, *Quelque part en Barbarie*, Paris, L'Harmattan, 1993. *Ombres* was published under the name Arriz Tamza. For his other works, the author has used the name Maya Arriz Tamza.

51. Ramdane Issaad, *Le Vertige des Abbesses*, Paris, Denoël, 1990; idem, *Pégase*, Paris, Denoël, 1991; idem, *Laisse-moi le temps*, Paris, Denoël, 1992; idem, *L'Enchaînement*, Paris, Flammarion, 1995.

52. Stories written by Begag specifically for children are *Les Voleurs d'écritures*, Paris, Seuil, 1990; *La Force du berger*, Geneva, La joie de lire, 1991; *Jordi ou le rayon perdu*, Geneva, La joie de lire, 1992; *Les Tireurs d'étoiles*, Paris, Seuil, 1992; *Le Temps des villages*, Geneva, La joie de lire, 1993; *Une semaine de vacances à Cap Maudit*, Paris, Seuil, 1994; *Ma Maman est devenue une étoile*, Geneva, La Joie de lire, 1995; *Mona et le bateau livre*, Lyon, Le chardon bleu, 1996.

53. Azouz Begag, *Le Gone du Chaâba*, Paris, Seuil, 1986; idem, *Béni ou le Paradis Privé*, Paris, Seuil, 1989; idem, *L'Ilet-aux-vents*, Paris, Seuil, 1992.

while in *Quand on est mort, c'est pour toute la vie* he presents a more naturalistic but again invented narrative set amidst the hazards of the quasi-civil war raging in Algeria in the mid–1990s.[54]

Renewal and diversity are clearly visible in the growing corpus of writing produced by writers of immigrant origin. These works are of variable quality, as is true of practically any body of writing, be it that of 'French', 'Algerian' or any other conventionally defined literary space. While informed to a greater or lesser extent by their shared ethnic origins, the writings of second-generation Maghrebis move in a variety of directions and include many distinctive voices. A decade and a half after they first began to enter print, there is no sign of any weakening in the quantity or quality of their output.

54. Begag, *Quand on est mort, c'est pour toute la vie*, Paris, Gallimard, 1994; idem, *Les Chiens aussi*, Paris, Seuil, 1995.

Select Bibliography

Unpublished Sources

Manuscripts

ARRIZ TAMZA, Maya, 'Les Enfants de Marseille'
——, 'L'Héritage'
——, 'Quelque part en Barbarie'
BEGAG, Azouz, 'Le Gone du Chaâba'
——, 'Beni ou le Paradis Privé'
——, 'L'Ilet-aux-Vents'
BELGHOUL, Farida, 'L'Enigme'
——, Georgette!'
——, 'La Passion de Rémi' (extracts)
BOUKHEDENNA, Sakinna, 'Journal'
HOUARI, Leïla, 'Zeida de nulle part' (extracts)
ISAAD, Ramdane, 'Dernier roman'
KALOUAZ, Ahmed, 'Le Pluriel d'espoir n'est-ce pas désespoir . . .'
LALLAOUI, Mehdi, 'Les Beurs de Seine' (extracts),
——, 'La Colline aux oliviers'
RAÏTH, Mustapha, 'Et le bonheur en prison . . .?'
——, 'Douleur ensemencée'
——, 'Houria'
TOUABTI, Hocine, 'Rue de la rive'
YACINE, Jean-Luc, 'La Messe dans la porcherie'
——, 'Les Années de brume'

Interviews and correspondence

ARRIZ TAMZA, Maya, 28 Aug. 1989; 27 Jan. 1991
BEGAG, Azouz, 2 Dec. 1987; 18 Apr. 1988; 21–6 Nov. 1988; 1–5 May
    1989; 16 Dec. 1990; 29 Jan. 1992; 22 Aug. 1996
BELGHOUL, Farida, 23 Apr. 1988; 23–8 Sept. 1988
BOUKHEDENNA, Sakinna, 21 Apr. 1988

CHAREF, Mehdi, 17 Sept. 1987

DJURA, 18 Aug. 1990

HOUARI, Leïla, 15 Sept. 1987; 10 June 1988; 15 Apr. 1993; 22 Nov. 1995; 22 Aug. 1996

IMACHE, Tassadit, 18 Nov. 1989

ISAAD, Ramdane, 9 July 1990

KALOUAZ, Ahmed, 23 July 1987; 2 Dec. 1987; 13 June 1988; 21 Jan. 1991; 15 Jan. 1995

KARA, Mme (mother of Bouzid Kara), 25 Nov. 1989

KENZI, Mohammed, 5 Mar. 1990

KESSAS, Ferudja, 12 May 1990

KETTANE, Nacer, 26 Sept. 1988; 12 July 1989

LALLAOUI, Mehdi, 14 Sept 1987; 17 Apr. 1988; 25 Apr. 1988; 27 Sept. 1988; 29 Sept. 1996

LEBKRI, Moussa, 26 Jan. 1991

MOUNSI, 14 Dec. 1990

NINI, Soraya, 1 June 1994. 2 Nov. 1996

RAÏTH, Mustapha, 19 Apr. 1988

TADJER, Akli, 26 Apr. 1988; 21 Apr. 1991; 7 Jan. 1994

TOUABTI, Hocine, 17 Sept. 1987; 27 Nov. 1987

YACINE, Jean-Luc, 16 Sept. 1987; 30 Nov. 1987; 11 Dec. 1988; 24 Oct. 1990; 2 Dec. 1991

ZEMOURI, Kamal, 30 Sept.–1 Oct. 1988

Published Sources

Narrative works

ARRIZ TAMZA, Maya [pseud. BOUSSELMANIA, Messaoud; see also Tamza, Arriz], *Lune et Orian: conte oriental,* Paris, Publisud, 1987

——, *Zaïd le mendiant,* Paris, Publisud, 1989

——, *Quelque part en Barbarie,* Paris, L'Harmattan, 1993

BEGAG, Azouz, *Le Gone du Chaâba,* Paris, Seuil, 1986

——, *Béni ou le paradis privé,* Paris, Seuil, 1989

——, *Les Voleurs d'écritures,* Paris, Seuil, 1990

——, *La Force du berger,* Geneva, La joie de lire, 1991

——, *L'Ilet-aux-vents,* Paris, Seuil, 1992

——, *Jordi ou le rayon perdu,* Geneva, La joie de lire, 1992

——, *Les Tireurs d'étoiles,* Paris, Seuil, 1992

——, *Le Temps des villages,* Geneva, La joie de lire, 1993

——, *Quand on est mort, c'est pour toute la vie,* Paris, Gallimard, 1994

——, *Une semaine de vacances à Cap Maudit,* Paris, Seuil, 1994

——, *Les Chiens aussi,* Paris, Seuil, 1995

——, *Ma Maman est devenue une étoile,* Geneva, La Joie de lire, 1995

——, *Mona et le bateau livre,* Lyon, Le chardon bleu, 1996

BELADE, *Et Dieu créa l'ANPE,* Paris, IM'média, 1994

BELGHOUL, Farida, *Georgette!,* Paris, Barrault, 1986

BENAÏCHA, Brahim, *Vivre au paradis: d'une oasis à un bidonville,* Paris, Desclée de Brouwer, 1992

BOUDAOUD, Adda, *Renaître: j'ai vaincu mon alcoolisme,* Mulhouse, Salvator, 1985

BOUKHEDENNA, Sakinna, *Journal. 'Nationalité: immigré(e)',* Paris, L'Harmattan, 1987

BOUZID, *La Marche,* Paris, Sindbad, 1984

CHAREF, Mehdi, *Le Thé au harem d'Archi Ahmed,* Paris, Mercure de France, 1983

——, *Le Harki de Meriem,* Paris, Mercure de France, 1989

DJURA [pseud. ABOUDA, Djouhra], *Le Voile du silence,* Paris, Michel Lafon, 1990

HOUARI, Leïla, *Zeida de nulle part,* Paris, L'Harmattan, 1985

——, *Quand tu verras la mer...* Paris, L'Harmattan, 1988

IMACHE, Tass, *Le Rouge à lèvres,* Paris, Syros, 1988

IMACHE, Tassadit, *Une Fille sans histoire,* Paris, Calmann-Lévy, 1989

——, *Algérie: filles et garçons,* Paris, Albin Michel Jeunesse, 1991

——, *Le Dromadaire de Bonaparte,* Arles, Actes Sud, 1995

ISSAAD, Ramdane, *Le Vertige des Abbesses,* Paris, Denoël, 1990

——, *Pégase,* Paris, Denoël, 1991

——, *Laisse-moi le temps,* Paris, Denoël, 1992

——, *L'Enchaînement,* Paris, Flammarion, 1995

ISTACE-YACINE, Jean-Luc [see also Yacine, Jean-Luc], *La Mauvaise Foi,* Paris, L'Harmattan, 1993

K., Ahmed [pseud. KALOUAZ, Ahmed], *L'Encre d'un fait divers,* Paris, L'Arcantère, 1984

KALOUAZ, Ahmed, *Point kilométrique 190,* Paris, L'Harmattan, 1986

——, *Celui qui regarde le soleil en face . . .* Alger, Laphomic, 1987

——, *Leçons d'absence,* Paris, Blandin, 1991

——, *De Barcelone au silence . . .,* Paris, L'Harmattan, 1994

KEDADOUCHE, Zaïr, *Zaïr le gaulois,* Paris, Grasset, 1996

KENZI, Mohammed, *La Menthe sauvage,* Lutry, Bouchain, 1984

KESSAS, Ferrudja, *Beur's Story,* Paris, L'Harmattan, 1990

KETTANE, Nacer, *Le Sourire de Brahim,* Paris, Denoël, 1985

LALLAOUI, Mehdi, *Les Beurs de Seine,* Paris, Arcantère, 1986

LEBKIRI, Moussa, *Une Etoile dans l'oeil de mon frère,* Paris, L'Harmattan, 1989

——, *Bouz'louf!...tête de mouton,* Paris, Lierre et Coudrier, 1991

——, *Règlements de contes,* Paris, L'Harmattan, 1995

MOUNSI [pseud. MOUNSI, Mohand Nafaa], *La Noce des fous,* Paris, Stock, 1990

——, *La Cendre des villes,* Paris, Stock, 1993

MOUZAIA, Laura, *Illis u meksa (la fille du berger),* Algiers, Entreprise Nationale du Livre, 1994

NINI, Soraya. *Ils disent que je suis une beurette . . .,* Paris, Fixot, 1993

RAÏTH, Mustapha, *Palpitations intra-muros,* Paris, L'Harmattan, 1986

SMAÏN [pseud. FAIROUZE, Smaïn], *Sur la vie de ma mère,* Paris, Flammarion, 1990

——, *Rouge baskets,* Paris, Michel Lafon, 1992.

——, *Ecris-moi ,* Paris, NiL Editions, 1995

TADJER, Akli, *Les ANI du 'Tassili',* Paris, Seuil, 1984

TAMZA, Arriz [pseud. BOUSSELMANIA, Messaoud; see also Arriz Tamza, Maya], *Ombres,* Paris, L'Harmattan, 1989

TOUABTI, Hocine, *L'Amour quand méme,* Paris, Belfond, 1981

——, *Dans la ville aux volets verts,* Paris, Challenges d'aujourd'hui, 1994

WARDAN, Habib, *La Gloire de Peter Pan ou le récit du moine beur,* Paris, Nouvelle Cité, 1986

YACINE, Jean-Luc [see also Istace-Yacine, Jean-Luc], *La Béotie,* Paris, Editions Saint-Germain-des-Prés, 1977

——, *L'Escargot,* Paris, L'Harmattan, 1986

——, *Amghrar, la vérité voilée,* Paris, L'Harmattan, 1995

ZEMOURI, Kamal, *Le Jardin de l'intrus,* Algiers, Entreprise Nationale du Livre, 1986

Others works by or about individual authors

AHMED [pseud. KALOUAZ, Ahmed] *Je vois ce train qui dure,* Paris, La pensée universelle, 1975

ASSOULINE, Florence, 'Azouz Begag écrivain: "Khomeiny et Rushdie ont blessé mon pére"', *L'Evénement du jeudi,* 2 Mar. 1989, p. 14

AYARI, Farida, '*Le Thé au harem d'Archi Ahmed* de Mehdi Charef', *Sans Frontière,* May 1983, pp. 36–7

BACHIRI, Khadidja, 'Le produit des circonstances', *Cinémaction,* no. 24, 1983, pp. 126–7.

BEGAG, Azouz, *L'Immigré et sa ville,* Lyon, Presses Universitaires de Lyon, 1984

——, *La Ville des autres,* Lyon, Presses Universitaires de Lyon, 1991

——, *Espace et exclusion: mobilités dans les quartiers périphériques d'Avignon,* Paris, L'Harmattan, 1995

——, with BURGELIN, Claude and DECOURTRAY, Monseigneur, *Les Lumières de Lyon,* Lyon, Horvath, 1993

——, with CHAOUITE, Abdellatif, *Ecarts d'identité*, Paris, Seuil, 1990

——, with DELORME, Christian, *Quartiers sensibles*, Paris, Seuil, 1994

BELGHOUL, Farida, 'La Gifle', *Im'média magazine*, no. 2, Spring 1985, pp. 15, 16, 39

——, '*Le thé au harem d'Archiméde* de Mehdi Charef', *Cinématographe*, May 1985, pp. 32–3

CHAREF, Mehdi, 'La Nouvelle Culture des migrants: d'abord ne pas oublier', *La Croix*, 3–4 July 1983

——, 'Mères patries', *La Croix*, 25 Nov. 1983

——, 'J'ai écrit mon premier roman pour eux', *Migrants Formation*, no. 56, Mar. 1984, pp. 52–3

CRESSOLE, Michel, 'Le Gone du Chaâba réédite ses exploits', *Lyon-Liberation*, 25–6 Oct. 1986

——, 'Béni soit un beur obése', *Libération*, 10 Jan. 1989

CUAU, Bernard, 'Mehdi Charef: La tendresse dans le béton', *Jeune Afrique Magazine*, May 1985, pp. 26–7

DAZAT, Olivier, 'Mehdi Charef', *Cinématographe*, July 1985, pp. 10–12

DJURA, *La Saison des narcisses*, Paris, Michel Lafon, 1993

HORVILLEUR, Gilles, 'Farida Belghoul', *Cinématographe*, July 1985, pp. 18–19

HOUARI, Leïla, *Les Cases basses*, Paris, L'Harmattan, 1993

——, *Et de la ville je t'en parle*, Brussels, EPO/IDI, 1995

——, *Poème-fleuve pour noyer le temps présent*, Paris, L'Harmattan, 1995

ISSAAD, Ramdane, and GREMILLON, Michel, *La Dictature d'Hippocrate*, Paris, Denoël, 1992

JAY, Salim, 'Mehdi Charef: *Le Thé au harem d'Archi Ahmed*', *L'Afrique littéraire*, no. 70, Oct.–Dec. 1983, pp. 106–9

KALOUAZ, Ahmed, *Cette cité coincée*, Honfleur, Oswald, 1977

——, *A mes oiseaux piaillant debout . . .*, Paris, Mots d'homme, 1987

——, *Double soleil*, Grenoble, Les Inachevés/Cynara, 1989

——, *Foulée bleue*, Seyssel-sur-Rhône, Editions Comp'Act, 1992

——, *Péninsule de Valdès*, Paris, Arcantére, 1992

KENZI, Mohammed, *Temps maure*, Sherbrooke, Naaman, 1981

KETTANE, Nacer, *Droit de réponse à la démocratie française*, Paris, La Découverte, 1986

KOCOUREK, Frédéric, "*Point kilométrique 190*', *Plurielle*, nos 5-6, July 1987, pp. 12–15

LALLAOUI, Mehdi, *20 ans d'affiches antiracistes*, Bezons, Association Black Blanc Beur, 1989

——, *Du bidonville aux HLM*, Paris, Syros, 1993

——, *Kabyles du Pacifique*, Bezons, Au nom de la mémoire, 1994

LALLAOUI, Mehdi, and ASSOULINE, David *Un siècle d'immigrations en*

France, première période: de la mine au champ de bataille, 1851-1918, Bezons, Au nom de la mémoire, 1996

LEBKIRI, Moussa. *Il parlait à son balai*, Paris, L'Harmattan, 1992

——, *Prince Trouduc en panach'*, Paris, L'Harmattan, 1993

LECLERE, Thierry, 'Mehdi Charef: Contre-plongée dans l'univers des HLM', *Murs, murs*, Mar. 1985, pp. 38–9

MESTIRI, Ezzedine, 'Une mémoire vivante et grave de l'immigration', *Tribune immigrée*, nos 24–5, Jan.–Mar. 1988, pp. 127–30

MOUNSI, *Territoire d'outre-ville*, Paris, Stock, 1995

RAÏTH, Mustapha, 'Seconde Génération: les problémes d'identité, la crise, le réve' *Algérie-Actualité*, 21 Aug. 1986, p. 2

SCHMITT, Olivier, 'L'Homme qui marche', *Le Monde*, 29 Dec. 1987

YACINE, Jean-Luc, *Mélancolie*, Paris, Editions Saint-Germain-des-Prés, 1976

——, *Les Chemins de ma mémoire*, Paris, Editions Saint-Germain-des-Prés, 1977

General literary studies and related works

ACHOUR, Christiane, *Anthologie de la littérature algérienne de langue française*, Algiers, ENAP/Paris, Bordas, 1990, pp. 173–231: 'Ecritures de la migration'

Actualité de l'émigration, 11 Mar. 1987, pp. 22–7: 'L'Expression "*beur*": esquisse d'une littérature'

ALAOUI ADBALAOUI, M'hamed, 'Entraves et libération: le roman maghrébin des années 80', *Notre Librairie*, no. 103, Oct.–Dec. 1990, pp. 14–30

ANGENOT, Marc, 'L'"Intertextualité": enquéte sur l'émergence et la diffusion d'un champs notionnel', *Revue des sciences humaines*, vol. 60. no. 198, Jan.–Mar. 1983, pp. 121–35

APPIGNANESI, Lisa (ed.), *Postmodernism: ICA Documents*, London, Free Association Books, 1989

BAKHTIN, M.M., *The Dialogic Imagination*, trans. Caryl Emerson and Michael Holquist, Austin, University of Texas Press, 1981

BENARAB, Abdelkader, *Les Voix de l'exil*, Paris, L'Harmattan, 1994

BENVENISTE, Emile, *Problémes de linguistique générale*, vol. 1, Paris, Gallimard, 1966

BHABHA, Homi, 'The Commitment to Theory', *New Formations*, vol. 5, 1988

BOEHMER, Elleke, *Colonial and Postcolonial Literature: Migrant Metaphors*, Oxford/New York, Oxford University Press, 1995

BOKOBZA, Serge, *Contribution la titrologie romanesque: variations sur le titre 'Le Rouge et le Noir'*, Geneva, Droz, 1986

BONN, Charles, *La Littérature algérienne de langue française et ses lectures*, Ottawa, Naaman, 1974

——, 'La lecture de la littérature algérienne par la gauche française: le "cas" Boudjedra', *Peuples méditerranéens*, no. 25, Oct.–Dec. 1983, pp. 3–10

——, *Le Roman algérien de langue française*, Paris, L'Harmattan/ Montreal, Presses de l'Université de Montréal, 1985

——, 'Roman maghrébin, émigration et exil de la parole', *Annuaire de l'Afrique du Nord*, vol. 24, Paris, CNRS, 1987, pp. 399–415

——, 'Lectures croisées d'une littérature en habits de médiation', *Hommes et migrations*, Apr. 1993, pp. 27–31

——, *Littératures francophones de l'émigration maghrébine: petite bibliographie*, supplement to *Etudes littéraires maghrébines*, no. 9, 1994.

BONN, Charles (ed.), *Anthologie de la littérature algérienne (1950-1987)*, Paris, Livre de poche, 1990

——, *Littératures des immigrations*, 2 vols, Paris, L'Harmattan, 1995

BOUCHEDDA, Ahcène, 'Culture, au diapason de l'Algérie', *Actualité de l'émigration*, 29 June 1988, p. 26

BOULAL, Jamila, 'Introduction la littérature française d'expression immigrée', unpublished doctorial thesis, UER de Sciences des textes et documents, Université de Paris VII, 1989

BOURAOUI, Hédi, 'A New Trend in Maghrebian Culture: the Beurs and their Generation', *Maghreb Review,* vol. 13, nos 3–4, 1988, pp. 218–28

Cahiers FIC, [no.1], Mar. 1984, pp. 34–47: 'Quand nos parents nous ont perdus: Un déjeuner-débat au FIC'

CHIKH, Chérif, and ZEHRAOUI, Ahsène (eds), *Le Théâtre beur*, Paris, Arcantère, 1984

DÉJEUX, Jean, 'Romanciers de l'immigration maghrébine en France', *Francofonia*, vol. 5, no. 8, Spring 1985, pp. 93–111

DELEUZE, Gilles, and GUATTARI, Félix, 'What is a Minor Literature?', *Mississippi Review,* vol. 11, Spring 1983, pp. 13–31

DELVAUX, Martine, 'L'Ironie du sort, le tiers espace de la littérature beure', *French Review*, vol. 68, no. 4, March 1995, pp. 681–93

DESPLANQUES, François, 'Quand les Beurs prennent la plume', *Revue européenne des migrations internationales*, vol. 7, no. 3, 1991, pp. 139–52

DJAOUT, Tahar, 'Une Ecriture au "Beur" noir', *Notre Librairie*, no. 103, Oct.–Dec. 1990, pp. 35–8

DJEGHLOUL, Abdelkader, 'L'Irruption des Beurs dans la littérature française', *Arabies,* May 1989, pp. 80–7

DJEGHLOUL, Abdelkader (ed.), *Kateb Yacine: le provocateur . . . provoqué!*, Paris, Actualité de l'émigration, 1987

GADANT, Monique, 'La Littérature immigrée', *Les Temps modernes*, nos. 452–4, Mar.–May 1984, pp. 1988–99

GENETTE, Gérard, *Figures III*, Paris, Seuil, 1972

——, *Nouveau discours du récit*, Paris, Seuil, 1983

——, *Seuils*, Paris, Seuil, 1987

HARGREAVES, Alec G., '*Beur* Fiction: Voices from the Immigrant Community in France', *French Review*, vol. 62, no. 4, Mar. 1989, pp. 661–8

——, 'Resistance and Identity in *Beur* Narratives', *Modern Fiction Studies*, vol. 35, no. 1, Spring 1989, pp. 87–102

——, 'Language and Identity in Beur Culture', *French Cultural Studies*, vol. 1, no. 1, Feb. 1990, pp. 47–58

——, *La Littérature beur: un guide bio-bibliographique*, New Orleans, CELFAN Edition Monographs, 1992

——, 'Perceptions of Place Among Writers of Algerian Immigrant Origin in France', in Russell King, John Connell and Paul White (eds), *Writing Across Worlds: Literature and Migration*, London/New York: Routledge, 1995, pp. 89–100

——, 'Resistance at the Margins: Writers of Maghrebi Immigrant Origin in France', in Alec G. Hargreaves and Mark McKinney (eds), *Post-Colonial Cultures in France*, London/New York: Routledge, 1997

HARLOW, Barbara, *Resistance Literature*, New York, Methuen, 1987

Hommes et migrations, Apr.–May 1988: 'Le Livre et l'immigration'

IRELAND, Susan, 'Writing at the Crossroads: Cultural Conflict in the Work of *Beur* Women Writers', *French Review*, vol. 68, no. 6, May 1995, pp. 1022–34

Itinéraires et contacts de cultures, vol. 14, no. 2, 1991, pp. 137–92: 'Ecritures des deux rives'

JAKOBSON, Roman, 'Two Aspects of Language and Two Types of Aphasic Disturbance', in Roman Jakobson and Morris Halle (eds), *Fundamentals of Language*, The Hague, Mouton, 1956, pp. 55–82

JANMOHAMED, Abdul R., 'Humanism and Minority Literature: Toward a Definition of Counter-Hegemonic Discourse', *Boundary 2*, nos 12–13, Spring–Fall 1984, pp. 281–99

KEIL, Regina, 'Entre le politique et l'esthétique: littérature "beur" ou littérature "franco-maghrébine"?', *Itinéraires et contacts de cultures*, vol. 14, no. 2, 1991, pp. 159–68

KERMODE, Frank, *The Sense of an Ending: Studies in the Theory of Fiction*, New York, Oxford University Press, 1967

KRISTEVA, Julia, *Etrangers à nous-mêmes*, Paris, Fayard, 1988

LACHMET, Djanet, 'Une Composante de l'underground français', *Actualité de l'emigration*, 11 March 1987, p. 26

LARONDE, Michel, 'La "Mouvance beure": émergence médiatique', *French Review,* vol. 62, no. 4, March 1989, pp. 661–8

——, *Autour du roman beur: immigration et identité,* Paris, L'Harmattan, 1993

LEJEUNE, Philippe. *Le Pacte autobigraphique,* Paris, Seuil, 1975

——, *Je est un autre,* Paris, Seuil, 1980

LIONNET, Françoise, and SCHARFMAN, Ronnie (eds), *Yale French Studies,* no. 82, 1993: 'Post/Colonial Conditions: Exiles, Migrations and Nomadisms'

LODGE, David, *The Modes of Modern Writing: Metaphor, Metonymy, and the Typology of Modern Literature,* London, Edward Arnold, 1977

LYONS, John, *Semantics,* 2 vols, Cambridge University Press, 1977

MAATOUK, Frédéric, 'Le Théâtre des travailleurs immigrés en France', unpublished doctorat d'état, UER Sciences de l'Homme, Université François-Rabelais, Tours, 1979

MCHALE, Brian, 'Free Indirect Discourse: A Survey of Recent Accounts', *PTL,* vol. 3, 1978, pp. 249–87

MDARHRI-ALAOUI, Abdallah, 'Place de la littérature "beur" dans la production franco-maghrébine', in Charles Bonn (ed.), *Littératures des immigrations,* vol. 1, *Un espace littéraire émergent,* Paris, L'Harmattan, 1995, pp. 41–50

MEHREZ, Samia, 'Azouz Begag: Un di Zafas di Bidoufile (Azouz Begag: Un des enfants du bidonville)', in *Yale French Studies,* no. 82, 1993, pp. 25–42

OLLÉ, Jean-Michel, 'Les Cris et les rêves du roman beur', *Le Monde diplomatique,* Oct. 1988, p. 27

PRINCE, G., ' Introduction l'étude du narrataire', *Poétique,* no. 14, Apr. 1973, pp. 177–96

——, *Narratology,* Berlin/New York/Amsterdam: Mouton, 1982

ROSELLO, Mireille, 'The "Beur Nation": Toward a Theory of "Departenance"', *Research in African Literatures,* vol. 24, no. 3, Fall 1993, pp. 13–24

SAID, Edward W., *Beginnings: Intention and Method,* Baltimore, Johns Hopkins University Press, 1975

TODOROV, Tzvetan, *Nous et les autres,* Paris, Seuil, 1989

VOLOSINOV, V.N. [pseud. BAKHTIN, M.M.], *Marxism and the Philosophy of Language,* trans. Ladislav Matejka and I.R. Titunik, New York/London: Seminar Press, 1973

Social and historical studies

ABOU-SADA, Georges, and MILET, Héléne (eds.), *Générations issues de l'immigration: 'mémoires et devenirs',* Paris Arcantère, 1986

AICHOUNE, Farid, *Nés en banlieue*, Paris, Ramsay, 1991

AISSOU, Abdel, *Les Beurs, l'école et la France*, Paris, CIEMI/L'Harmattan 1987

AMAR, Marianne, and MILZA, Pierre, *L'Immigration en France au xxᵉ siècle*, Paris, Armand Colin, 1990

BOULOT, Serge and BOYZON-FRADET, Danielle, *Les Immigrés et l'école: une course d'obstacles*, Paris, CIEMI/L'Harmattan, 1988

Club de l'Horloge, *L'Identité de la France*, Paris, Albin Michel, 1985

COSTA-LASCOUX, Jacqueline, and TEMIME, Emile (eds), *Les Algériens en France: genèse et devenir d'une migration*, Paris, Publisud, 1985

ERIKSON, Erik H., *Identity: Youth in Crisis*, London, Faber and Faber, 1986

Espaces Quatre-vingt-neuf, *L'Identité française*, Paris, Editions Tierce, 1985

FERENCZI, Thomas, 'Le Burnous sous le béret', *Le Monde* 22–3 Dec. 1985

GILLETTE, Alain, and SAYED, Abdelmalek, *L'Immigration algérienne en France*, 2nd edn, Paris, Entente, 1984

GONZALEZ-QUIJANO, Yves, 'Les "Nouvelles" Générations issues de l'immigration maghrébine et la question de l'islam', *Revue française de science politique*, vol. 37, no. 6, Dec. 1987, pp. 820–31

GRIMMEAU, J.P., 'Les Derniers Immigrés? Maghrébins et turcs en Belgique: quelques considérations géographiques et démographiques', *Tribune immigr*ée, no. 21, Dec. 1986, pp. 5–9.

HARGREAVES, Alec G. *Immigration, 'Race' and Ethnicity in Contemporary France*, London/New York: Routledge, 1995

HARGREAVES, Alec G. (ed.), *Immigration in Post War France*, London, Methuen, 1987

HERVO, Monique, and CHARRAS, Marie-Ange, *Bidonvilles*, Paris, Maspéro, 1971

INSEE, *Recensement général de la population de 1982, sondage au 1/20, France métropolitaine: Les Etrangers*, Paris, La Documentation Française, 1984

——, *Recensement de la population de 1990: nationalités, résultats du sondage au quart*, Paris, 1992

JAZOULI, Adil, *L'Action collective des jeunes maghrébins de France*, Paris CIEMI/L'Harmattan, 1986

——, *Les Années banlieues*, Paris, Seuil, 1992

KEPEL, Gilles, *Les Banlieues de l'Islam*, Paris, L'Harmattan, 1987

KHELLIL, Mohand, *L'intégration des Maghrébins en France*, Paris: Presses Universitaires de France, 1991

LAPEYRONIE, Didier, *L'Individu et les minorités: La France et la Grande-Bretagne face à leurs immigrés*, Paris, Presses Universitaires de France,

1993

LEFORT, François, and NÉRY, Monique, *Emigré dans mon pays*, Paris CIEM/L'Harmattan, 1985

MALEWSKA-PEYRE, Hanna, et al., *Crise d'identité et déviance des jeunes immigrés*, Paris, La Documentation Française, 1982

MELA, Vivienne, 'Parler verlan: règles et usages', *Langage et société*, no. 45, Sept. 1988, pp. 47–72

MORSEY, Magali (ed.), *Les Nord-Africans en France,* Paris, CHEAM, 1984

NOIRIEL, Gérard, *Le Creuset franéais: histoire de l'immigration, xixe-xxe siècles,* Paris, Seuil, 1988

RODRIGUES, Nelson, et al. (eds), *La Ruée vers l'égalité*, Paris, Mélanges, 1985

Le Point, 29 Apr. 1985, pp. 46–7: Les Français et le racisme'

Population, vol. 29, no. 6, Nov.–Dec. 1974, pp. 1015–69: 'Attitudes des Français à l'égard de l'immigration étrangère: nouvelle enquête d'opinion'

SILVERMAN, Maxim, *Deconstructing the Nation: Immigration, Racism and Citizenship in Modern France,* London, Routledge, 1992

STORA, Benjamin, *La Gangrène et l'oubli,* Paris: La Découverte, 1991

TALHA, Larbi, et al., *Maghrébins en France: émigrés ou immigrés?,* Paris, CNRS, 1983

Index

Index

Index